"Old Favorite: This book is back again . . . and Tobias remains the funniest of financial writers."   — *Newsweek*

"Books that say 'you can do it' are popular—and some sell very well. That's why they're written. Read and enjoy them as entertainment. But don't believe them. Andrew Tobias's *The Only Investment Guide You'll Ever Need* is different—particularly worth reading as a primer. It's full of sensible advice and useful information."   —Charles D. Ellis, author of *Investment Policy*

"Required reading."   — *Seattle Times*

"Cheerfully irreverent . . . This book delivers useful, right-to-the-point advice."   — *Mutual Funds*

What Readers Say

"Five stars. Very informative."
—R. Thomas Ross, November 4, 2015

"Entertaining and practical ideas you can put in place now to make a difference for yourself."
—Andy Anderson, July 22, 2015

"Far and away the most practical money management and investment book I've ever encountered. Have purchased two editions over the years, gifting five family members both times. This is not how to be a day-trader or how to 'get rich.' It is simply a practical guide to money management; how to grow savings/investments with reasonable safety and gain the satisfaction of meeting one's life goals."   —J. K. Standish, May 17, 2015

"Truly a breath of fresh air in a murky arena. I read and appreciated an earlier version. I wanted to get Mr. Tobias's views after the 2008/9 Recession so bought his latest edition. I wasn't disappointed."   —David Phelps, December 14, 2014

"I have purchased each edition of this guide since the first was published in the late 1970s. Having read other investment books over the years, I can say that this is STILL the only one that I have actually needed."   —Joey Belize, November 27, 2014

"Bought two copies for our grown children. Great advice that never goes out of style."   —Marji D., November 10, 2014

"So much I wish I'd known as a young adult. Distilled to basics with a variety of life-management hints too. Overall great read."
—Jeff Pickens, June 22, 2014

"**Written in a way that does not scare away those, like me, who are intimidated by all things money.**"

—Giggirl, February 8, 2014

"**Exactly what the title implies.**"

—Bennett Nelson, February 5, 2014

"This is the book I give to my kids when they turn 18. It's truly the only investment guide they'll probably ever read, so **it needs to cover the bases. And does.**"   —DMac, February 3, 2014

"This is **probably the 10th copy I've purchased.** This time I gave it to a college student learning to work in the economy."

—John E. Rockwell III, October 28, 2013

"I bought the first paperback edition in the spring of 1978 at the Keesler AFB Base Exchange. Still have it, and **make it a point to re-read the latest edition every time it is updated.**"

—TopCat19, September 7, 2013

"Just **as informative and witty as when I read it 20 years ago!** I will give copies to both my young adult children."

—R. Simmons, July 8, 2013

"**It really is** the only investment guide you'll need. Covers all the basics, and the principles behind them. It's also fun to read."

—Edward Klemm, April 25, 2013

"**Much more readable than almost all the investing books I have read, and I have read dozens.**"

—Wanderer977, December 30, 2012

"Entertaining, practical, accurate, solid content, no hype . . . **that's all there is to say about this book.**"

—Sam Torode, April 27, 2012

"I followed the advice and systematically deposited each month in my children's savings accounts. The money grew and my daughter had a nice down payment for a house. My son is using his money to start a business. I also saved for my own retirement. I am not very good at investing but this book laid down a path for me and I was able to follow it. Inspiration is a rare and precious gift. **Andrew Tobias has been a blessing to me and my family and he doesn't even know us!**"

—LoveAmazon, January 14, 2012

"**If I had to go with one single guidebook** for someone starting out and needing finance advice, this would be the book."

—Michael Taylor, January 10, 2014

"**Not only a great investment guide but a fun read.** The author makes the whole managing your money, your life, doable from a down-to-earth perspective. I bought it for my husband for Christmas and I've given it to people I care about."

—J. Tussing "Sales Coach," January 12, 2012

"Bought an early edition years ago and still refer to it. **Tobias's advice has been a great help to us in our saving and investing.** I have given later editions to several young people who've asked for advice." —Atlanta Bob, December 23, 2011

"**I wish I'd read this book 30 years ago.** The younger you are when you read this book the longer you will benefit from it."

—J. Salay, December 4, 2011

"Whether you own none, one, or several books on investing, this one should be featured **front-and-center** in that collection."

—kthdimension, November 2, 2011

"I bought this book's first printing in 1978. Following its advice, I was able to retire at 59. Tobias is fun to read. **If you've thought about investing, this is the first book you should read.**"

—Russ Newell, September 3, 2011

"Andrew Tobias is smart, witty, sensible, and self-deprecating. If you have a son or daughter who is embarking on young adulthood, or a newly divorced friend who knows nothing of finances, this is **an ideal book for you to give** to him or her to encourage financial independence and stability."

—GatorFan, January 20, 2011

"When my husband and I married, **we were completely broke.** We heard about Andrew's book and started following the advice. That was 20+ years ago. I'm always uncomfortable saying the number, but here goes . . . Can you say a net worth of $800K? We have never had CEO incomes. My husband drives a truck, and I work in the medical field. Buy the book. Andrew Tobias will show you the way."

—Liebchi, July 31, 2011

"I bought this book when it first appeared in the late 70s and it was a bestseller then for good reason. **This time I got copies for my three kids and you should, too.** It's a cheap investment in good advice."

—P. Church "50s Guy," June 9, 2011

"**I read the original edition of this book when I was just starting out, and it did change my life.** I retired in my 40s and now live in a paid-off house, drive an old Toyota, and happily live within my means. With humor and wit, Tobias zeros in on broad commonsense approaches to managing your finances (and your life). Perhaps not for a really sophisticated investor, but it worked for me!"

—Amazon Customer, July 5, 2011

"I have been reading the various editions of this book since the first one. Tobias is a terrific writer. So much so that this book would make entertaining reading even if you completely ignored the advice it offered. Ignoring the advice, though, would be a bad idea because Tobias gives an overview of just about everything the average person needs to know about managing his or her money . . . **If you are looking for a comprehensive introductory guide to managing your money, look no further."**
— Hal Jordan, December 24, 2011

And from prior editions . . .

"I'm a professor at the Harvard Business School and a big fan. Before virtually every class, I think of your 'The Greatest Moment of My Life' story." — Terry Burnham, Boston, MA

"I studied finance at **a top business school** and understand the theory of investing from some of the top investors in the country. But in terms of netting it out into something usable and understandable, this was **better than all of that combined."**
— KC, Stamford, CT

"Incredibly helpful." — Russil Wvong, Vancouver, Canada

"Regularly hilarious." — Todd Schmeltz, Oak Harbor, WA

"This is the only investment book I have read that truly made sense." — Dallas Mavericks owner Mark Cuban

THE ONLY
INVESTMENT GUIDE
YOU'LL EVER NEED

ANDREW TOBIAS

MARINER BOOKS • HOUGHTON MIFFLIN HARCOURT

Boston   New York

For information about permission to reproduce selections from this book,
write to trade.permissions@hmhco.com or to Permissions,
Houghton Mifflin Harcourt Publishing Company, 3 Park Avenue,
19th Floor, New York, New York 10016.

www.hmhco.com

Library of Congress Cataloging-in-Publication Data is available.
ISBN 978-0-544-78193-1

Printed in the United States of America
DOC 10 9 8
4500648099

The prices and rates stated in this book are subject to change.

Quotation by John Templeton on page 142 reprinted
courtesy of *Mutual Funds* magazine.
Graph on page 80: Courtesy of the author.
Graph on page 197: Courtesy of www.macrotrends.net.

To my broker—even if he has,
from time to time, made me just that.

CONTENTS

ACKNOWLEDGMENTS

I would like to thank Sheldon Zalaznick and Clay Felker, the wonderful editors, much missed, with whom I worked most closely at *New York* magazine when this book was first written . . . the estimable Less Antman, for persuading me to revise it — and for providing, over the years, a tremendous amount of invaluable help, insight, and good humor in the bargain . . . Carol Hill, my editor on the original edition, and Ken Carpenter, my editor on this one . . . Sheldon Richman, Barbara Wood, and Rachael DeShano, for their close readings . . . Ibbotson Associates for their market statistics . . . Jerry Rubin and Bart Barker, among many others from the computer software world . . . John Kraus, Laura Sloate, Martin Zweig, Burton Malkiel, Alan Abelson, Ken Smilen, Yale Hirsch, Charles Biderman, Paul Marshall, Robert Glauber, Murph and Nancy Levin, Jesse Kornbluth, Jack Egan, Marie Brenner, Peter Vanderwicken, Eugene Shirley, Walter Anderson, David Courier, John Koten, Joel Greenblatt, Jane Berentson, Bryan Norcross, Brandon Fradd, Steve Sapka, Chris Brown, Zac Bissonnette, Bob Tortora, Brian Gatens, Victor Jeffreys II, and Charles Nolan (who, though departed, remains in charge) . . . *Forbes,* Google, the *Wall Street Journal,* and the *New York Times.* Although much of what I know I have learned from these people and institutions, whatever egregious faults you — or they — may find with this book are strictly my own.

If it is brassy to title a book *The Only Investment Guide You'll Ever Need,* it's downright brazen to revise it. Yet not to do so every few years would be worse, partly because so many of the particulars change, and partly because so many people, against all reason, continue to buy it.

In the 38 years since this book first appeared, the world has spun into high gear. Back then, there were no home-equity loans, no 401(k) retirement plans or Roth IRAs . . . no variable annuities to avoid or index funds to applaud or adjustable rate mortgages to consider . . . no ETFs, no 529 education funds, no frequent-flier miles (*oh, no!*), no Internet (can you imagine? *no Internet!*) — not even an eBay, Craigslist, or Amazon. (How did anyone ever *buy* anything?)

The largest mutual fund family offered a choice of 15 different funds. Today: hundreds. Stock prices were quoted in fractions and New York Stock Exchange volume averaged 25 million shares a day. Today: 3 billion shares would be a slow day.

The top federal income tax bracket was 70%.

The basics of personal finance haven't changed — they never do. There are still just a relatively few commonsense things you need to know about your money. But the welter of investment choices and the thicket of jargon and pitches have grown a great deal more dense. Perhaps this book can be your machete.

THE BIG PICTURE

NOT LONG AFTER this book first appeared in 1978, the U.S. financial tide ebbed: stock and bond prices hit rock bottom (the result of sky-high inflation and interest rates) and so did our National Debt (relative to the size of the economy as a whole). Investing over the next three decades—as difficult as it surely seemed at times—was actually deceptively easy, as the tide just kept coming in.

Now we're in (roughly, vaguely) the opposite situation—very *low* inflation, very *low* interest rates, and an uncomfortably *high* National Debt—making the years ahead a particular challenge.

Understanding that challenge—seeing the big picture—will help you put events and decisions in context.

Take a minute to consider the National Debt and interest rates; then another minute to consider "the good stuff."

National Debt

In 1980, the National Debt—which had peaked at 121% of Gross Domestic Product in 1946 as a consequence of the need to borrow "whatever it took" to win World War II—had been worked back down to 30%.

It's not that we repaid any of it, just that the economy gradually grew to dwarf it.

Whether for a family or a business or—in this case—a nation, having a low debt ratio is healthy. It gives you wiggle room if you ever run into trouble, like a recession, and need to borrow.

Indeed, that had long been the big idea: that in bad times governments should lean into the wind and run deficits . . . borrowing to boost demand and ease the pain while excess business inventories were gradually worked down . . . and then, in good times, *not* borrow much, or even run a surplus, to build borrowing capacity back up.

Yet in the mostly good years since 1980, our National Debt has ballooned. From 30%, when the Reagan-Bush team took over, it topped 100% in the fiscal year George W. Bush passed it on to his successor. (Only between Bush Senior and Junior was the annual deficit tamed, as Clinton handed off what *Fortune* called "surpluses as far as the eye could see.")

Although the deficit has once again been tamed as of this writing — meaning that the National Debt is once again growing more slowly than the economy as a whole — the wiggle room is largely gone.

I wrote in this space five years ago, with the unemployment rate hovering just under 10% and home foreclosure rates peaking, "We will get through this and emerge more prosperous than ever. But the decade ahead will be more about hunkering down and retooling than about jet skis and champagne." And, indeed, the unemployment rate has fallen to 5.0%, as I write this in early 2016; foreclosures are running at their lowest rate since 2007; and the stock market is more than double its March 2009 low. So we did "get through it."

Even so, the nation's infrastructure has been allowed to decay badly; the National Debt may require 35 years to shrink back to 30% of GDP, as it gradually did in the 35 years following World War II; and many of the "new" jobs don't pay nearly as well as the ones they've replaced. So it's still too soon for the champagne.

Interest Rates

In 1981, Uncle Sam said: Lend me $1,000 for two years and I'll pay you $336 in interest. In early 2016, Uncle Sam was saying, Lend me that same $1,000 and I'll pay you $20. And people were rushing to take it.

So it is a very different world.

In 1981, investors willing to take a risk on stocks or long-term bonds knew that—if inflation didn't spin entirely out of control—interest rates would eventually fall, making the prices of both stocks and bonds rise.

In 2016, investors have to understand that—whatever may come first—interest rates eventually will *rise,* making bond prices *fall* (see Chapter 5) and stocks relatively less attractive as well. (The more interest you can get from safe bonds, the less reason to take a risk with stocks.)

None of this is to say stocks can't go up if interest rates do. They absolutely can if rates don't go too high and sit atop healthy economic growth. But as a general rule, falling rates boost profits and stock prices. And for nearly 35 years, long-term interest rates generally *were* falling: wind beneath the market's sails.

At this point, if rates were to start falling again in any major way, it would only be because economic conditions are terrible —and that's not likely to drive enthusiasm for stocks. So either way, up or down, we face a bit of a headwind.

The Good Stuff

For all our problems, there is the astonishing onrush of technology.

People look at the last 50 years of technological progress and they are dazzled. And they think to themselves, "The next 50 years may be equally dazzling! Won't *that* be something!" But no, says futurist Ray Kurzweil, they are wrong. Technological progress over the next 50 years will *not* be "equally dazzling"—it will be *32 times* as dazzling, *32 times* as fast, *32 times* as great.

The implications are both thrilling and scary. Cyberterrorism? Don't get me started. There's no guarantee that, whether as a nation or a species, we'll keep from hurtling off the rails. That is, indeed, the central challenge of the century.

But if we can manage to keep from blowing it, the implications are amazing. Imagine, for example, a world of "nearly free" clean renewable energy, much as we now have nearly free communications. (When I was a kid, a hushed, urgent *"I'm on long distance!"* meant get the hell away from the phone. And that was for a call to Chicago. Today, the same call — even if it's to China, and even if it's a video call — is nearly free.) Nearly free energy would make everything dramatically less expensive — including materials, like energy-intensive aluminum — allowing most people to enjoy a terrific boost in their standard of living.

And that's just energy. The rate of advance in medical technology is another thing, already dazzling, that's likely to speed up — with astonishing implications.

It's getting from here to there that is the challenge. At best, it will be a bumpy ride. But making sensible economic and financial choices, and getting into sensible habits, will at the very least tilt the odds in your favor to enjoy as much of the upside as possible while avoiding the pitfalls.

OK. Let's get started.

PART ONE

MINIMAL RISK

There is no dignity quite so impressive,
and no independence quite so important,
as living within your means.

— CALVIN COOLIDGE

If I'm So Smart, How Come This Book Won't Make You Rich?

> *You have to watch out for the railroad analyst who can tell you the number of ties between New York and Chicago, but not when to sell Penn Central.*
>
> — NICHOLAS THORNDIKE

HERE YOU ARE, having just purchased a fat little investment guide we'll call *Dollars and Sense,* as so many investment guides are (although the one I have in mind had a different title), and you are skimming through idea after idea, growing increasingly excited by all the exclamation marks, looking for an investment you would feel comfortable with. You page through antique cars, raw land, mutual funds, gold — and you come upon the section on savings banks. Mexican savings banks.

The book explains how by converting your dollars to pesos you can earn 12% on your savings in Mexico instead of 5½% here. At 12% after 20 years, $1,000 will grow not to a paltry $2,917, as it would at 5½%, but to nearly $10,000! What's more, the book explains, U.S. savings banks report interest payments to the Internal Revenue Service. Mexican banks guarantee not to. Wink.

The book does warn that if the peso were devalued relative to the dollar, your nest egg would shrink proportionately. But, the author reassures, the peso is one of the stablest currencies in the world, having been pegged at a fixed rate to the dollar for 21 years; and the Mexican government has repeatedly stated its intention not to devalue. Now, how the heck are you, who needed to buy a book to tell you about this in the first place, supposed to evaluate the stability of the Mexican peso? You can only assume that the author would not have devoted two pages to the opportunity if he thought it was a poor risk to take—and *he's* an expert. (Anyone who writes a book, I'm pleased to report, is an expert.) And, as a matter of fact, you do remember reading somewhere that Mexico has *oil*—pretty good collateral to back any nation's currency. Anyway, what would be so dreadful if, as your savings were doubling and tripling south of the border, the peso *were* devalued 5% or 10%?

So, scared of the stock market and impressed by the author's credentials, you take *el plunge*.

And for 18 months you are getting all the girls.* Because while others are pointing lamely to the free clock radios they got with their new 5½% savings accounts, you are talking Mexican pesos at 12%.

Comes September, and Mexico announces that its peso is no longer fixed at the rate of 12.5 to the dollar but will, instead, be allowed to "float." Overnight, it floats 25% lower, and in a matter of days it is down 40%. Whammo. Reports the *New York Times:* "Devaluation is expected to produce serious immediate difficulties, most conspicuously in heavy losses for Americans who have for years been investing dollars in high-interest peso notes." How much is involved? Oh, just $6 or $8 *billion*.

You are devastated. But you were not born yesterday. At least you will not be so foolish as to join the panic to withdraw your funds. You may have "bought at the top"—but you'll be damned if you'll sell at the bottom. The peso could recover somewhat. Even if it doesn't, what's lost is lost. There's no point taking your diminished capital out of an account that pays 12% so you can get 5½% in the United States.

And sure enough, in less than two weeks the float is ended, and the Mexican government informally repegs the peso to the

---

* Or boys.

dollar. (Only now one peso is worth a nickel, where two weeks ago it was worth 8 cents.) You may not know much about international finance (who does?), but you know enough to sense that, like a major housecleaning, this 40% devaluation in Mexico's currency ought to hold it for a long, long time. In fact, you tell friends, for your own peace of mind you're just as glad they did it all at once rather than nibbling you to death.

And then six weeks later the peso is floated again and slips from a nickel to less than 4 cents. Since Labor Day, you're down 52%.

Aren't you glad you bought that book?

(Everything changes and nothing changes. That was 1976. In 1982 the peso was devalued again—by 80%. By mid-2010 it was back to its 1976 value of 8 cents, but only because three zeros had been lopped off the currency in 1993. A thousand pesos purchased in 1976 for $80 and kept in a mattress . . . albeit an unlikely repository . . . would 34 years later have become one new peso worth 8 cents. And now, in 2016, just 6.)

This immodestly titled book—the title was the publisher's idea; in a weak moment I went along—is for people who have gotten burned getting rich quick before. It is the only investment guide you will ever need *not* because it will make you rich beyond any further need for money, which it won't, but because *most* investment guides you *don't* need.

The ones that hold out the promise of riches are frauds. The ones that deal with strategies in commodities or gold are too narrow. They tell you *how* you might play a particular game, but not whether to be playing the game at all. The ones that are encyclopedic, with a chapter on everything, leave you pretty much where you were to begin with—trying to choose from a myriad of competing alternatives.

I hasten to add that, while this may be the only investment guide you will ever need, it is by no means the only investment guide that's any good. But, sadly, reading three good investment guides instead of one will surely not triple, and probably not even improve, your investment results.

The odd thing about investing—the frustrating thing—is that it is not like cooking or playing chess or much of anything else. The more cookbooks you read and pot roasts you prepare, the better the cook—within limits—you are likely to become. The more chess books you read and gambits you learn, the more opponents—within limits—you are likely to outwit. But when it comes to investing, all these ordinarily admirable attributes —trying hard, learning a lot, becoming intrigued—may be of little help, or actually work against you. It has been amply demonstrated, as I will document further on, that a monkey with a handful of darts will do about as well at choosing stocks as most highly paid professional money managers. Show me a monkey that can make a decent veal parmesan.

If a monkey can invest as well as a professional, or nearly so, it stands to reason that you can, too. It further stands to reason that, unless you get a kick out of it, you needn't spend a great deal of time reading investment guides, especially long ones. Indeed, the chief virtue of this one (although I hope not) may be its brevity. This one is about the forest, not the trees. Because if you can find the right forest—the right overall investment outlook—you shouldn't have to worry much about the trees. Accordingly, this book will summarily dismiss investment fields that some people spend lifetimes wandering around in. For example: It is a fact that 90% or more of the people who play the commodities game get burned. I submit that you have now read all you ever need to read about commodities. (Or at least about *playing* with them; in the last chapter I will offer a prudent way to use a broad-based commodities *fund* to increase your diversification and decrease your overall portfolio risk.)

This thing about the forest and the trees—about one's degree of perspective—bears further comment, particularly as for many of us it is second nature to feel guilty if we "take the easy way out" of a given situation. If, for example, we read the flyleaf and first and last chapters of a book, to get its thrust, instead of every plodding word.

I raise this not only because it could save you many hundreds of hours stewing over investments that will do just as well un-stewed, but also because it leads into the story of The Greatest Moment of My Life.

The Greatest Moment of My Life occurred in the Decision Analysis class at Harvard Business School. Harvard Business School uses "the case method" to impart its wisdom, which, on a practical level, means preparing three or four cases a night for the following day's classroom analysis. Typically, each case sets forth an enormous garbage dump of data, from which each student is supposed to determine how the hero or heroine of the case—inevitably, an embattled division manager or CEO—should ideally act. Typically, too, I could not bring myself to prepare the cases very thoroughly.

The format of the classroom discussion was that 75 of us would be seated in a semicircle with name cards in front of us, like United Nations delegates, and the professor would select without warning whomever he thought he could most thoroughly embarrass to take the first five or ten minutes, solo, to present his or her analysis of the case. Then everyone else could chime in for the rest of the hour.

On one such occasion, we had been asked to prepare a case the nub of which was: What price should XYZ Company set for its sprockets? Not coincidentally, we had also been presented with a textbook chapter containing some elaborate number-crunching way to determine such things. The theory behind it was simple enough—charge the price that will make you the most money—but the actual calculations, had one been of a mind to do them, were extremely time-consuming. (This was just before pocket calculators reached the market.)

The professor, a delightful but devious man, noting the con-spicuous absence of paperwork by my station, had the out-and-out malevolence to call on me to lead off the discussion. I should note that this occurred early in the term, before much ice had been broken and while everyone was still taking life very seriously.

My instinct was to say, with contrition: "I'm sorry, sir, I'm not prepared"—a considerable indignity—but in a rare moment of inspiration I decided to concoct a bluff, however lame. (And here is where we get, at last, to the forest and the trees.) Said I: "Well, sir, this case obviously was meant to get us to work through the elaborate formula we were given to determine pricing, but I didn't do any of that. The case said that XYZ Company was in a very competitive industry, so I figured it couldn't charge any *more* for its sprockets than everyone else, if it wanted to sell any; and the case said that the company had all the business that it could handle—so I figured there would be no point in charging *less* than everyone else, either. So I figured they should just keep charging what everybody else was charging, and I didn't do any calculations."

Ahem.

The professor blew his stack—but not for the reason I had expected. It seems that the whole idea of this case was to have us go round and round for 55 minutes beating each other over the head with our calculations, and *then* have the professor show us why the calculations were, in this case, irrelevant. Instead, the class was dismissed 12 minutes after it began—to thunderous applause, I might add—there being nothing left to discuss.*

Now, let me return to commodities.

My broker has, from time to time, tried to interest me in commodities.

"John," I ask, "be honest. Do *you* make money in commodities?"

---

* Herewith a list of all my other triumphs at Harvard Business School: I graduated.

"Sometimes," he says.

"Of course, *sometimes*," I say, "but overall do you make money?"

"I'm making money now. I'm up $3,200 on May bellies." (Pork bellies—bacon.)

"But overall, John, if you take all the money you've made, minus your losses, commissions, and taxes, and if you divide that by the number of hours you've spent working on it and worrying about it—what have you been earning an hour?"

My broker is no fool. "I'm not going to answer that," he sort of gurgles.

It turns out that my broker has made around $5,000 before taxes in four years of commodities trading. Without a $10,000 profit once in cotton and a $5,600 profit in soybeans he would have been massacred, he says—but of course that's the whole idea in this game: a lot of little losses but a few enormous gains. He can't *count* the number of hours he's spent working on and worrying about commodities. He went home short sugar one Friday afternoon after it had closed limit-up (meaning that he was betting it would go down, but instead it went up so fast he didn't have time to cover his bet, and now he stood to lose even more than he had wagered) and spent the entire weekend, and his wife's entire weekend, worrying about it. So maybe this very smart broker, with his very smart advisors, and their very smart computer, has made $2 or $3 an hour, before taxes, for his effort. And he wants *me* to play? He wants *you* to play?

If 90% of the people who speculate in commodities lose (and 98% may be a more accurate figure), the question, clearly, is how to be among the 10% (or 2%) who win. If it is not just a matter of luck, then it stands to reason that the players who have the best chance are insiders at the huge firms—Hershey, Cargill, General Foods, etc.—who have people all over the world reporting to them on the slightest change in the weather, and who have a minute-to-minute feel for the market (whether it be the market for cocoa, wheat, or what-have-you). You are not such an insider, but those who are would be delighted to have you sit down at the table and play with them.

If, on the other hand, it *is* just luck, then you have just as good a chance as anybody else for the jackpot, and all you're doing is gambling, plain and simple, and paying commission after commission to a broker who, friend or brother-in-law though he may be, cannot bring himself to give you the right advice. He'll give you advice on October broilers or the frost in Florida or the technician's report he claims somehow to have seen before anybody else. Gladly. What he won't tell you—or it will cost him dearly if he does—is that you shouldn't be in the game at all.

Class dismissed.

Similarly: antique cars, wine, autographs, stamps, coins, diamonds, art. For two reasons. First, in each case you are competing against experts. If you happen already to be an expert, then you don't need, and won't pay any attention to, my advice anyway. Second, what most people fail to point out as they talk of the marvelously steady appreciation of such investments is that, while what you would have to *pay* for a given lithograph might rise smartly every year (or might not), it's not so easy for the amateur to turn around and sell it. Galleries usually take half the retail price as their cut—so a print that cost $500 and appreciated in five years to $1,000, retail, might bring you all of $500 when you went back to the gallery to sell it. Yes, eBay can narrow the spread and is the preferred way to trade Beanie Babies. But is this investing? Meanwhile, neither print nor wine nor diamonds would have been paying you dividends (other than psychic); indeed, you would have been paying to insure them.

I gave a speech to this effect in Australia many years ago, just as the first faint flaws were beginning to appear in what was then a very hot diamond market. Nothing is forever, I suggested, not even the 15% annual appreciation of diamonds. When I finished, a mustachioed gentleman with a bushy head of previously owned hair came up to say how much he agreed with my remarks. "Diamonds!" he scoffed (you could see the disgust in his face). And for a minute there I thought I had met a kindred spirit. "*Opals!*" he said. "*That's* where the money is!" The fellow, it developed, was an opal salesman.

As a child, I collected "first-day covers" (colorful, specially post-marked envelopes to commemorate the issuance of a new stamp). Sure enough, every year they cost me more and more. Decades later, discovering them in the back of a closet, I called a local collector I had reason to know was on the acquisition trail. (I saw his notice on the supermarket bulletin board.) Knowing you always do better if you can cut out the middleman, I figured on selling them to him direct. These are beautiful first-day covers we are talking about, from the forties and fifties—hundreds of them. They had cost anywhere from 25 cents on up (although, in those days, so had a week in the country).

"How much does your collection weigh?" the buff asked, once I had suitably whetted his interest.

"How much does it *weigh*?" I asked. "Is your collection on a diet? It weighs a few pounds, I guess."

"I'll give you $25 for it," he said. Checking around, I found this was not an unfair price.

Commemorative medallions (and so forth) issued ad nauseam as "instant collectors' items" by the Franklin Mint served to make the original shareholders of the Franklin Mint rich but are much less likely to do the same for you. Their silver, gold, or platinum content is only a fraction of the selling price.

Gold itself pays no interest and costs money to insure. It is a hedge against inflation, all right, and a handy way to buy passage to Liechtenstein, or wherever it is we're all supposed to flee to when the much-ballyhooed collapse finally materializes. But if you're looking for an inflation hedge, you might do better with stocks (even a gold stock or two) or real estate. In the long run, they will rise with inflation, too. And in the short run, they pay dividends and rent.

Broadway shows are fun to invest in, but even if the show you back gets rave reviews, you are likely to lose. A show can linger on Broadway for a year or more, with packed houses on the weekends, and not return its backers a dime.

Chain letters never work.

Things that look like cosmetics companies but are really chain letters in disguise, where the big money to be made is not in selling cosmetics but in selling franchises to sell franchises (to sell cosmetics), don't work either.

Things that involve personal salespeople who are full of enthusiasm at the prospect of making you rich don't work. The richer they hope to make you, the faster you should run.

There are, in fact, very few ways to get rich quick. Fewer still that are legal. Here's one: take $5,000 (borrow it if you have to), place it on 22 at the nearest roulette table, and win $175,000. Don't laugh. Many complicated schemes, if they were stripped of their trappings and somehow reduced to their underlying odds, would be not much less risky. It's the trappings — the story, the pitch — that obscure the odds and persuade people to ante up the $5,000 they'd never dream of betting at roulette.

Anyway, enough of the things that won't do you much good and on to some things that might. The goal of the next chapter is to save you $1,000 a year. Maybe more.

A Penny Saved Is
Two Pennies Earned

"I walked home to save bus fare."
"Gee, you could have saved a lot more by not taking a taxi."

— Old Joke

You are in a higher tax bracket than you think. At least, most people are. And this number — your tax bracket — is critical to understanding your finances.

If you earn $40,000 and pay $4,000 in tax, that does *not* mean you are in the 10% tax bracket (any more than if you earn $240,000 and pay $24,000). On *average,* you are paying 10% of your income in tax, but that's not what's important. What's important in making financial decisions is how much tax you pay on the margin — on the last few dollars that you earn.

Because the income tax is graduated, you pay little tax on the first few dollars you earn but a lot on the last few. That may average out to 10%; but, in the case above, if you earned another $1,000 and you're single, nearly a third of it would go straight to the government ($250 in federal income tax, another $76.50 in Social Security tax), and *that's* your tax bracket: 33%. Unless you happen to be self-employed (add another 7.65%) and/or subject to local income taxes as well (add some more). In New York City, it's not hard to find subway riders, never mind guys in limos, in close to the 50% tax bracket.

To figure your own tax bracket, should you be of a mind to, just haul out last year's federal and local tax returns and calculate how much more tax you'd have had to pay if you had earned an extra $1,000.* If you'd have had to fork over $350 of this hypothetical $1,000 bonus in taxes, you're in the 35% tax bracket. Or thereabouts.

Add in sales tax and property taxes, of course, and the bite is even worse. But such taxes, which are not directly tied to what you earn, don't count in figuring your tax bracket. (Neither does Social Security tax when making many decisions, since it is not levied on investment income and is not reduced by charitable or other "deductions.")

For the sake of simplicity, even though it's an exaggeration for most people, let us assume you are in the 50% bracket, or not far from it. Do you know what that means?

It means that if your boss gave you a $1,000 bonus or raise, you would get to keep $500.

It means that "time-and-a-half for overtime," since it's all earned on the margin, is not such a posh deal after all. After taxes, it may be no more valuable to you than any other "time."

It means, above all, that a penny saved—not spent—is *two* pennies earned.

Consider: If you were planning to go out for dinner tomorrow night, as you do every Thursday night, for around $50 with the tip . . . but you ate at home instead for $10 . . . you'd have saved $40. To *earn* an extra $40, you'd actually have had to earn $80: half for you, half for the tax men.

My point is not that we pay too much in taxes. For whatever comfort it may provide (not much), we get off pretty easy relative to the citizens of most other nations. My point, rather, is that when Ben Franklin said, "A penny saved is a penny earned," there *was* no income tax. There *was* no Social Security tax.

---

* If you use a computer to do your taxes, this calculation is easy. Otherwise, you can get a general idea just by looking at the tables the IRS prints each year—or by checking **irs.gov.** (Note that any additional local taxes could be partially offset by a federal tax deduction —if you itemize your deductions . . . but might not be if you get clipped by the Alternative Minimum Tax. *Promise me you will not try to figure this out.*)

The updated adage would read: "A penny saved is *two* pennies earned." Or nearly so.

So if you want to pile up a little nest egg, or a big one, the first thing you might consider—even though you've doubtless considered it before—is spending less rather than earning more. Which is what this chapter's about. If you're in the 50% tax bracket, it's twice as effective—and often easier.

Charles Revson, the late cosmetics tycoon, bought his mouthwash by the case. By doing so, although it was the furthest thing from his mind, he did better investment-wise than he ever did in the stock market. In the stock market, with his Revlon-made fortune, Revson perennially blew tens of thousands of dollars on one or another speculation. But on Cepacol he was making 20% or 30% a year, tax-free.

He made it two ways: the discount he got for buying the super-economy size, in bulk; and the discount he got, in effect, by beating inflation. He got a year's worth, or two, at last year's price. If he had kept the money he spent on Cepacol in a savings account at 5%—for him back then, 1.5% after tax—and taken it out bit by bit to buy Cepacol in the one-at-a-time $1.19 size, where would he have been?

The lesson is clear, even if you are one of those people with naturally pleasant breath.

Say you're a couple who drink one bottle of red wine every Saturday night. And say, to keep the math simple, you go for the fancy stuff—$10 a bottle. Say, finally, your wine shop is like mine: it offers a 10% discount if you buy by the case. What kind of "investment return" can you "earn" buying by the case? Ten percent? No, it's better than that.

The old way, you paid out $10 every week. Buying by the case, you lay out $108 ($120 for twelve bottles, minus the 10% discount). That means tying up an extra $98, but "earning" a $1 discount on every bottle for doing so. In the course of the year, that comes to $52. That's quite a reward for keeping, at most, an extra $98 tied up throughout the year! It works out to better than a 53% return — tax-free, no less, since the IRS doesn't tax you for smart shopping.*

The goal is not to save $12 on a case of wine, but to do as much of your buying this way as is practical. In the aggregate, it might tie up an extra $1,000. But between beating inflation by buying now and buying in bulk when items are on sale (or getting a by-the-case discount), you could easily stretch $1,000 to buy $1,400 of the very same stuff you'd have bought in the course of the year anyway. And that's a 40% tax-free return on your money — $400 you've managed to save in the course of the year — *with no sacrifice whatever.* It's not enough to make you rich, but neither is $1,000 in a savings account.

This is the chickenhearted way to play commodities, guaranteed safe for all but compulsive eaters. Forget pork bellies on 10% margin and all those other near-surefire ways to get fried. I am "long," as of this writing, several cases of Honest Tea, a case of private-label bathroom tissue, a virtual lifetime supply of trash-can liners, several kegs of Heinz ketchup, and much more. I was "short" sugar years ago, when it ran up to the moon, which is to say I wouldn't buy any. I just ate down my inventory. Wholesale sugar prices subsequently fell from 64 cents back down to 9 cents and I went "long" a few pounds.

Where to put this mountainous investment? Besides the obvious, like a pantry or basement, if you have such spacious digs, you might also consider stashing your hoard under a bed or table, with a bedspread or tablecloth over the top. I know this is absurd, but I'll bet you can fit 30 cases of staples under just one table. Or make it a bench and put a board over it, with a cushion. Water jugs, bouillon cubes, a can opener (don't forget that!) — plan your portfolio, which doubles as a disaster hoard, and buy it on sale, in bulk. (If you're hoarding tuna, you've obviously got to hoard mayonnaise, too.)

---

* Well, actually it works out to 177% — see the appendix for details.

This idea of a disaster hoard, by the way, is not such a foolish one. Nor is it "gloom and doom." Disasters do occur . . . floods, earthquakes, power outages . . . and it does make sense for every household to accumulate—now, when there's no need to, at sale prices—enough nonperishables to last a while. Such a modest stockpiling not only protects individuals, it serves the social interest as well. Just as the nation is stronger if it has strategic stockpiles, so is the social fabric a little less susceptible to disruption or panic if everyone has an added layer of security.

Don't tell me about botulism, either—out of 1.43 trillion cans of food sold between 1926 and 1994 (when I stopped counting), only eight produced fatal cases of botulism. Canned food lasts for years (though soda does tend to go flat).* And if you rotate your cases of food and drink, the way you used to rotate the sheets on your bed in summer camp—top to bottom, bottom to laundry, fresh one on top—you'll never let anything get too far out of date.

If this sort of investment takes up space, it also takes less effort: fewer trips to the store. And you are less likely to run out of things. I don't think there was a day in Charles Revson's life that his breath did not smell medicine-fresh.

What amazes me is that when I first wrote this, in 1978, almost no one did it. Sure, there were thrifty shoppers, and lots of people clipping coupons to get 25 cents off. But there was no Costco or Sam's Club—barely a Walmart—no Trader Joe's or Amazon. By now, who *hasn't* shopped at one of these places? (You? If there's one near you, try it. Anyone can now pay $55 for an annual Costco membership—money back if not satisfied—or $110 for an "executive" membership that gives you a 2% credit at the end of the year. Pay with a Citibank Costco Visa card and you can be earning further cash back at the same time. Just don't assume Costco prices are always lowest. Shop around.)

---

* The guidance you'll find at **stilltasty.com** is way too conservative, if you ask me. I have a case of tuna I expect to be emergency-ready, if I ever need it, *decades* from now.

Herewith, a few more ways to save money (feel free to skim!):

◆ **Fly now, pay now.** The simplest, safest, most sensible way to earn 18% or 20% on your money is to pay off your credit cards. Not having to pay 18% or 20% is as good as earning 18% or 20%. Tax-free! Risk-free! It's folly to pay credit-card interest if you can possibly avoid it.

Still, more than 60% of credit-card holders fail to pay them off within the grace period. In fact, many people keep money in a savings account, earning 1% or 2% after tax—if that—at the same time as they are paying 20% to buy on time. They're earning 2 cents on each dollar with their left hand while paying out 20 cents with their right. That's a loss of 18 cents on every dollar—or, if theirs is a family perpetually $8,000 in hock, $1,440 a year, year after year. Wasted. Credit cards are great for convenience, but terrible for borrowing. Either cut them up, if you can't pay on time; or—if you *can* pay on time—**make your credit cards pay *you*.** Use cards that give you cash back at the end of the year or frequent-flier miles or some other goodie. Check out **bankrate.com, cardoffers.com, creditcards.com,** and especially, if you fly, **milecards.com** to find the best deals.

Frequent-flier cards give you a "mile" for each dollar you charge. If you have an American Express card, sign up for their Membership Rewards program. The miles you earn accumulate in a "bank" for transfer to your frequent-flier accounts at airlines and hotels.

(You should have seen me fighting with the sales manager when I bought my last car. He required a deposit and said I could put it on a credit card. So I naturally tried to put the *whole thing* on the card. An upside-down negotiation ensued, with me trying to give him the biggest possible deposit and him trying to take the smallest.)

Many people go through life paying 18% extra for everything they charge because they don't pay their cards off on time . . . and getting nothing back because they use the wrong cards.

If you have a $3,000 balance at 19.8% and you pay the required monthly minimum (which with some cards remains as low as "2% of the balance or $15, whichever is greater"), *it will take 39 years to pay off the loan*—years longer still if you occasionally suffer a $39 late fee. And you'll pay more than $10,000 in interest. Be one of the smart ones who *earn* 1% or 2% on your cards instead.*

• **Fly now, pay less.** Especially if you find yourself wanting or needing to take a trip on short notice, when the best fares are gone, visit **priceline.com**. You just might save $300 at the cost of having to lay over for an hour in Chicago. And you may not even have to do that. Priceline offers the option of booking the specific flight you want at a set price (instead of "naming your own price"). Just remember: no refunds; so if you think you might need to change your plans, try carriers like JetBlue (**jetblue.com** or 800-JETBLUE), Southwest (**southwest.com** or 800-I-FLY-SWA), and Airtran (**airtran.com**). The one thing *not* to do with Southwest—or any other airline, really, if you can possibly avoid it—is visit a ticket counter. Traveling "ticketless," with an e-ticket, is usually a breeze. Trying to buy, let alone adjust, a ticket at the airport is almost guaranteed to ruin your trip.

Among the sites that make fare-shopping relatively painless: **kayak.com, farechase.com,** and **farecompare.com. Matrix .itasoftware.com** shows you which travel days of the month will be cheapest, if you don't care exactly when you go. **Theflightdeal .com** is great if you don't care exactly *where* you go—you just want to pounce on a crazy "mistake" fare to a place that sounds cool and have an adventure.

(**Skiplagged.com** finds cheap "hidden-city" fares, where the connecting city is your destination so you just skip the second leg of the trip. But this is a breach of the ticket contract and may

---

* Quick tip: Photocopy the contents of your wallet. In case it ever gets stolen, you'll know just what cards—and everything else—you lost.

result in your losing your frequent-flier account, or other penalties. I'd steer clear.)

Finally, two tips on the fee airlines charge for changing a nonrefundable ticket (which can range from zero on Southwest to several hundred dollars on an international fare):

First, if you know nine months in advance that you're going to either Rio or Paris for Christmas (say), consider buying tickets—now—to both. Better to spend $569 each for two tickets bought months in advance, knowing that you'll suffer a $250 penalty for changing the one you don't use—bringing the true cost up to $819—than to wait until the last minute and pay $1,540. Likewise, those winter fares down to Florida. Not sure which weekends you'll be able to get away? Consider buying tickets for four weekends—now—at $269 each, knowing that you'll likely suffer penalties on a couple of them. All four combined could cost less than one would cost if purchased just a few days before you fly.

Second, even though it takes a little more effort, it generally makes sense to book two one-way tickets rather than a single round trip. That way, if you need to change the outbound flight, at least the cheap return flight will still be valid.

• **Stay cheap.** You can save a fortune through the aforementioned **priceline.com.** The only time I don't use Priceline is when I think I may have to change the dates of my trip—Priceline offers *no refunds* when you "name your own price"—or when I need to stay at a specific hotel (because that's where the convention is). Otherwise, I specify the city and neighborhood, the number of "stars" I want—I like four-star hotels—and then bid really low. Many is the time I've stayed in a $300 room for $89. If you're not as spoiled as I am, specify two or three stars.

To decide how much to bid, go to **expedia.com, orbitz.com,** or **hotels.com** to see what kinds of deals they're offering; then bid at least 30% less at Priceline.

The part I love is where Priceline comes back with a message to the effect of, "Are you *kidding*?" Hold firm—and minutes later, the room may well be yours.

If you do bid too low, Priceline generally makes you wait a day before rebidding—unless you make some change in your request, which is very easy to do. Just add a second neighborhood you'd be willing to consider, or change the number of stars. (To become a pro, visit **biddingfortravel.com.** You'll learn all the tricks of the Priceline trade and see recent prices at which bids have been accepted.)

Hotwire.com offers excellent hotel deals, like Priceline concealing the hotel name until you've booked it. **Newyorkhotel .com** represents the Empire Hotel Group. All their hotels have oversize rooms by Manhattan standards and reasonable prices. Though you won't get as good a deal as you would bidding blind through Priceline, you'll know your hotel *and* be able to cancel without penalties.

For the more adventuresome, there are hostels (**hostelz.com**), couches (**couchsurfing.org**), and of course **airbnb.com.**

And if you're not one to plan ahead, try **hoteltonight.com** for a great last-minute price.

♦ **Avoid the mini-bar,** room service, or even the hallway Coke machine. Instead, give the next wide-mouthed plastic beverage container you empty a permanent spot in your overnight bag along with a few Crystal Light On the Go packets. Total weight added to your luggage? Minimal. Homeland Security issues? Zero. (Neither liquid nor gel.) So now you check in to your hotel, fill the ice bucket with complimentary ice, empty a Crystal Light packet into the plastic container, add water and ice, shake like crazy—and you've just saved anywhere from $3 to $12 depending on how you travel. (The packets themselves run around 33 cents* and make the equivalent of two glasses of a cold drink

---

* I do understand you could just . . . drink water. And save even the 33 cents. But I need to taste something. Hey: live large.

that room service would send up at $4 each plus service charge, tax, tip, and the time it takes to *wait* for room service.) Over a three-day stay, even if you'd otherwise just go down the hall to use the $1.50-a-can vending machine, you save a fortune — and avoid having to get dressed again to go down the hall. The nutritional value is questionable, I grant you. But could Crystal Light be any worse for you than soft drinks that corrode car bumpers?

• **Rent cars cheap.** If you are going on a long road trip, consider **priceline.com** (yet again) for a bargain-priced rental to spare wear and tear on your own car, and so that in the event of a breakdown you're not stuck 600 miles from home.

• **Vacation cheap.** Priceline lets you build a package where you can see the resort hotel, the flights, and the rental car *before* you commit to purchase.

(This may be an appropriate place to mention that I have no connection to, or ownership interest in, Priceline.)

And consider lower-cost "alternate" locales. For a tropical getaway, *Kiplinger's* suggests trading Costa Rica for Fiji. For Old World European charm: Budapest for Vienna. Wine tasting? California's Sierra Foothills region over Napa Valley. French cuisine and architecture? Quebec.

• **Don't finance your car.** As with credit cards, not paying 5% on a car loan is as good as earning 5%. Risk-free! Tax-free!

"Ah," you are thinking. "Surely he is not now going to tell me I should pay off my mortgage." And I am not — although if it was taken out at 7%, and 4% mortgages are available as you read this, why, then, surely it has crossed your mind to refinance. And even paying down a 4% mortgage is not a *bad* investment. It's simply the equivalent of a completely safe 4% return. The difference between a house and a car is that a car depreciates, while a house, over time, may appreciate. Plus, the interest on a mortgage is tax-deductible, while the interest on a car loan is not.

Can't afford to buy a car for cash? Well, then . . .

◆ **Buy a used car.** It could be really depressing to *have to* do this. But when it's *your* decision, to reach *your* goals, that's another story. And it will save you thousands of dollars. That "new-car smell" is the most expensive fragrance in the world.

◆ **Buy an economical car.** If you purchase a car that averages 36 miles to the gallon instead of 18 . . . and if an average gallon of gas over the next few years costs four bucks . . . then after having driven 36,000 miles you'll have saved $4,000, cash, on gas alone. What's more, the cars that get the best gas mileage often cost the least. This despite the fact that in terms of their most important feature—getting you where you're going—they are identical to the higher-priced models. By buying an "economy car" you save substantially on the purchase price, substantially on your insurance bill (the less expensive the car, the lower the theft and collision premiums), substantially on gas, substantially on maintenance, and substantially on interest (if you finance the purchase). In all, the financial decision to be "automotively frugal"—while it is a decision you have every right not to make—could easily mean as much to you, after tax, as a $5,000 raise.

◆ **Resist the temptation to lease.** First off, it generally means a new car, so you're paying for that smell. Second, it means financing almost the entire thing—but with a hidden interest rate. (Hint: They're not hiding it because it's low.) Third, it's just a lot more complicated, with more potential pitfalls, than buying a car outright. If you're a budding salesperson, light on cash, who needs a new car to impress clients and who can deduct the cost for tax purposes, leasing may make sense (in that case, check out LeaseWise at CarBargains, discussed below). But if you're just driving to work or school or the supermarket, leasing is ordinarily the most expensive way to go.

◆ **Finance your car (if you must) with a home-equity loan.** One way to pay off your credit-card debt and your car loan is to borrow against the equity in your home, if you own one. Home-equity loans are like huge credit cards you can draw on and pay back, in full or in part, as often as you like. They generally carry much lower interest rates than credit cards and somewhat lower rates than car loans; and the interest you pay is generally tax-deductible. If you currently pay $3,000 a year in credit-card and car-loan interest, replacing all that debt with a home-equity loan could save you $1,500, between the lower interest rate and the value of the tax deduction.

The risk: you'll hock your home and then—credit junkie that you are—run those credit cards right back up again. If this sounds like you, take out the home-equity loan but *cut up* all your credit cards.

And even then there are risks. What sense is there in taking out a 20-year loan to pay for a six-year automobile? (Or a two-week vacation?) With nothing forcing you to pay off the loan over the life of the car, it's quite possible you won't. When it comes time to buy a new one, you'll just go deeper into debt. Instead of owning your home free and clear at retirement, you could find yourself mortgaged to the hilt. Wise use of a home-equity loan requires self-discipline.

If a home-equity loan doesn't work for you—perhaps you don't *own* a home—your best bet will be a credit union loan. If you don't belong to one, your regular bank will often have a better rate than the dealership. Either way, buy the car based on its *total price,* not by comparing monthly payments. You'd be amazed how many people unwittingly pay $1,000 more than they need to for the car—and perhaps another extra $1,000 in interest—because the 60-month car loan made the payments lower than the 36-month loan. **You want to borrow as little as possible, as cheaply as possible, for as short a time as possible.**

If you do opt for a home-equity loan, seek a lender offering "no points" and minimal up-front fees.* That saves a chunk of

---

* Each point is 1% of the loan. Three points on a $100,000 loan equals $3,000, cash, up front. And on refinancings, points are *not* deductible all at once, but rather over the life of the loan—just $100 a year in the case of a 30-year loan with $3,000 in points.

cash, and you'll have lost less if you ever decide to move or refinance.

• **Don't be fooled by 1.9% financing.** When you see one of those deals offering 1.9% financing—or $1,500 cash back—*take the cash.* Otherwise, you're buying a $19,500 car for $21,000, albeit at a good low rate of interest. It's just one more way to lull you into paying more than you should.

• **Haggle**—at least when it comes to buying or leasing cars. Among the websites that offer helpful tools and free quotes: **auto bytel.com, autoweb.com, intellichoice.com,** and **autos.msn .com.** You will only get quotes from dealers who have worked out referral agreements with that website, and if you live in a rural area, you may not even find one of those. But it's worth a shot.

Or try **carbargains.com,** a buying service operated by a nonprofit consumer group. For $200, they solicit bids from at least five dealers in your area. Even when the fee is taken into account, CarBargains frequently wins online comparative shopping tests. They also operate **leasewise.com,** for leases.

Or visit the no-haggle buying service at **costcoauto.com.**

Visit **edmunds.com** to find out what you should pay—or the value of the vehicle in your driveway. Also, Kelley Blue Book —**kbb.com.**

• **Skip the trade-in.** Sure it's easier just to leave the old car there and drive off in the newly purchased one. Dealers know that and use it to their advantage. If you separate the buying and the selling, you are likely to come out ahead. Your goal: get the best deal you can on the car you buy. Then get a decent deal on the car you sell, perhaps to a neighbor or through the classifieds or **craigslist.com.**

• **Drive smoothly.** Rapid accelerations are murder on gas mileage; unnecessary braking converts energy, through friction, to heat. "Good driving habits," properly inflated tires, and a well-tuned engine can save as much as a third of a family's gasoline bill.

◆ **Beat traffic.** That saves gas. The app, as you probably know, is **waze.com.**

◆ **Buy *no* car.** Seriously: if you're a city-dweller (or live on campus), check out **zipcar.com** to see whether it could work for you. You pay $7 a month to "borrow" cars—and pickup trucks—for an hourly rate, starting at $8, that includes gas and insurance. Compared with the $9,000 a year you could easily spend on parking, insurance, maintenance, and—of course—car payments, even liberal use of Zipcar could save a fortune.

◆ **Better still, get chauffeured around.** That's what I do. I haven't owned a car in years. **Uber.com** and **lyft.com** are so easy—and in many cities cheaper than cabs. With never any need to search for parking, get inspected, get repaired, fight tickets, stop for gas . . . or even remain awake. Text all you like while someone else is driving.

◆ **When buying auto or homeowner's insurance, shop around**—call GEICO (800-861-8380) or visit **geico.com,** among others, for a quote. Progressive Insurance (**progressive.com**) offers not just its own quote over the phone (800-288-6776) but, in many states, rates for State Farm and two others as well—even when the competition is cheaper. So one call does the work of four. Try, also, **insweb.com.**

◆ **Self-insure** by choosing the highest "deductible" you can comfortably afford. This usually means eating the first $500 or $1,000 of loss yourself, instead of $100 or $250. But unless you're dreadfully unlucky, your savings in premiums over a lifetime will more than cover the extra unreimbursed losses. This is especially true because even people who are fully insured hesitate to hit their insurance companies for small claims, knowing that their rates may rise if they do. Why pay for coverage you may not even use? Generally, there's no point in paying someone else to take a risk that you can afford to take yourself. After all, they're not doing it as a favor. They plan to make a profit even after paying all their overhead, marketing, and sales costs. Why not keep all that yourself? Besides money, you'll save yourself the hassle and aggravation of making claims.

The ultimate deductible, of course, if you've bought a ratty old used car—my favorite kind—is to skip collision and theft coverage altogether. Who would steal it?

◆ **When buying life insurance, it's the same advice:** *Shop around.* There are two basic kinds: "term" and "whole life" (also called "straight" or "ordinary" or "permanent" or "universal" or "variable"). With term insurance all you pay for—and get—is protection. If you die, they pay. With whole life you are buying a tax-sheltered savings plan as well. Your policy accumulates "cash values."

Term insurance rates start very low but go up every year. Whole-life rates start high but remain constant.

Insurance reps are eager to sell whole-life policies because their commissions are so much higher. But you would be wiser to buy renewable term insurance and do your saving separately. (With a renewable policy you are assured of continuing coverage even if your health deteriorates.)

The problems with whole life:

◆ Many policies pay low interest.

◆ It is impossible for a nonexpert to tell a good policy from a bad one.

◆ There is a tremendous penalty for dropping the policy, as many people do, after just a few years.

◆ Most young families can't afford the protection they need if they buy whole life. The same dollars will buy five or six times as much term insurance.

◆ In later years, and particularly beyond the age of 50 or 55, term insurance premiums rise rapidly. But by then you may have a less urgent need for life insurance. The kids may be grown, the mortgage paid off, the pension benefits vested. You will still need to build substantial assets for retirement, and to protect your spouse; but there are better ways to save for old age than whole life.

To find a good low rate on term life insurance, try **accu quote.com, findmyinsurance.com,** or **insweb.com.**

To determine how much life insurance you need—if any—see the appendix we've artfully titled "How Much Life Insurance Do You Need?"

If you already have a whole-life policy, don't feel bad—and don't necessarily drop it. With hindsight, you might have done better buying term insurance and, say, putting the difference into a Roth IRA. But you are building a valuable tax-advantaged nest egg, nonetheless. What's more, you've already *paid* the upfront charges; dropping the policy won't get them back. For an expert $100 evaluation of an investment-type policy you currently own or are considering, visit **evaluatelifeinsurance.org,** a website of the Consumer Federation of America.

Insurance agents hate the phrase "buy term and invest the difference." They counter it by arguing people *won't* invest the difference—they'll squander it. And that is definitely a risk. But who's to say, if you're a squanderer, you're not also one of the great number of policyholders—something like 25%—who will let their expensive whole-life policies lapse within the first few years? That's *really* squandering it.

• **Beware variable universal life.** I'm sorry to make you keep reading about this boring stuff, but there's a whole army of personable, well-intentioned salespeople lurking out there, and you need to be forewarned. (Look! Over there! Behind that tree!) If you do want an "investment type" whole-life policy for some reason, fine—check out **tiaa-cref.org, usaa.com, ameritas.com,** and **northwesternmutual.com.** But beware variable universal life.

Every life insurance salesperson seems to have learned the same script (you'll know it's the script the moment you hear the phrase "Swiss army knife"). Supposedly, you can put as much or as little as you want into one of these plans, pay with pretax dollars, invest in lots of different tax-free ways, and withdraw the accumulated cash value tax-free whenever you want. Unfortunately, the much-touted tax advantages are usually exaggerated. And they are dwarfed, in most cases, by the various charges and hidden expenses. Consider:

- There will be roughly 6% in sales fees and state premium taxes on each dollar you invest. With the best policies, it's as low as 3%, but these are not the ones being promoted by commissioned salespeople—and why lose even 3%?

- There will usually be a contract charge averaging $400 to establish the policy, and periodic administration charges averaging $100 a year.

- There will be overblown "insurance" charges on the money invested in stock and bond funds comparable to those of variable annuities, decried in a later chapter.

- There will be the management expenses (usually around 1% per year—five times what an index fund might charge).

- The cost of the life insurance you're buying—as separate from the investment component—is typically too high.

- The implication that you can raise or lower the amount of life insurance coverage at will is misleading. To raise it, you may need to prove that you are still insurable. To lower it, you bump into the IRS's "corridor" rule, which requires coverage until you're 95, whether you need it or not.

- The implication that you can withdraw funds tax-free is also often overblown. You can't withdraw tax-free any more than you actually contributed in premiums. Above that, the only way to get at the money "tax-free" is to borrow it, paying nondeductible interest. Yet the IRS requires that you keep the policy in force. If your much-touted "tax-free withdrawals" and loans deplete the account too much to keep up with the premiums, the policy will collapse, all previous loans will become withdrawals—and you'll owe ordinary income tax on anything you took out above your contributions.

- When the growth in your investments is withdrawn, it's taxed at ordinary income rates, even if that growth resulted from long-term capital gains. Congratulations: you've just paid the insurance company all these fees to convert what would have been lightly taxed long-term gains into heavily taxed ordinary income.

Buy term life insurance and invest the difference.

- **Skip insurance you *don't* need,** including life insurance for children (a good buy only if your child is a movie star and you depend on his or her earning power); credit life insurance, offered as an option when you take out a loan (a good buy only for the elderly or terminally ill); flight insurance (a good buy never —only about a nickel of each dollar it costs goes to pay claims; the rest is marketing expense and profit); cancer insurance (it makes no sense to buy health insurance one disease at a time); car rental insurance (if your credit card or your own auto insurance policy covers you, as many do).

Skip particularly "appliance insurance"—extended warranties on your refrigerator or washer/dryer. Even if you remember you have this insurance years from now, when the appliance breaks, and even if the time you have to spend collecting on it is minimal—two big ifs—why pay someone to insure a risk you can afford yourself? Over the years, you will come out way ahead by resisting the salesperson's attempts to sign you up.

- **Phone free.** You don't use **skype.com**? Seriously? It's free when calling other Skypers, nearly free calling traditional landlines and cell phones—all over the world.

- **Cut your cell phone bill.** If you need a cell mainly for emergencies, short chats, and texting, buy a TracFone (**tracfone .com**). There are no contracts and, since this is prepaid cellular, no danger of your tween texting you out of house and home. If you're a heavier user, Walmart's **straighttalk.com** may save you money—as I write, $45/month for unlimited service.

- **Drop your landline.** Check out **magicjack.com, ooma.com,** and **vonage.com.** (But if your Internet goes out, so does your phone; so perhaps keep a single landline with the cheapest, absolute most basic service, for emergencies.)

- **Go Prime.** Where would I be without **amazon.com**? I buy so much stuff there, the $99-a-year "Amazon Prime" free shipping pays for itself over and over; not to mention the time and expense previously required to actually, physically *shop,* nor to mention the million songs and thousands of books, movies, and TV shows you get free access to, or the unlimited photo storage.

- **Use the Internet. (Well, duh!)** In the first edition of this book I suggested everyone get a copy of the Sears catalog—not necessarily to shop from, but as a handy reference point for what everything cost. Ah, brave new world: that iconic catalog is long gone and now, to buy—or sell—*anything,* new or used, there's **ebay.com** and **craigslist.com** and the aforementioned Amazon.

  Angieslist.com's million members review service companies, contractors, and doctors (rejecting anonymous reviews, for more reliability).

  Pricegrabber.com can help with comparison shopping.

  Retailmenot.com will tell you whether there are promotional coupons to use at checkout.

  Great cheap clothes? **Uniqlo.com.**

  For most financial products, like insurance or a mortgage refinancing, **quicken.com** is worth a visit. Don't miss **fairmark .com** to help you with tax questions . . . **hsh.com, bankrate .com,** and **banx.com** for locating good home and auto loan rates

. . . **moving.com** for quotes on moving expenses and help selecting local realtors . . . **move.com** for tips on home maintenance, repairs, and improvements, and ways of reducing costs other than the mortgage . . . **nolo.com** before spending money on a lawyer.

Money-saving blogs include **wisebread.com, dealseeking mom.com,** and **frugaltraveler.blogs.nytimes.com.** Every week **carnivalofpersonalfinance.com** showcases its favorite blog posts from around the Web.

◆ **Use the government. (It invented the Internet!*)** Use **usa .gov** to find almost anything—from contact info for your local state representative to food-safety tips to help starting a business to help finding a new job to passport issues to buying stuff at government auctions . . . take a minute or two now just to see the huge range of resources it makes available.

◆ **If you use a discount broker, use a *deep-discount* broker** instead (see page 273). You'll save even more.

◆ **Double-check your bank.** I had an adjustable-rate mortgage on an apartment building. OK, a very small apartment building in a very modest part of town. OK, a slum. The point is, it started out in February 1992 as a $400,000 mortgage at 7.5%, to be paid off ("amortized") over ten years. After 12 months, I got a notice lowering my rate to 7% and telling me to pay $4,670.51 instead of the $4,748.07 I had been paying. In entering this into my computer, I noticed they were asking for $17.22 a month more than they should. But on such a large loan, I figured I'd just chalk it up to not wanting to start "a thing."

After 12 more months, I got a notice that the interest rate would still be 7%—unchanged—yet telling me to pay a *different* monthly amount. Hello? I took a closer look and found that they showed my unpaid principal—the amount I still owed

---

* Well, DARPA did, and that's part of the government.

—as being about $7,000 higher than my computer thought it should be. Now this was getting serious. Seventeen bucks is one thing. Seven thousand is another. But the point I want to make here is: Without checking, who would have known? Who possibly has the kind of instincts that would tell him the unpaid principal on a loan like this should be $341,091.50 by April 1994, not $348,940.01? Dustin Hoffman in *Rain Man*? Forget it! The man counted toothpicks.

Brought to the bank's attention, it developed that they had hit me up for $6,800 plus interest in "force-placed insurance." The way that works: Their computer looks for confirmation that your insurance has been renewed. If no one tells it "yes," then it sends you a notice telling you that the bank, to protect its interest, has "force-placed" a policy on the property at your expense, and, incidentally, this is the most expensive insurance policy in the history of the world. So you call and tell them, politely, to get their greedy little hands off your property—you *did* renew the insurance—and you fax them the renewal to prove it. They politely assure you that they won't hit you up for the insurance, after all. But, in this case, they did anyway. When I complained, I got a nice letter from the bank adjusting my unpaid balance down by $7,098.85.

Banks make mistakes. (Years ago, along with my bank statement, I once got the checks of a Chinese laundry. "What do you want me to do?" I asked the bank. "Send them to the laundry," answered the bank.) Especially with adjustable-rate mortgages, errors sometimes do creep in. Be sure to double-check your statement each time the payment is adjusted. **Myamortizationchart .com** may help with that. Note: Banks sometimes force-place insurance on car loans, too. Beware.

♦ **For help with college tuition,** visit **finaid.org.** And as you contemplate loan options, heed the words of my friend Less Antman: "Never, never, never take out a private loan to finance college costs." Federal loans offer far more flexible options for reducing required payments or even canceling loan balances in the event of hardship or ten years of government service.

• **If you have student loans,** you may be able to save money and/or make your life easier by consolidating them: **loancon solidation.ed.gov.** If your payments are high and your income low, don't miss **ibrinfo.org** to learn about income-based repayment. If your credit is good and/or prospects bright, use **sofi .com** to refinance at what could be a much lower rate.

• **To *avoid* student loans,** check out *Debt-Free U: How I Paid for an Outstanding College Education Without Loans, Scholarships, or Mooching Off My Parents* by Zac Bissonnette. (High concept: the expensive private colleges aren't worth going into debt for, and there are lots of ways to make money while still in school.)

Another way to avoid borrowing for college is not to go. You won't find *me* advocating that; but from a strict financial perspective note, first, that if you compare apples to apples—kids *with comparable SAT scores* who have or lack college degrees—the vaunted wage gap narrows somewhat. One study shows it at 22% a decade or so out from high school graduation . . . which must be balanced against the *cost* of college plus what they might have *earned* during those years. Second, it's the *degree* that counts most in boosting your future income—don't go unless you really plan to finish. (And consider a two-year community-college degree which, by your demonstrating seriousness of purpose and the discipline to reach a goal, could be worth more in the job market than *three* years of study someplace *without* completing the degree. You could always then transfer to a four-year school.) Third, try to finish on time. Not to say you shouldn't go nuts partying, switching majors, and all the other things that could stretch four years to six—but financially, that's a killer.

If you do have to drop out for a while, or transfer schools, there are, at this writing, three fully accredited colleges in the United States that accept virtually all transfer credits from previous schools. They also allow you to test out of nearly all the classes needed for many basic bachelor's degrees. Remaining classes can be taken online. In fact, you can earn degrees at these colleges for under $10,000 and complete your work in far less than four years if sufficiently motivated.

They are: Charter Oak State College—part of the Connecticut state college system; Thomas Edison State College—part of the New Jersey state college system; Excelsior University—a nonprofit college that began as part of the New York state college system before being split off.

"Don't confuse these three with for-profit colleges that advertise heavily and offer degrees that are not regionally accredited," writes Less Antman. Nor with diploma mills. "While they are incredibly flexible, all three require clear demonstration of competence before awarding credits and ultimately a degree. The difference from traditional colleges is that they award credits based solely on demonstrated mastery of the material without requiring class attendance. This is known as Competency-Based Education."

In a sense, earning a traditional college degree involves attending classes and passing 40 final exams. Competency-based education involves just passing the 40 final exams. See **home schoolcollegeusa.com** for more on *becoming* competent.

All that said: if you think you want to and can afford it (some of the best schools will make sure you get the aid you need), go to college! Life is not a business!

♦ **Save energy.** Simple insulation (and even simpler weather stripping) may be the best "investment" you can make, returning as much as 35% or more, tax-free, in annual savings on heating and cooling. Why put $1,000 into the stock of some utility and earn $40 in annual taxable dividends if you can put the same money into insulation and save $350—tax-free—on your utility bill? Check, also, the various credits that may be available to encourage such energy-saving investment. Your electric company will know about these and may offer a free "energy audit" to show you how to cut your bills most effectively.

Want to earn a phenomenal return on $25 or $50? Go buy a six-pack of LED light bulbs. I used to light my kitchen with four 100-watt dimmable floods—400 watts. Now four much-longer-lasting 6-watt dimmable LEDs serve just as well—24 watts. Saves 94%! And the planet. The $4 60-watt-equivalent LED I'm looking at as I type this comes with a manufacturer's claim of $113 in lifetime savings—almost surely an exaggeration. But if $4 saves you even *$20* over a decade, what kind of stock or bond could possibly match that? Tax-free, no less!

◆ **Reverse your airflow.** Why do we need it to be 78 degrees in the winter, when it's cold outside, and 70 degrees in the summer, when it's hot? A willingness to reverse these two settings can save a heap of dough.

Ceiling fans can be a good investment—in the summer, obviously, for their wind-chill effect; but also—if you flip a switch in the winter to reverse their flow—forcing the hotter air, that wants to rise, back down toward your toes. (Or flip the angle of the blades; most ceiling fans make it easy to do one or the other.)

◆ **Buy a pool blanket**—an enormous sheet of bubble wrap. Mine cost $125 and, left on when the pool is not in use, raises the water temperature by at least 10 degrees, extends the swimming season by several weeks, and even saves on the cost of water (less evaporation). Compare that to the $300 a week my neighbor spends on propane.

◆ **Diamonds are . . . ridiculous.** Beautiful, yes, but diamonds are also a lot more expensive than they would be if DeBeers hadn't organized the world diamond cartel so efficiently, and hadn't persuaded starry-eyed young men that, to *be* men, they have to devote two months' pretax pay to the purchase of an engagement ring.

I never thought I would actually write the words "cubic zirconia," but visit **diamond-essence.com** and be dazzled by the possibilities. You could do worse than to risk $139 on a two-carat ring that could otherwise cost $20,000.

And, OK, yes, these are fake diamonds. But about the only way for a layperson to *tell* they are fake is to scratch them with real diamonds. And what kind of people go around at parties doing that? Especially since *their* real diamonds are locked away in a safe-deposit box, and they're wearing fake ones, too.

Do you remember Moh's Hardness Scale? I do! It runs from 1 to 10, with TALC being softest, at 1, then GYPSUM, CALCITE, FLUORITE, SOMETHING, FELDSPAR, QUARTZ, BERYL, RUBY, DIAMOND. Ta-da! (Ah, those endless, lonely childhood hours.) Diamond is 10. But quartz, at 7, is pretty darn hard, as you surely know, so if these $139 suckers are 9, and can scratch *quartz,* for crying out loud . . . can scratch *beryl* . . . can hold their own against *rubies* — well, surely such a ring, along with matching his-and-her $5,000 Roth IRAs, is the wiser way to demonstrate your love and commitment.

On your 50th anniversary, she'll still have the ring. But you'll also have — just by accepting a 9-hardness stone instead of a 10 — an extra $114,000, after-tax, in today's buying power to help make your golden years joyous. (This assumes a return 5% above inflation, and from just one investment of $5,000 apiece in the matching his-and-her Roth IRAs. Contribute $5,000 apiece *every* year at that rate, and on your 50th anniversary you will have, between the two of you, an extra $2.2 million.)

You take the trinkets; I'll take Manhattan.

♦ **Stagger your tax deductions.** A lot of people find that they have almost enough deductions to make itemizing worthwhile — but not quite. If you fit this category, or if you have barely enough deductions to itemize and thus save very little by doing so, consider bunching your deductions into every second year. Plan to itemize in 2017 and 2019, for example, but to take the standard deduction in 2016 and 2018. *Don't* make the year-end charitable gifts you normally would in 2016—make them in January 2017. (Likewise, local tax payments and any other potential deductions you may be able to push into 2017.) Come December 2017, *do* make your charitable contributions, prepay local taxes, and so forth. In half the years, you'll have the same standard deduction you would have had anyway. But in the other half you might find yourself with an extra $4,000 or $5,000 in deductions. That will save $1,000 or $2,000 on your tax bill every second year.

◆ **Prepare your *own* taxes.** If you've been paying $100 or more to do your taxes, do 'em yourself and save all that money. Easier than you think. See page 133.

◆ **Save on software.** Two things worth paying for are a computer (if you can't get one free through **freecycle.org**) and a high-speed Internet connection. But software? If you just bought your computer, head over to **ninite.com** and select the programs you want to install to get going. (Don't miss Dropbox, for backing up your work and syncing it with your other computers; and check out Evernote, a tool to store and retrieve everything that interests you.) For an extraordinary list of free software and expert reviews, visit Gizmo's Freeware at **techsupportalert.com.** Or go to **osalt.com,** search on the name of any popular commercial software, and it will list free alternatives.

In prehistoric times, my face was on a fantastic set of floppy disks (you're too young to know what those were) called Managing Your Money. List price: $199 a copy. Today you can keep all your finances organized at **mint.com.** Free.

◆ **Get free tech support.** Before you pay Microsoft, try **tech guy.org.**

◆ **Trim your *own* hair.** ("And tuck in your shirt," advises Mom. "*Look* at you!") You can have your hair cut every three weeks at $25 a clip—$425 a year—or you can get one of those $5 stainless-steel razor-blade Tinkle haircutting doohickeys (they look like combs with razor blades safely out of reach) and save, over five years, $2,125 plus maybe 100 hours of getting to, sitting in, and returning from the barber's chair.

Or have it cut professionally a few times a year and touch it up yourself the rest of the time.

• **Walk.** Save a dollar by not taking the bus—or ten by not taking a cab.

• **Crunch.** If you love your gym membership—great. But if the real goal is to stay fit, not to meet people, then consider this: you can be a man or woman of steel if you do no more than push-ups and crunches (little half sit-ups) on a towel on your floor —everyone has a floor—and you can have a healthy heart if you take a vigorous walk or run every day or two. Canceling the gym membership doesn't mean you can *never* visit. But for some, paying the occasional day rate will cost less than the full fare.

• **Listen.** The two biggest obstacles to exercise are laziness and boredom. The biggest obstacle to reading books is finding time. The biggest problem with *listening* to books while exercising is the cost. **Audible.com** solves all these problems. For about $20 a month you get your choice of two books—so they cost $10 each instead of $30. I have walked across America with Lewis and Clark listening to *Undaunted Courage* (while I shopped for groceries) and built the Panama Canal listening to *The Path Between the Seas* (while loping around my neighborhood). How long is Ayn Rand's (ridiculous but fun) *Atlas Shrugged*? I'll tell you exactly: for me, it was 347 miles.

• **Use the library.** Even cheaper than Audible or Amazon are the books and audio books you can borrow from the local library. Instead of a movie, popcorn, and Coke for the four of you —$80—how about a trip to the library where everyone has an hour to explore and meet up back at the checkout? Then hot fudge sundaes at home? We all know that if something is free, it's perceived to have little value. And few people love movies more than I do. But how often have you heard people say of a movie, "It wasn't as good as the book"?

So read the book!

If this ruse worked with your kids once a month, you'd be saving $900 a year, not to mention the educational possibilities. (Seriously: don't mention them.)

◆ **Get TiVo** or one of the cheaper cable-company-provided alternatives. It's a life-changer. Just by fast-forwarding through the commercials and an occasional segment that doesn't interest me, I watch the evening news in 20 minutes instead of 30. That *alone* saves 60 hours a year. Sixty hours! Time is money! There are a million other reasons to love TiVo (*60 Minutes* in 45, *Seinfeld* reruns in 23, the ability to watch on your schedule, not theirs); but on the evening news alone, if my time is worth $3 an hour, that's $180 a year.

(Of course, if you're really struggling to get out of credit-card debt, *no* unnecessary expense is worth making until you've met your goal—even TiVo.)

◆ **Get Netflix.** For $9 a month, you can watch all the movies (and TV shows) you want. If it saved you one $80 movie night a month, you'd net an $852 annual savings.

◆ **At the movies,** for the nights you do go, share your popcorn (one medium costs pennies more than two smalls) and, depending on whom you're with—and your morbid fear of "backwash" —consider $4.75 for one large soda and two straws instead of $9 for two mediums.

◆ **Cancel cable.** Not me—I'm old. But kids these days? *They don't even have TVs!* (That's the problem with kids these days! They don't watch enough television!) They stream everything —and if you do, too, that can save you $1,000 a year. Visit **can celcable.com.**

+ **For family vacations,** give each child a predetermined sum that has to last the whole trip. You'd still pay all the basics—travel, meals, tickets to the water park. This allowance would be for the completely optional extras. Your kids will learn to make the money last over the specified number of days and to weigh each purchase more carefully. Good life lessons. Meanwhile, you may be spared the begging for trinkets and candy, because that's now all at *their* discretion. If, under this system, your kids turn suddenly frugal and actually end up with some leftover cash, good for them. It's theirs to keep. Indeed, as a life lesson in delayed gratification, you might even offer, up front, to *double* whatever they have left over at the end.

+ **Avoid lottery tickets.** They pay barely 50 cents in prizes for every dollar sucked in; and since all the big prizes are heavily taxed, the odds are even worse. Heads you win 30 cents, tails you lose $1.

+ **Bargain down your credit-card fees.** If yours charges an annual fee, call to see whether they'll match those that don't. It's cheaper for them to say yes than to replace you.

+ **Quit smoking.** At a pack a day, there's $2,000 to $4,000 a year right there. Tell your teenager you don't *care* about her health or soon-to-yellow teeth, you care about her *money*. The decision to develop a saving rather than a smoking habit makes a huge difference. One way, she puts $2,000 a year into Newports and, at age 65, has cancer. The other way, she puts it into a mutual fund that compounds at 7.5% a year and, at 65, has $1 million.*

And guess what: *Allen Carr's Easy Way to Stop Smoking* really *has* helped millions of people quit without cost or pain.

---

* Smokers also spend more on life insurance, cold remedies, and health care. The Tobacco Institute may not have been convinced smoking kills, but the three life insurers *owned* by tobacco companies long have been. All three charge smokers about double for term life insurance. Meanwhile, a division of Dow Chemical found that smokers averaged 5.5 more days of absence from work each year and took eight more days of disability leave.

◆ **Buy the store brand.** Private-label merchandise is often made on the same production line, with the same ingredients, as the more expensive advertised brands. Aspirin is aspirin, no matter how elaborate the commercials get.* Bleach is bleach. It is a sad fact of American consumer patterns that poor people in particular avoid private-label brands, despite the potential savings — so persuasive is national advertising. For example, private-label shaving cream is occasionally on sale at $1.29. Believe me, it works just as well as the name brands on the next shelf that sell for $2.79.

Granted, not all private-label merchandise is as good as its name-brand competition. None of it, presumably, is better. You will never find *me* eating any ketchup other than Heinz. But is it really worth 80% more to you to sneeze into a genuine Kleenex-brand "kleenex"?

◆ No matter what you buy, **pay attention as your order is rung up.** Make sure you weren't charged for more than you received.

◆ **But wait!** Lisa B of Atlanta suggests **"the 48-hour rule."** She writes: "My husband and I have lived the principles in your book as long as we've been married. We've never lived cheap. Just smart. No unnecessary debt. Live below the paycheck. Don't pay interest, *receive* interest. The 48-hour rule before purchases means if we find something we like, like a sweater or a pair of boots, we wait 48 hours before we buy it. If we still want it, go get it. Most of the time, I don't even remember what it was that I considered buying."

◆ **Eat cheaper** — register one of your credit cards with **rewards network.com** and get some *extra* miles or hotel points or cash

---

* *Consumer Reports* has been devastating in comparing such brands as Bayer, Bufferin, Anacin, and Excedrin with plain private-label aspirin. The difference is almost entirely in price, with here and there some caffeine or a trace of antacid or an aspirin-like analgesic thrown in. At one store, they found a 100-tablet bottle of generic aspirin for 99 cents versus Bayer for $4.99.

back each time you dine. Just remember that it's still a lot cheaper to have Pepsi and pasta at home.

◆ **Eat less meat.** Beef? Consider pork. Pork? Consider chicken. Chicken? Try the rigatoni. The further down the food chain you go, the less it costs and, often, the better it is for you (and the planet).

◆ **Eat *less.*** The average male American waistline has grown nearly 5 inches, from 35 to 39.7, since 1960; the average female waistline, 7 inches. The standard 9-inch dinner plate is now often 11 or 12 inches—with (finally! a reason to multiply pi by *r*-squared! I've waited all my life for this!) 78% more area for potatoes. Forget the fact that diabetes is no fun; think of the cash you'd save on food—and on diet programs—if you served smaller portions and just ate less.

◆ ***Waste* less.** Americans waste 30% to 40% of the food we grow each year—and the water we use to grow it—scraping it off the plate, discarding it for a blemish, or chucking it once it's past an often-meaningless "best-by" date. Those dates are *not* expiration dates . . . as the frozen creamed spinach dated October 27, 2007, that I consumed with no ill effects in late 2015 attests. (It had gotten sort of buried at the bottom of my freezer.)

◆ **But keep the freezer full.** The more nearly full you keep your refrigerator and freezer, the *less* energy they burn (just be sure to leave room for air to circulate). Rather than toss them, I fill empty plastic containers with water and stick them in the freezer. Nice big blocks of ice for the cooler. (Why *buy* ice for parties?)

◆ **Skip Starbucks.** Brewing coffee at home and taking it with you in a travel mug saves big. When you're out of debt and rich, go to Starbucks twice a day.

◆ **Try an Andy Burger.** Once, anyway. An Andy Burger is a fully loaded cheeseburger, with lettuce, tomato, and pickle on a grilled bun—hold the meat but slather on the ketchup. It contains no burger, yet has the burger smell and taste from being toasted on the grill, and all the taste of the ketchup, which is, let's be honest, the whole point of the burger in the first place. Mmmm, *mmmm!* Every bit as good as the traditional burger but less expensive, lighter on the land, healthier, and much easier on the cow. No? Well, it works for me.

♦ **Do the math.** Whenever you spend money on an incidental, do the math. **It's not a $5 Starbucks, it's a $2,000 mocha grande**—which is to say five times a week = $25 times 52 weeks = $1,300, which is all you have left, after withholding, from a $2,000 paycheck.

It's not a $125 massage, it's a $9,000 massage, because you get one almost every week = $6,000, which is what you have left after earning $9,000.

This is not to say you shouldn't have the mocha grande or the massage. It's just to give you the big picture, which might make you *want* to bring a thermos of coffee to work or take a really nice hot bath when you get home, instead—*want* to go for $4 beers instead of $10 vodka tonics.

Investing $5,000 a year that might otherwise have gone for bottled water (buy *one* bottle, refill thereafter from the tap), books (use the library), and phone charges (Skype)—and earning 6% after inflation, which isn't easy but should be possible—will grow, if you're 25 now, to $794,000, in today's buying power, by age 65. Which could then provide you with an extra $57,000 a year through age 95.

Not to mention that frugal people tend not to need to borrow at high rates against their credit cards, often saving 8% or 18% or even 29% on everything they charge. That could easily be another $2,000 a year on interest alone, which with the same assumptions as above bumps the retirement nest egg past $1 million and your annual payout, age 65 to 95, past $80,000.

One of the joys of being rich, or even just rich-ish, is that you don't have to think about relatively small things like this. Think twice about buying a yacht, yes—but a latte? A massage? Yet unless you've inherited your wealth (which brings with it its own set of demons) or married it (potential ditto), you first have to *get* rich. And doing *that* means living beneath your means for a decade or three and investing the difference.

• **Split your pills.** Ask your doctor to prescribe the much-less-expensive generic drug when he or she thinks it's appropriate, and then—whatever the brand—ask about pill splitting. Thirty 80-milligram Lipitor tablets cost the same $135.99 when last I checked **drugstore.com** as 30 of the 40-milligram pills.

Buy the higher dosage, cut it in half (if your doctor has prescribed 40 milligrams a day), and you've just cut a $1,632 annual Lipitor bill in half, saving $816 a year. More power to Bob Dole, but if you're ten or 20 years his junior, you might find that cutting each Viagra tablet four ways is all the pep you need. (Do not attempt this with time-release capsules—or anything else you haven't gotten your doctor's OK to subdivide.)

• **Get them free.** Your doctor may have samples. And you can even get free antibiotics at some pharmacies, including those at Giant, Stop & Shop, Publix, Meijer, and Wegmans. Free prenatal vitamins at Meijer and Schnucks.

• **Or at least get them cheap.** Load the free **onerx.com** app onto your phone to find the cheapest price or copay for your medication—and, sometimes, on-screen discount coupons. Try, also, **goodrx.com**.

• **Read—and possibly dispute—your medical bills.** I know; I know. But they could contain costly mistakes. If you need help, the Patient Advocate Foundation (**patientadvocate.org**) can review your medical bills for free . . . and possibly help you bargain them down or resolve disputes.

• *Shop* **for your MRI or new knee.** Visit **newchoicehealth .com** to possibly save big—or a country like Malaysia or Costa Rica to possibly save even bigger. (And soon, perhaps, Cuba?) Check out **medretreat.com** to learn about "medical tourism."

• **Ask for a discount.** There's no shame in asking whether someone "can do any better." AARP reports that only 15% of hearing-aid shoppers ask for a deal; yet—because the markups are so high—most of those who do, get one.

• **Ice water** has at least as much nutritional value as Diet Coke, and it's free. Drinking lots of water is supposed to be good for you. Sipping it continuously keeps you feeling cool even with the thermostat set a few degrees higher. That's a $300 annual saving on the Coke, a $300 saving on the a/c.

"Fill some cool-looking **resealable bottles** with water and store them in the fridge," suggest Camp Wigwam owners Bob and Jane Straus. "The kids will grab these instead of a soda. Much cheaper, much healthier."

• **Tap water.** Listen: unless you live in a typhoid swamp, I don't ever again want to catch you buying bottled water. What an easy way to save money—and avoid dumping plastic into the ocean, which is where a lot of it ultimately floats. It's a crazy waste of oil (used to make the plastic and to truck those bottles to the store). Just get a single plastic container and keep refilling it from the tap. If need be, get a Brita water pitcher (**brita.com**) or some similar filtration solution. I am deeply ashamed to have bought hundreds of bottles of water for our water volleyball guests over the years. Now I just put out a pitcher of ice water and some of those big red plastic cups (which we reuse dozens of times—why would you even *think* of throwing them out?).

It's not a 75-cent bottle of water twice a day, it's a $547 annual bottled-water bill and 730 plastic bottles that you add to the 30-odd billion we Americans throw out each year.

• Scotch drinkers can tell one scotch from another,* but show me the man who can tell what vodka was used to make his

---

* Or not. As research for this book, I placed before a Johnnie Walker Blue Label aficionado three unlabeled jiggers—one from a $220 bottle of the Blue (a gift, needless to say), two from a bottle of Glenlivet at one-fifth the price—and watched delightedly as he picked the wrong one.

vodka tonic. If status symbols are important to you, buy *one* bottle of Grey Goose and a 59-cent plastic funnel. They should last a lifetime.

♦ **Paper towels?** Have you people not heard of a *sponge*? Google "cotton rags" and buy a few dozen for $20 or so; or make your own next time you're about to discard a tattered old towel or terry-cloth robe. Just cut them up instead.

♦ **Forget wrapping paper.** I use newspaper—makes a nice gray background for a Magic Marker sentiment ("Arnie and Sue, this is for you!"), spares the environment, saves money. For special occasions, I use the *New Yorker* covers I save throughout the year and tape them together for the same purpose.

With each gift should come a poem. Preferably in the form of a riddle. "Come rain or come shine / You're my kinda fella / So I went out and got you / This brand new um ———!"

How hard is that?

♦ **Forget the newspaper.** I know I just suggested you wrap things with it, but what if you skipped the physical newspaper and read it online instead? You save money, spare trees, and don't have to remember to suspend delivery when you're on vacation. Indeed, you don't even have to wait until morning to read it. You can read it the night before. It's always yours wherever you have access to the Internet.

I love the *New York Times* and want to see it thrive, so I occasionally buy the Sunday paper—one of the luxuries a lifetime of serving guests cheap vodka allows—but willingly pay the $35 a month to have it ever present online. That's still a lot cheaper than the $600 a year I was paying before.

♦ **Improve your credit rating.** Most people think theirs is higher than it actually is—I did—and are surprised at some of the reasons their score is lower than they expected. To find yours, visit **annualcreditreport.com** (lots of important information on your account from each of the three rating agencies, all free *except* for the score, which requires you then to enter a credit card, if you want to, and pay $7.95) or **creditreport .com,** which provides the score "free" (well: $1) but only if you remember to cancel the $14.95-a-month membership within the trial period.

Your score can matter. The average rate charged on a 30-year fixed-rate home mortgage when I tried this was 4.49% for someone with a FICO score of at least 760, versus *4.89%* for someone just a couple of notches down at 690 — an extra $17,000 in interest on a $200,000 mortgage over the life of the loan. Drop the score to 630 and, if you can even qualify for a loan, the rate rises to *6.08%* and you'll be paying, not $17,000, but $71,000 more.

The fastest way to boost your credit score is by demonstrating responsible use of credit cards. (Not debit cards or "charge cards.") Basically: Visa, MasterCard, or Discover — and those American Express cards that don't require full payment each month. The trick to building your credit score is to use them actively — but (a) don't get anywhere close to your credit limit (anything above 30% or so can make the FICO algorithm nervous) and (b) pay them off in full each month (the algorithm loves that). After six or eight months like this, maybe apply for a second card based on that history, and then use each of them regularly — but, again, sparingly, rarely using more than 20% of your limit. Pretty soon, people will be beating down your door to lend you money. (Resist their entreaties.)

If your credit score is so bad you can't *get* a credit card, visit **beverlyharzog.com** to find a good "secured credit card" (because some are awful), where you put up $1,000 in cash (say) to secure a card with a $1,000 limit. It's still considered a credit card, and your responsible use of it will be reported to the credit-rating agencies.

Until you do fix your credit: rent.

♦ We've already talked about Cepacol. **Consider buying *services* "by the case," too.**

I got my flood insurance renewal notice recently and a choice: one year at $429 or three years for $1,147. Which would you choose?

It's the kind of choice we face frequently, perhaps most often with magazine subscriptions. Here's how you might go about making a rational decision:

In the example above, you're "investing" an extra $718 up front to save $140 (paying $1,147 instead of $429 three times — $1,287). But what kind of return is that?

The trick is to figure out how long you're tying up the money. Your first inclination may be to say "three years," but that's wrong. If you had paid annually instead of all at once, the second $429 would have been due just a year from now, so *that* portion of the $718 — fully 60% of it — is only being tied up one year. And the rest ($289) is only being tied up two years.

If 60% of your $718 is being tied up for one year and 40% for two years, then the whole thing, taking a weighted average, is being tied up for 1.4 years. (How'd I get that? I multiplied one year by 60% and got .6 years; then multiplied two years by 40% and got .8 years; then added .6 and .8 years together to get 1.4 years.)

What kind of return is it to earn $140 on $718 in 1.4 years? If you're not into computers or higher math, just divide the $140 return by the $718 investment and you get a 19.5% gain. Divide *that* by 1.4 years and you get a wrong, but close, answer of 13.9% gain per year. The precise answer — easily obtained with a pocket calculator or computer program that includes "present value" functions with irregular time periods — is "about 13%."* And it's tax-free.

---

* I no longer carry such a calculator — why get lost in the weeds? But yes, if you plugged in $718 as your investment, with a "return" of $429 a year later, when the second payment would have been due, and $429 a year after that, when the third payment would have been due, such a calculator would tell you it was a 12.73% annual rate of return.

And there's the saving if, by locking in today's price, you avoid price increases in years two and three. So the after-tax return may wind up being even better.

On the other hand, you should consider whether there might be some cancellation fee if you decided to terminate your insurance (or magazine subscription) in mid-term, and whether the insurer (or magazine publisher, or health club, or exterminating service) might go broke before the end of the three years, leaving you uninsured (or with nothing to read, no place to work out, or rats).

◆ **Live light on the land.** If your shirts come back from the dry cleaner folded in **plastic bags,** use them in place of sandwich bags for storing leftovers. It saves a little money, saves a little planet. (Plastic bags are made from oil.) When you need to **boil water,** don't boil more than you need (and use a lid). You'll save water, time, and fuel. Skip the **dishwasher.** I have a patented "non-stack method" for which I hereby waive the royalties: just rinse the tops of plates and bowls as you clear the table *without stacking them* (which needlessly soils their undersides), then put them in one of those cheap vertical drying racks. You're done. Seriously.

Want a hobby? Fire up your Google and research **"residential heat pump water heaters."** Make sense for you? Take a couple of minutes to explore **low-flow showerheads** (Kramer: "Low flow? Well I don't like the sound of that.") like the $8.14 "Niagara Earth Massage" that could cut your hot water shower use by 75%. Pipes at risk of freezing in the winter? Search **"autocirc pump"** to solve that problem *and* save on hot water. Research **"residential solar panels."** I have a little 3.6-kilowatt power plant on my roof. Even when it's cloudy, the electric meter generally runs *backwards,* as I'm generating more power than I use. Without federal, state, and utility-company incentives, solar is still at best a marginal investment. But the incentives are there for a reason (known as "externalities"), and *with* them, in some parts of the country, the return is outstanding.

The list goes on! You'll get lots of good ideas at **eere.energy .gov/consumer/tips** (the website is friendlier than the URL).

One of my website readers cut her family's peak quarterly electric bill from $447 to $243 just by switching to more efficient light bulbs, installing power strips to make it easy to switch off TVs that draw power when not in use, buying an efficient front-loading washing machine that also saves on drying (because the clothes are nearly dry when the washer finishes), and installing an on-demand water heater. "We're saving 45% with some simple changes and no sacrifice," she reports.

It becomes a game. Could I afford to keep my aforementioned 400 watts burning to light my kitchen? I could. But, quite apart from the investment return, cutting that consumption by 94% to just 24 watts makes me smile every time I switch on the lights.

If all this penny-pinching sounds niggling, don't miss the larger point: the suggestions in this chapter can very likely save you $1,000 a year—and possibly much more—with very little effort. And that's important, because the typical American doesn't save enough.* When this book was first published in 1978, personal saving as a percentage of disposable income in the United States was 10%. By 2005, it was down to 2%. Hard times reminded people to prepare for rainy days, so it spiked some in the Great Recession. But in the summer of 2015 it was back under 5%.

Most people need to do better for themselves—and can.

---

* A century ago, in 1916, "with the First World War looming imminently on the horizon, the leaders of America's major civic organizations launched an ambitious education campaign designed to ready the American public for a wartime economy"—National Thrift Week. According to the good folks at **bringbackthriftweek.org**, it was sponsored primarily by the YMCA and kicked off on January 17 each year, Ben Franklin's birthday (the "American apostle of thrift"). It died in 1966—the same year Bank of America launched the nation's first general-purpose credit card. Out with thrift, in with plastic. National Thrift Week sounds hopelessly old-fashioned—what's next, gingham dresses? But it just *might* be time to bring it back.

You *CAN* Get By
on $165,000 a Year

A penny saved is—impossible.

— OGDEN NASH

MANY OF US spend a great deal of time worrying about our money; few of us use that time to make a sensible plan. Where am I? Where do I want to be? How do I get there?

If you already have a budget, or are too rich or frugal to need one, skip ahead. But if like many successful people you have trouble making ends meet, let alone overlap, *listen up*. This is important, because it's not just a budget you'll end up with; it's an overall plan.

First, get a pencil and a yellow legal pad (or the planning tool on **mint.com**). Next, tell your secretary to hold your calls. If you are a secretary, get a smaller legal pad. If you neither are nor have a secretary—if you've got a *man's* job, like operating a crane —do this at home, in your favorite chair, late at night, when no one can see you. (Real men make bets, not budgets.)*

If you have a significant other, sit him or her down, too, and work on this together.

1. **Tally your net worth.** Add up everything you own, subtract everything you owe, and that's your net worth.

In other words, before you even start to make the budget, take a few minutes to see where you stand. Down the left side

---

* Do I really need a footnote to let you know *I'm kidding*? Yes, notes my editor, it's 2016. I do.

of the first sheet of your yellow legal pad, list all your assets and their approximate value—the house, the car, the savings account. Down the right, list all your debts—the mortgage and car loan and credit-card balances. Which list totals more?

If you own more than you owe, you have a positive net worth. You're already three steps ahead of the game.

If you have a negative net worth—you owe more than you own—you can see why your mother is worried about you. (What's that? You think just because she's deceased she's not worried?)

Subtract what you owe from what you own and write the total at the bottom of the page.

2. **Set goals.** Where would you like to be a year from now? "Out of debt" might be an appropriate goal. And two years from now? "Out of debt with $5,000 in an IRA and $2,000 in the bank and a sound system that will wake up the dead." And five years from now? "A net worth of $60,000 headed for a million."

It is to reach these goals that you make your budget. Write them down on the second page of your yellow legal pad. Don't make them too aggressive. Try to set goals that, after going back and forth with your budget for a while, you secretly think you'll be able to exceed. If you aim too high, you'll never feel you're doing well enough. You can still have unwritten goals and hopes and dreams—by all means!—but think of them (and not too often, if you can help it) as icing on the cake. Sure you want a BMW. Everybody seems to want one (not me—I want to be invisible and to fly). But it's really nuts to want one so much you're unhappy you don't have one.

3. **Figure your annual earnings.** At the top of the third yellow page, list all your sources of annual income: your take-home pay (multiply your paycheck by the 12, 24, 26, or 52 times a year you receive it), payments from Grandpa's trust, the $20 a week you pick up reffing Little League, dividends, and so on.

Note that for most folks, it's not a long list. "Take-home pay: $28,400." End of list.

Note also:

◆ Precision is not the goal. Ballpark estimates are fine.

◆ When in doubt, estimate low. That way, any surprises are likely to be pleasant ones.

4.   **Take a first pass at your expenses.** This is like naming all the states. If you picture the map and start with Maine, gradually working your way south and west, you will come up with 43 states. Then you'll remember Kansas (if you're from Kansas, you'll remember Delaware) and a few others and get to 48. The last two are murder, though you know them perfectly well (Nebraska—of course! Alabama!), and you may even have to sneak a look at the map to find them.

So it goes with budget categories. You'll quickly come up with headings to cover most of your expenditures, although with budget categories, unlike states, there are no preset boundaries. You might have one broad category for Entertainment or several narrower categories all summing to it: Restaurants, Movies & Music, Books & Magazines, Theatrical & Sporting Events. Whatever makes sense for you.

Nor is there a specific number of budget items the way there's a specific number of states, so you won't know with quite the same certainty whether you've missed any. You'll *think* you've thought of everything, just as, until you count up your list of states, you think you've hit them all. But chances are, you have not. (Gasoline—of course! Lawn Care!) If you get stuck, sneak a look at the map—last year's checkbook and credit-card statements. Under what headings would last year's expenditures have fallen? (Miscellaneous! Of course!)

Next to each category, estimate what you currently spend. If you haven't any idea what you currently spend—well, all the more reason to be going through this exercise. Two nights out a week at $100 apiece? (Not hard to do, between dinner, a movie, and ice cream on the way home.) That's $10,400 a year.

Some categories, like this one, are best thought of in weekly terms and multiplied by 52. Your rent or mortgage payments and electric bill are naturally thought of in monthly amounts and multiplied by 12. Your semiannual trips to the dentist are multiplied by two—but don't include them at all if you're reimbursed for dental care by insurance. Reimbursable expenditures don't affect your financial plan, so ignore them.

Ignore, too, items that are automatically taken out of your pay, because it was only your net take-home pay that you listed as income. Or, if you prefer, list your *gross* pay as income and list each of the deductions—taxes, health insurance, and so on—as an expense item. Either approach is fine.

Don't include Credit Cards as a budget category. Only the annual credit-card fee itself and, more important, credit-card interest ought to be budget items. The rest—the clothing and dinners and such that you charge to the cards—should go into categories like Clothing and Dinners.

On your first pass, jot down both the annual expenditure and the way you figured it ("$100 2/wk = $10,400"). Make no effort to economize. When in doubt, estimate high. Round up. Your auto insurance runs $950? Call it $1,000.

Leave for the end of your list those "expenditures" that aren't really expenditures at all: investments. The $5,000 you voluntarily contribute to an IRA is not like the $5,000 you blow on a hot tub. It's cash that merely moves from your front pocket to your back pocket. Similarly, spending $20,000 on an Oriental rug, if it's really worth $20,000 (as the ones that fly clearly are), isn't spending money at all. It's merely shifting funds from one investment, like a savings account, to another, like a rug. (If the rug would fetch only $10,000 were you immediately to resell it—and that may be optimistic—then you have in effect invested $10,000 in a rug and spent $10,000 on your living room.)

If you buy a new car every four years, for cash, don't budget zero for the first three and then $26,000 for the fourth. Budget $6,500 a year (plus maintenance, plus insurance).

If you own your home, include an allowance for maintenance and repairs even though you can't be sure what might need fixing or when. If you budget $2,500 a year, planning to repaint, but the roof starts to leak—well, this year you might patch the roof and, if funds are scarce, hold off repainting until next year.

5. **Take a second pass at your expenses.** What have you forgotten? Furniture? Appliances? Gifts? Inevitably you'll think of other things as you go along, but that's why you do this in pencil.

6. **Refine your plan.** Add up your expenditures, not counting things that are really investments, like IRA contributions. How does what you expect to shell out compare with what you expect to rake in? Ideally, you're raking more than you're shelling, and by enough to meet the goals you've set for yourself on the second page of this legal pad. Usually, though, you're not.

What's the shortfall? Are you living a $50,000 lifestyle on a $45,000 income?

You have three ways to close the gap:

- Spend less.
- Earn more.
- Set less-aggressive goals.

Go back over your budget and, without being unrealistic, see what you can trim. ("There are several ways to apportion family income," counseled Robert Benchley, "all of them unsatisfactory.") Before, scrimping this way was a chore. Now it's still a chore, but a chore that's part of a grand plan.

So first trim your budget. But don't trim it unrealistically. Don't set yourself up to fail.

Then, if your expenditures and goals for saving still exceed your income, think about increasing your income.

Sadly, this often involves doing more work. But if you don't already work two jobs or live rent-free by acting as super for your building or bartend on weekends, wait tables, or design websites—and if you want to achieve your goals and work less hard in the future—you should consider it. For one thing, you'll earn more money. For another, you'll spend less. You'll be too busy and tired to spend.

If you can't get or don't want more work, take yet another pass through your expenses—but a radical one this time. You could, for example, move to a cheaper home. You could give up skiing for jogging or take in a roommate.

Your other choice is simply to set lower goals.

Round and round you go, juggling income, expenses, and goals, brushing eraser crumble to all corners of your kitchen table or clicking the heck out of your budgeting software, until you arrive at an earning-spending-saving plan that adds up. The process itself is useful. It helps you set priorities. It helps you see where your finances are headed and, if you like, redirect them. What's involved here, really, is taking control of your life.

By estimating your income low and your expenses high, you set yourself up to succeed. That makes your budget a game that's fun to play instead of a constant burden of guilt and discouragement that you'll soon abandon.

(Speaking of discouragement, if you've got three small kids, don't be discouraged that you're unable to save much. For many, it's only before the kids are born and after they've graduated that any serious saving is possible. But even just funding an IRA as they're growing up, though hard, can put you $250,000 or $500,000 ahead of the game in your later years. So try to set *something* aside.)

In setting your goals, spend a little time thinking about the things you have (like your health, and a smartphone that puts *the whole world* in your pocket) and not just about the things you don't.

7. **Once you've settled on a plan, find a congenial way to track your progress.** Blow $10 on an old-fashioned 12-month budget book (down at the local stationery store) — or, much better, 99 cents on a budget app on your smartphone or something similar (see **mint.com,** page 59). It doesn't much matter what method you choose, so long as you use it. Nor need you wait until January to start. The government budgets on a fiscal year; so can you. Most budgeting tools are set up to record 12 months' expenditures but let you fill in the names of the months. The first can be April just as easily as January.

Before you go to bed each night, be sure you've entered all the day's expenditures. Indeed, budget or no budget, you'll likely reduce expenditures that make you feel foolish when you have to record them this way.

Is all this too tedious for words? Here's a simpler system: Destroy all your credit cards. Deposit the first 20% of each paycheck in one or more investment accounts that you never, ever touch (the "don't-touch-it budget," as budget counselor Betty Madden calls it). Put the remaining 80% in a single checking account and make do, no matter what, with the balance in that account.

It's an unconventional financial discipline, but better than the Visa budget system most people use. Under that system, Visa tells you exactly what you can afford to spend (your available credit) and exactly how much to pay each month (your minimum monthly payment), all the while collecting 12% or 20% or 29.9% for its trouble.

8. **Give yourself a break.** If you do take the time to plan your financial future and to track your progress as it unfolds, don't be slavish about it. Who cares if you forget to jot down every last

expense? Who cares if you go over budget from time to time? The idea isn't to account for every penny (although it could be an intriguing experiment for three months to see exactly where the money goes). The idea is to spend less than you earn each year, get out of debt, and build a secure, comfortable future.

Doing It by Computer

Remember checks? And bills? And postage stamps? Here's how I pay my condo maintenance each month: I don't. It's automatically debited from my bank account. Likewise, almost all my other bills — debited from either my checking account or one of my credit cards (so I get the miles).

If you already use Quicken or some other program to track all this (and even to print the occasional check), you already know what I'm talking about and are already set up to track your budget and expenses.

If not, consider a free website, **mint.com,** that can pull together information from all of your bank accounts, credit cards, loans, and brokerage accounts (assuming you have online access). Mint grabs the information daily, so the only thing it won't know about are the cash expenses — but you can track those, too, most conveniently on the Mint iPhone or Android app.

The beauty of this brave new world, besides the ease of use, is that your information is retained. Want a quick list of all the times you've paid the housekeeper if there's a dispute? Bang — it's there. Want to compare what you've spent on clothes this year with last? Bang. Want to reconcile your checkbook quickly and easily? Bang.

The advantage of the computer is that it makes budgeting, and tracking your budget, *fun*. It puts you in control of your finances. You become chairman of the board. Where before you had no convenient way to track your finances throughout the year, now it's all kept track of *for* you. Personal finance software has been credited with saving more than one marriage.

If you have a computer and aren't using it to pay your bills and prepare your taxes . . . to make a budget and then track your progress . . . you're missing something good.

Getting By on $165,000 a Year

Most of us feel we couldn't get by on a penny less. But all a family struggling to get by on $190,000 a year needs do is look down the street to see a family that—somehow—manages to get by on $165,000 a year. (They do their own pool maintenance.) A family struggling on $28,000 need only look down the street to see one surviving—don't ask me how—on $22,500.

The point is that you *can* save money if you're willing to make some sacrifices. And it's wise to do so. Because even forgetting retirement needs, "rainy days," and all that, if you can arrange things to come out a little *ahead* each year instead of falling a little further behind, you will quickly find your financial security and, not long afterwards, your standard of living improving. Money *does* make money. The rich *do* get richer.

And they sleep better.

A lot of people manage to dig themselves into a big hole of debt. Some go bankrupt; most just muddle through life, juggling their bills and praying that an unexpected expense or job loss doesn't put their finances over the edge.

But there are success stories. One fellow I know of managed to pull back from a lifestyle that peaked at nearly $70,000 in credit-card debt—substantially more than a year's take-home pay—and he did it without bankruptcy. Here's how:

◆ Not having the heart to cut up all his credit cards, he just cut up one (which was at its limit anyway). Every day, he looked in the mirror and said, "Today, I will cut up another credit card." Although most days he couldn't bring himself actually to do it, a month of incantations finally got him down to the one card he felt he had to keep for identification and business use.

- He generally made only the minimum monthly payments on his cards, but (and this was the key) he racked up no *new* debt. (Heavy debtors start solving their problems when they just stop adding new debts. Debtors Anonymous—with local chapters throughout the country that you can find through **debtors anonymous.org**—uses the same one-day-at-a-time approach as Alcoholics Anonymous, urging its members to resolve not to borrow any money today.)

- So, gradually, he paid them all off. At the same time, he put $50 a month into the stock market, via a mutual fund.

It might have made more sense, mathematically, to apply that $50 to paying off more debt, "earning" 18% tax-free by doing so. But psychologically, he wanted to start building something, however small. And he found that he didn't really miss that $50. He still felt broke all the time, he said—"but no broker." So he raised the contribution to $100 per month, then $150. As one credit card after another got paid off, his monthly debt payments decreased and his monthly investments increased. After five years he was saving 20% of every paycheck. And still does. He now has an investment portfolio that dwarfs his former debts.

If you have reached the point where late payments or even bankruptcy are considerations, visit **nfcc.org** or call 800-388-CCCS day or night to locate an accredited Consumer Credit Counseling Service near you. Sponsored by many of the largest creditor groups in the country and usually charging little or nothing for its advice, such a service can act as a go-between to help negotiate debt repayment plans and, sometimes, interest waivers on your debt. Some of these services are offered online or by phone, without your even having to show up. One I like is provided by the Lutheran Social Service of Minnesota, which helps folks nationwide—**lssmn.org** or 888-577-2227.

Consider the words offered to Charles Dickens by his father, a financial failure (words Dickens later put into the mouth of another financial failure, Mr. Micawber, in *David Copperfield*): "Annual income, twenty pounds; annual expenditure, nineteen pounds; result, happiness. Annual income, twenty pounds; annual expenditure, twenty-one pounds; result, misery." That's pretty much it. Spend less than you earn. Live a little *beneath* your means.

Saving is difficult, but less so when you have a goal and a plan. To sacrifice any given night-out-on-the-town makes little sense. What's another 60 bucks? But as part of a plan to pay off all consumer loans within the year or build a net worth of $25,000 in five, a sacrifice that would otherwise seem pointless —and perhaps depressing—can be purposeful indeed. Satisfying, even.

No one wants to pass up something because she can't afford it. But to pass it up because she *wants* to—because her eye is on a higher goal—well, that is quite a different thing.

The day your paycheck comes, put 10% or 20% of it, automatically, without question, into a separate savings vehicle. It can be a savings account or a mutual fund or an IRA or some combination of accounts—but do it. (Your employer may be able to do this for you, which is ideal, because the best way to avoid temptation is never to see the cash in the first place.) Simply live as if you are making $22,000 instead of $26,000; $44,000 instead of $52,000; $125,000 instead of $150,000.

There are loads of competent financial planners to help you make sense of your finances. But until you internalize the plan, whether you worked it out with a 79-cent legal pad or a $2,500 financial planner, it won't mean anything. You've got to make it *your* plan, and you're not likely to if you simply rely on someone else once a year to work it out for you. Buying fancy exercise equipment is fine, but it's not enough. You've got to *pedal*.

As with any regimen, the hardest part is getting into the habit. As your pile mounts, it becomes much easier.

But what to do with your pile?

4

Trust No One

Trust everybody, but cut the cards.

— FINLEY PETER DUNNE

IF YOU OR anyone you know is over 50, *I urge* you to get pencil and paper ready."

So began the celebrity life insurance commercials we used to see on TV. Dick Van Dyke did them (and he starred in *Mary Poppins*!). Johnny Carson's trusty sidekick Ed McMahon did them. Even Gavin MacLeod — good ol' Murray on *The Mary Tyler Moore Show,* remember him? — did them.

Murray, Murray, Murray.

But the plans sounded good, didn't they? No matter how bad your health, *you could not be turned down* for this "top-quality, big-dollar" protection. Yet amazing as it seems — well, this is why I told you to get your pencil and paper ready — Murray's plan cost just $5 a month. And — get this! — your premiums were guaranteed never to rise as you got older.

Said Murray: "I can't tell you what a relief it is to know that we won't be a burden on our children." Here the kids thought they stood to inherit a pretty penny — Murray did go on to captain the *Love Boat,* after all — but had it not been for this insurance, they'd have been left with nothing but the funeral bill. *Thank heavens for this insurance.*

If you're 50, Murray said, just $5 a month would buy you $10,000 in protection.

Catch #1: If you died of an illness, your heirs got $2,800, not $10,000. The bulk of the insurance benefit was for *accidental* death only. Yet accidents are a minor cause of death among older people. (Dick Van Dyke's pitch called them "one of the leading causes of death for people over 45." But actually, fewer than 3% of deaths among people over 45 are caused by accidents. So more than 97% of the time the payoff would be $2,800, not $10,000.)

It was true, you couldn't be turned down for this coverage; but — Catch #2 — only after you'd paid premiums for two years were you actually covered. Die of an illness before then, and your heirs got nothing but a refund of the premiums.

True, too, your rates were guaranteed not to rise (well, sort of) but — Catch #3 — as you got older, your coverage would fall. Say you paid $5 a month, month after month, for 25 years. Then, at 75, having paid in a total of $1,500, you had a heart attack and died. This policy paid your heirs a grand total of $225. Period. (Die after age 79 and they got no benefit at all.) This is what Murray endorsed as BIG-DOLLAR protection. He couldn't tell you what a relief it was to know that $225 would be there when his loved ones needed it.

If at age 79 you died not of an illness but, say, hang gliding into a utility pole, your heirs would get an extra $775, except that — Catch #4 — death while hang gliding didn't qualify for the accidental death bonus. Neither did death in a war (declared or undeclared), in a private plane, by suicide, during surgery, or while intoxicated, if intoxication caused the accident. (If you were merely three sheets to the wind in the bar car of your commuter train when it derailed and flew off a cliff, you'd be OK.)

Catch #5: Your rates were guaranteed never to rise *only so long as the insurance company didn't raise them*. They couldn't single *you* out and raise just *your* rate. But if the company decided *everybody* should pay $6 a month instead of $5, or to cancel all the policies altogether because it wasn't making money on them, the company was free to do so.

Catch #6: Five bucks a month was the least you could pay; but this was portrayed as *such* a good deal for "folks like us," as Murray put it — you know, lovable, bald guys who make $80,000 an episode — that many signed up for the full $40-a-month's worth, to cover both them and their spouses four times over. Five dollars a month was nothing when Murray was making this pitch. But $40 a month, in the budgets of many older Americans — $480 a year — was a hefty sum.

The pitchmen freely acknowledged they were paid to endorse these insurance plans, but Dick Van Dyke said, in his follow-up letter: "P.S. I'm sure you know I would never speak out for anything I didn't personally believe in." Gavin MacLeod, in *his* P.S., wrote: "I want you to know I would never speak out for anything I didn't believe in with my whole heart." The cash that Continental American Life paid him to endorse this plan had nothing to do with it.*

Trust no one. It kills me to say that, and I'll admit there are exceptions — but the list is shorter than you think. I mean, my God: if you can't trust *Murray*! If you can't trust the *Beardstown Ladies*!

(You mean you hadn't heard? These sweet, sweet ladies, who became world famous for their down-home recipes and shrewd stock-picking — who sold millions of books up through 1998 based on their extraordinary market-beating performance† — turned out to have been calculating their results in an unusual way. Say you or I started the year with $40,000, added $5,000 more, and saw our account total $50,000 by year's end. You or I might say our $45,000 had grown very nicely to $50,000. About 11%. Not bad. What the ladies apparently were figuring is that they started with $40,000, and now it's $50,000 — that's

---

* MacLeod and Van Dyke were both reportedly paid $25,000 to do the television commercials I refer to, plus a commission on each toll-free call the commercials produced. An executive close to the arrangement estimated the final take for each man to have been between $100,000 and $200,000.

† From the *American Bookseller*'s December 1997 list of recommended investment books: "*The Beardstown Ladies' Common-Sense Investment Guide.* A classic from the investment club that has outperformed Wall Street gurus three to one. It's easy to get investment advice these days. But in this volatile market, it's important to separate the faddish from the trustworthy." Uh, huh.

a 25% increase for the year. So instead of *beating* the market all those years, it turned out that—though sweet—they hadn't done particularly well at all. They received enormous publicity for earning returns averaging 23.4% per year for the first decade of their club's existence. But it turned out that the rate of return had actually been only 9.1%, at a time the market was growing at 15.3%. The ladies would have been far better off just putting their money into an index fund. As the late Emily Litella would have said, "Oh! That's different! . . . Never mind.")

Here is an ad for a mutual fund. It comes from a well-regarded investment firm, and this is its *special* fund. In fact, says the ad, this fund has appreciated at a rate of 21.5% a year for the past ten years. Compare *that* with what your local bank is paying. You're smart enough to know performance like that can't necessarily be repeated (if only you had thought to invest ten years ago!). And you imagine, given that they're trying pretty hard to sell this to you, there may be a sales commission involved (there is: only $4,575 of the $5,000 you were thinking of investing actually goes to work for you—the rest is an immediate loss). But never mind that. We're talking about 21.5% annual growth—enough, if it continued for another two decades, to turn a single $2,000 IRA contribution into $90,000!

You are all set to send in your money when you come across Jane Bryant Quinn's column in *Newsweek*. She has studied the prospectus—you could have studied it, too, but you would have been a rare investor if you did—and she has noticed that the big gains that the fund packs into its alluring yield of 21.5% came long ago. In the first six of those ten years, share values rose an average of 39% a year. But zigzag performance the last four brought an average annual *loss*.

No place in the ad do you see anything about an average annual *loss*. And guess what? In the hot stock market that followed (this ad actually appeared many years ago, giving us, by now, the benefit of hindsight), the fund did grow smartly—but underperformed the monkey throwing darts.

Trust no one. You've got to take responsibility for your own affairs.

Many people wish they could turn the whole mess over to someone else. Widows particularly express this wish, having in some cases been made to feel over many years of marriage that they can't possibly understand anything having to do with money. But the folks who do understand money, while many have your best interests at heart, have their own interests at heart, too. You have to take responsibility for your own money because no one cares about it as much as you. That doesn't mean you can't rely on a variety of experts to help—a good accountant, a good mutual fund manager, perhaps a good real estate or insurance agent, financial planner, or attorney. But ultimately it's you who are in charge.

If you don't understand what you're investing in, or haven't formed a broad spending/borrowing/saving/insuring/investing plan yourself, it's unlikely things will work out terribly well. (Most people wind up with nothing, says financial advisor Venita Van Caspel, "not because they plan to fail, but because they fail to plan."*) What's more, you *can* do it. The simple investments are very often the best. And that goes, too, for the simple loans, the simple insurance, and the simple financial plans.

Look at the trouble Wall Street got into with complex derivatives that even the rating agencies didn't understand. A migrant worker earning $13,000 a year somehow qualified for a

---

* Oh, gosh, and look at this: In 1989, Ms. Van Caspel—whose advice was quite helpful to people for the most part, and who for a while billed herself as "The First Lady of Financial Planning"—was accused of selling properties to limited partnerships owned by her clients *without telling her clients she had an interest in them.* When the partnerships tanked and the truth came out, her clients sued . . . only to have the court agree that the First Lady of Financial Planning had been acting as their stockbroker, not their financial planner, and thus had no duty to disclose the conflict. *Trust no one.*

$700,000 home mortgage, and that mortgage got bundled with thousands of other dubious ones into securities that Moody's and Standard & Poor's, as late in the game as 2008, rated triple-A. It very nearly brought down the entire global financial system. Or look at Bernie Madoff. No one could quite understand how he produced the results he did, but the results were great and *everyone else* was investing with him (and *he'd go to jail* if the results weren't real) so — what? — are you going to second-guess other, far more sophisticated Madoff investors and miss the opportunity to join them in these wonderful, steady gains? Realistically, you are not. But, because you can trust no one, at the very least you shouldn't put too many eggs into any one basket.

I can't fault the many investors who got caught up in the Madoff scheme; but I can fault (and feel deeply sorry for) those who put *all* their money with him.

And of course I've made these mistakes myself — just not with too many eggs. Back before the real estate market really heated up, I invested in several first mortgages arranged by a young mortgage broker who forwarded the monthly mortgage payments like clockwork — even *after,* unbeknownst to me, the mortgages had been paid off. (He had used a little of the payoff money to write me those checks, and much of the rest, it seemed, to support a drug habit.) But! But! But! He would *go to jail* if he did that! Except that he died first, of an overdose, which is how I learned of my loss.

So that's my own mini-Madoff story.

Meanwhile — and returning, now, from simple fraud to "investing in things you don't understand" — I had a friend who earned $2 million a year at Merrill Lynch executing a very complex, computer-assisted trading strategy. Around 1990, he went out on his own and offered friends the chance to participate. He labored mightily to explain exactly *what* he was doing, but all any of us could understand — even the head of an investment bank who also went in on this — was that a 50% annual gain was essentially guaranteed unless interest rates rose or fell more than 700 basis points in a single year. Which never happens—and didn't. Don't you wish you could get into deals like this? Don't you wish you knew what basis points were?* It was the most sophisticated, complex deal I've ever invested in. It sure wasn't available to "the little guy." And it lost money. Big time. My friend wasn't trying to fleece us. He meant well. He was just wrong—for reasons I could understand no better than what it was he was doing in the first place.

In stewarding your money, it's not enough to respond to advertising headlines or the salesperson's enthusiasm or the lavishly illustrated brochure. You've got to read between the lines—or at least read the prospectus. And since you won't—most prospectuses are unreadable—you've got to stick to sensible investments recommended by competent, disinterested parties. Not competent *or* disinterested, competent *and* disinterested—which certainly leaves out Murray, may very likely leave out tips from your hairstylist, and may even leave out advice from your accountant or financial planner, who could be getting a commission for steering you into a particular deal. ("Your purpose," a well-known San Francisco financial planner was quoted in the *Wall Street Journal* as having told a group of fellow financial planners years ago, "is to get up before [potential clients] and confuse them. And step two is to create a dependency." Step three, in many cases, is to start selling them things.)

If only you had access to an expert you could *trust*. Someone who did know how to read a prospectus.

With that in mind, pour yourself a beer and get out your letter opener, for what we have here—delivered by hand to our door—is a fat manila envelope from nothing less than the United States Trust Company, one of the oldest, classiest, most

---

* Each basis point equals one-hundredth of 1%. When the prime rate rises from 4% to 5%, it has climbed "100 basis points."

exclusive banks in the country. ("When you do something very well," its ads say, "you simply cannot do it for everyone.")*†

Inside is everything you'll need to evaluate and sign up for the Samson Properties 1985-A Drilling Program. U.S. Trust—which actually *is* a fine institution, this episode notwithstanding—describes Samson 1985-A as "a quality oil and gas investment with relatively moderate risk, inherent tax benefits, and the potential for significant upside economic gains." (As opposed to downside economic gains?)

The bank's cover letter outlines the deal and encloses a colorful Samson sales brochure, a deadly 165-page Samson prospectus, a huge U.S. Trust business reply envelope for your signed papers, and a form you sign agreeing to pay the bank a 5% "advisory fee" for bringing the deal to your attention. (There is already a 7.5% sales commission built into the deal, but the bank can't touch it—it's illegal for banks to sell securities like these‡—so, instead, it charges this 5% advisory fee. The bank's not *selling* anything—merely sending sales materials, recommending that you buy it, and enclosing all the papers you need to sign to send in with your check. See the difference?)

By paying the "advisory fee," you are in effect getting the deal at 105% of retail. You could avoid the fee by purchasing Samson units directly through a stockbroker, but when you deal with a classy bank—this is not a bank that's out hawking car loans—you should show a little class yourself.

Participation in Samson 1985-A runs $25,000 and up.

THESE ARE SPECULATIVE SECURITIES AND INVOLVE A HIGH DEGREE OF RISK, cautions the front page of the prospec-

---

* Oops. In the years since, it has been acquired by Charles Schwab, the discount broker, which is a little like Tiffany getting acquired by eBay. But at the time, especially, U.S. Trust was a big deal. (And no, Tiffany has not been acquired by eBay.)

† Oops, again. Since publication of the previous footnote, Charles Schwab sold it to Bank of America.

‡ Not anymore. The 1999 Financial Services Modernization Act allowed banks to engage in securities offerings. Run for your life.

tus. The SEC makes 'em say stuff like that. The bank prefers to describe it as "relatively moderate risk."

The brochure explains that by mid-1984, "Samson's 1973–1981 programs had distributed cash equal to 127% of total cash invested" and would distribute a further 226% over the life of those programs. The brochure says you shouldn't count on future programs all doing so well, but, hey, 127% and 226% — that's like three and a half times your money! Plus, U.S. Trust likes the program, and Samson must be getting more experienced each year, and drilling costs *are* really low these days, and boy, could I ever use the tax deduction — where do I sign?

At least that was my reaction.

The brochure did say, "These figures assume an equal investment in each of the programs offered from 1973 through 1981," but that sounds innocuous enough.

Hah!

It turns out that its very first program, a teeny-tiny deal in 1973 that involved a total of just $325,000 and 11 investors, has paid off like gangbusters. But all its subsequent programs, ranging from three to 30 times as big, have mostly bombed. (Funny how often that first deal, which helps sell all subsequent deals, is a lot more successful than the rest.)

If you *don't* assume "an equal investment in each of the programs," but assume instead the amounts that were *actually* invested, the return on those 1973–81 programs by mid-1984 would have been not 127% (all your money back and then some), but 45% (less than half your money back).

Of the nearly $30 million that investors handed Samson in 1981 (not to mention the $70 million in 1982, 1983, and the first part of 1984), less than $1 million had been paid back by September 30, 1984.

Of the three 1980 deals — one private, two public — one had paid back 74%, two had paid 17% and 9% respectively. Guess which one was the private deal.

And understand, these numbers are not return *on* investment (with luck, that comes later), they're return *of* investment.

If there were a cynic in the room—and I trust there's not —she might suggest that Samson raised $100 million in drilling investments from 1981 through 1984 on the strength of one crummy little $325,000 program it had drilled ten years earlier.

In fact, I eventually discovered, *that first deal wasn't drilled by Samson at all.* It was drilled by May Petroleum. Samson merely purchased the producing wells at $2-a-barrel-era oil prices and kept pumping as oil prices shot sky-high, apparently realizing that it had the makings of a great brochure.

One of the nice things about going through the bank was that you got the benefit of its independent analysis. "In addition to the information contained in the enclosed Offering Prospectus, supplied by [Samson]," wrote the bank in its cover letter, "certain other facts should be made known to you."

Oh, boy, I thought: the dirt.

"In particular, our analysis has established [Samson's competence and its track record]." Whereupon the bank simply restated the assertion of Samson's brochure: "Through June 30, 1984, Samson's 1973–1981 programs have distributed cash equal to 127% of total cash invested and had estimated future cash distributions equal to 226% of cash invested."

Somebody at U.S. Trust should have read the prospectus.

Yet if you can't blindly rely on U.S. Trust in such matters, on whom *can* you blindly rely?

No one.

5

The Case for Cowardice

This broker calls his customer for four straight years and each year puts him into some dreadful stock that drops right through the floor. The fifth year, the customer calls the broker and says, "Look: I don't know about all these stocks we've been buying—I think maybe I'd be better off in bonds."

"Yeah, sure," says the broker—"but what do I know about bonds?"

— OLD JOKE

I WENT TO THE track for the first (and last) time in my life some years ago. I went with a fellow who's been going twice a week since 1959. This is a man who knows horses. I know absolutely nothing about horses, but I brought $100 and figured I'd learn. About the only part I really understood was the hot dogs and beer, but the hot dogs weren't running and my midweek afternoon limit is three beers, so by the sixth race I was getting bored and decided it was time to place a bet.

My friend showed me the lineup for the race, explained why So-and-So would almost surely win, and just snorted when I said, no, I wasn't going to put my money on So-and-So, I was going to put my money on Willow. *Willow?* Willow, he chided, had never even raced before and had absolutely nothing going for her. (Or him. I never did get that straight.) She was the kind of horse they put in the race so none of the other horses feel bad. "You're missing the point," I explained. "Willow is going off at 25 to 1."

My friend tried to tell me about sucker bets (the odds at the track are always against you, but they're against you worst on the long shots), but I went and placed my bet and came back to our box and began trying to figure out where the race was going to start from. All the races had been starting from different points on the track, and I had been having some difficulty training my rented binoculars on the proper stretch of grass.

"And they're off!" announced the stationmaster (I recognized his voice from the Penn Station P.A. system), and I'm asking — "Where?"

Even after I found them I couldn't really tell the horses apart; but, according to the stationmaster, *Willow was in the lead*. I looked over at my friend, who had a knowing and slightly bored pucker to his face, and then back to try to find the horses. And Willow, according to the voice, *was still in the lead*.

I am ordinarily rather quiet among 15,000 strangers, but I had, after all, put my money on this horse, and I had, after all, consumed three fairly large beers. I began to shout, "Come onnnn, WILLow!" And Willow, at the half (or whatever they call it), was *still* in the lead.

Now, you think I'm going to tell you that with just a few yards to go, or furloughs or fathoms or something, Willow stumbled, or Willow punked out, or Willow got kicked by one of the other horses. But no — Willow won!

At 25 to 1, Willow won!

Unfortunately, I had bet only $3 of my $100 on Willow.

The point of all this — and I think you know it instinctively, but I'll spell it out anyway — is that if I had bet the full $100 on Willow, Willow would surely have lost. There is no way in the world she would have won.

Is there anyone who doubts this? Think about it.

People say, "One great speculation is worth a lifetime of prudent investing" — a terrific line, and true. The problem comes in finding the great speculation. Few people ever do, particularly if they are amateurs.

The line I prefer: "In the financial marketplace, you get what you pay for, if you're careful. If you try to get more, you get burned."

Savings accounts and money-market funds are for the chicken-hearted. But I respect the right to be chickenhearted. As you can perhaps tell from my Belmont stakes, I am rather chicken-hearted myself.

The challenge of chickenhearted investing isn't deciding where to put your money, but resisting the temptation to put it elsewhere. *Face it: sure things are boring.* Treasury bills have terribly predictable plots that make lousy cocktail party conver-sation (even if they do have some redeeming snob appeal), and they won't make you rich. If the United States Treasurer really wanted to sell those bills, she would issue them at slightly lower interest rates—and put the difference into a kitty for which there would be a daily drawing. The United States Lottery. That would give Treasury bill buyers something to check in the paper every day and a chance—however thin—to strike it rich.

Once in a long while you do find a sure thing with an outsize payoff, but it is very rare. The only time I was ever so fortu-nate was decades ago, with a stock called Nation Wide Nursing Centers. Of course, under normal circumstances nursing-home stocks are not fare for the chickenhearted. But this was one of those rare sure things. Through some remarkable good luck, on a day when this stock was selling for $22 a share over-the-counter —that was the price *you* would have paid—*I* was able to snag 500 shares at just $8 each "under-the-counter." The only hitch was that the shares were unregistered, which meant I couldn't sell them for a while. It was a virtual gift of $7,000, which was hard enough to believe, let alone turn down.

Ordinarily, however, there is no such thing as a financial bar-gain. The financial markets are too large and efficient for that. By and large, as I've said, if you're careful, you get what you pay for. Try to get more and you generally get what's coming to you.

I was told I would have to hold my nursing-home stock for three months, when it would almost surely be bought out by a merger-mad steel company at $40 a share. The head of research for one of Wall Street's most prestigious firms was in the deal for 4,000 shares, so I knew this was on the up-and-up.

The stock went to zero in under a year.

There are two kinds of money in the world, debt and equity. I find this easy to remember, because that's what a friend named his two golden retrievers: Debt and Equity. Debt is an IOU; equity is a piece of the action. Debt is bonds or bills or CDs —anything where you *lend* your money, whether to the U.S. government, a local government, a bank, a corporation— whomever. (Yes, when you deposit money in a bank, you are actually lending money. The bank is in your debt. You have taken their IOU in exchange for your cash.) Equity is where you *invest* your money, with no promise that your investment will be recouped, but with the idea that as the company prospereth or falleth into decline, so shall you prosper or fall. (Actually, it's not that simple. The company may prosper while its stock falls. But we'll get to that.)

A very basic thing to know about your money is that, over the really long run, people who buy equities—stocks —will almost surely make a lot more money (if they're at all sensible in how they do it) than people who make "safer" investments. Unfortunately, people tend to focus on this crucial knowledge and give it real credence only when the market is hitting record highs, losing faith when it's in the dumps, leading them to buy high and sell low. But it's true all the same. Especially when the market has tanked—a sorry condition that can last many, many years—*never lose sight of this basic fact.*

Yet until you have paid off your credit-card balances and have at least $10,000 or $20,000 someplace safe and liquid, like a savings account—unless you are so wealthy you don't have to worry about the contingencies of everyday living—you are crazy even to consider making riskier investments. Or more sophisticated ones. Relax; you are doing the right thing. You are *not* a sap.

There is a time and place for everything, and when cocktail party conversation turns to "investments" or "the market," I suggest the time has come for you to be smug. Let the others do what they do, say what they say—you are above it. They may gamble, they may speculate, they may talk of doubling their money (and not mention halving it); you are smug. (See page 271 for a set of smug rejoinders and harmless financial one-liners to keep up your end of the conversation.)

The first several thousand dollars of anybody's money (aside from equity in a home) should be in a checking or savings account (or a money-market mutual fund, which is essentially the same thing). And for many people, that's *all* their money.

In choosing among savings accounts that provide checks and checking accounts that pay interest (and money-market funds that do both but are not federally insured), the important thing to remember is: Who cares? It doesn't matter.

By and large, the going rate for safe, liquid funds will be about the same everywhere. One bank may offer a bit more than another for a while; money-market funds usually offer a bit more interest but entail very slightly more risk and may be a little less convenient; credit unions may offer a slightly better deal because they are nonprofit; an Internet bank might do better still because its costs are low.

But essentially, you just want your account, or accounts, someplace convenient that provides good service. (There's something to be said for doing much or all of your banking business with one institution in order to build a good relationship.)

The danger is that you will spend so much time trying to figure out whether the savings account that pays 1% more with the $4 monthly fee but no charge for checks is a better deal than the checking account that pays 1% less with no fee but a 25-cent charge for each check or deposit (answer: choose the one with the closest cash machine) that you will lose sight of the larger issues. For the real question is not how to wring an extra 1% out of the $10,000 or $20,000 you keep completely safe and liquid. An extra 1% on $10,000 or $20,000 comes to $100 or $200 a year. After taxes, even less. You are too busy to spend much time worrying about $100. The real question is overall strategy: What proportion of your assets do you want to keep completely safe and liquid? What proportion might you prudently tie up for a while to get a higher return? What proportion should you risk in the stock market in hopes of a still-higher return? What proportion should be in tax-free securities? Or in real estate? How well are you diversified?

The book that really used to get me, back in the days when all savings banks were paying 5½%, no matter what, and no saver of any size had even *dreamed* of double-digit rates, was the one that promised to tell you "HOW TO MAKE UP TO 13% OR MORE ON YOUR SAVINGS — ALL FULLY INSURED!" It went on to say how upset the savings banks were about this book, but there was nothing they could do, and the interest you earned could be even more than 13%, etc., etc. And when you sent for the book—could you really have expected differently?—you found that to earn these astounding rates of interest you had to spend most of your waking life transferring money with split-second precision from one bank on a Friday afternoon to another that handled its accounting a different way, and back and forth and around—*and even then you were only earning this rate a few days out of the year.* You did not earn 13% annually. Most of the time you earned just 5½%; *sometimes* you could jigger it to earn at a 13% annual rate over a long weekend. And for those extra dimes and nickels—*who cares?*

If, then, you have $10,000 or less, you know what to do with it. You've probably already done it: it's earning a tiny bit of interest someplace safe. If this book hasn't made you a dime, at least it's confirmed your good sense. And you can always start reading again when your fortunes swell. (Well, do read the next chapter, because you may be able to salt away and compound your savings tax-free.)

For those who have got enough money to make an extra point or two of interest worth worrying over, there are three things that will determine what you can get for it, three things the financial markets reward: volume, patience, and risk. To each of the three, the same refrain dolefully applies: the rich get richer.

- **Volume.** As with any product, financial or otherwise, if you buy in quantity, you generally get a better deal. It is well known that the odds are worst for the little guy—whether it be the dreadful odds of the state lotteries or the only slightly less dreadful odds of the nickel slot machines. The smaller the stakes, the larger the cut the house demands. (Happily, as I will explain, with things like deep-discount brokers, index mutual funds, and programs like Treasury Direct, there are ways to level the playing field.)

- **Patience.** The longer you are willing to tie up your money, the higher the interest rate you will ordinarily be paid for it. Only during occasional "credit crunches" will short-term rates temporarily exceed long-term rates.

- **Risk.** The more risk you take, the greater your potential reward (and the greater your chance of loss—see The Only Graph in This Book on page 80). But how much risk—even if it is, in your opinion, a "good" risk—can you afford to take?

If I offered you 2-to-1 odds on the flip of an honest coin— heads you win $20, tails you lose $10—wouldn't you take the bet? But what if the odds were the same, only you stood to lose $1,000? Or $50,000? Wherever you draw the line is a measure of your chickenheartedness—which is doubtless justified. There

The Only Graph in This Book

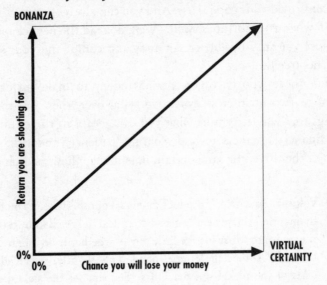

are a lot of excellent risks around that people of limited means simply cannot prudently accept.

One of them may be the stock market, but that's another chapter. For now, what are the alternatives for the investor who wants to take only minimal risk? Broadly speaking, these financial "instruments," also called "debt instruments" or "fixed-income securities," can be divided into short term and long term —just as your own credit-card borrowings are short term, while your mortgage seems to stretch on into eternity.

Not all make sense, as you'll see. But I run through them so you'll no longer glaze over when you hear the phrase "cumulative preferred." And so you'll understand *why* they don't make sense for you. The basics of this stuff, as it turns out, are really pretty simple. **If you get bored, or have no big bucks to invest, skip ahead to page 100 ("Loans to Friends")** and pick up from there.

Short Term

Money-Market Funds

Money-market funds invest your cash in blue-chip short-term government and corporate obligations, yet let you write checks, so they're really **like checking accounts that pay interest.** Generally, they pay a bit more than your bank. The tradeoff: they're not federally insured. The Money Fund Report at **imoneynet.com** maintains a current list of the top-yielding money-market funds, including funds that only invest in U.S. government securities (giving you something close to federal insurance) or municipal securities (if you want your interest tax-free).

Basically, you want a fund that's convenient and that has the lowest possible annual expense charges. The less they charge, the more you keep.

The most convenient money-market funds for substantial investors are the cash-management accounts—CMAs—offered by most brokers. Here your cash balances are automatically swept into a money-market checking account. And if you overdraw your cash balance, it triggers an automatic, relatively low-cost margin loan against the value of your stocks and bonds.

Safe as money-market funds are, whenever you venture beyond FDIC-insured bank accounts you ought to try to understand what you're investing in. Thousands of investors in the Piper Jaffray Institutional Government Income Portfolio (how's that for a safe-sounding name?) found out they had lost nearly 30% of their money in a few months in 1994 because it had reached for a higher yield by speculating on interest rates.

During the financial panic of 2008, the federal government stepped in and temporarily guaranteed virtually all money-market fund assets. But if you're going to rely on the feds, why not cut out the middleman and deal with them directly?

Treasury Bills

The safest short-term securities in the world — free of state and local income tax, to boot — are United States Treasury bills, now issued in $100 increments for three, six, and twelve months. You can purchase (and sell) them via Treasury Direct — **treasurydirect .gov.**

Even so, I have never bought a Treasury bill in my life. For me, it's easier just to use money-market funds.

LONG TERM

When you buy a bond you are lending money, whether to Uncle Sam, General Motors, or the City of Houston. There are three risks. The first is that you won't get paid back. The second is that you'll get paid back early. The third is that, should you want to sell the bond sometime before maturity (the payback date), you won't be able to get as much as you paid.

The first risk is a function of the creditworthiness of the borrower. It could go broke.

The second risk stems from the fact that many bonds are issued with provisions that allow the issuer to call them in before maturity. You thought you'd be getting a big fat interest rate for 20 years, but the particular bond you bought was callable — and when interest rates fell, sure enough, the issuer called them in. When this happens, you get back the full $1,000 face value of the bond — often with a small premium — but then have to go out looking for a new place to lend your money, presumably at a lower rate. Never buy a bond without first understanding its call provisions. (Fortunately, U.S. Treasury bonds are all noncallable.)

The third risk in buying bonds is that you may lose money when you go to sell them — even though if you held all the way to maturity you'd get full face value. That's because: **When interest rates rise, bond prices fall.**

There is a market for money just as there is a market for everything else—coffee, plywood, lemons—and when lots of people are trying to borrow but few are willing to lend, the price (namely, interest rates) goes up. When few are trying to borrow and many are eager to lend, the price (interest rates) goes down. Simple supply and demand, plus a good dose of government intervention. (The government controls the overall supply of money—which, unlike coffee, plywood, or lemons, does not grow on trees.)

The key to everything financial, and to nearly everything economic, is interest rates. When the going rate for money rises, bond prices fall. When the going rate for money falls, bonds rise.

There's nothing mysterious about this; it's simple arithmetic. If you paid $1,000 ("par") for a bond that paid $50-a-year interest, and then the general level of interest rates rose such that newly issued bonds were paying *$70* interest—who in his right mind would buy yours for $1,000? Why would anyone take 5% interest when the going rate had risen to 7%? If, however, you offered the bond at, say, $850, you might be able to sell it (depending on how long it had to run to maturity), because the buyer would be getting $50 interest on $850—5.88%—plus the prospect of a $150 profit when the bond matured.

It's like a seesaw. Rates up, bonds down; rates down, bonds up. It's just two ways of expressing the same thing, like the fullness or emptiness of a glass. The more full a glass gets, the less empty; the less full, the more empty.

(On stock prices, interest rates have a triple-barreled effect. For one thing, the higher interest rates go, the less attractive stocks look by comparison . . . so people sell stocks to buy bonds. Second, high interest rates discourage people from borrowing to buy stocks on margin. Third, high interest rates mean high borrowing costs to business, a drag on consumption, and, often, lower profits. It's definitely possible for stocks to rise despite rising interest rates if those rising interest rates accompany an upturn in economic activity—or to fall despite falling interest rates if the market foresees a worsening economy. The "seesaw" is not automatic with stocks, as it is with bonds. But it's a powerful relationship nonetheless.)

There are different interest rates for different kinds of borrowers and different kinds of loans, but they all move in rough tandem. If the rate banks charge their prime customers goes up, you can be sure the rates they charge their lesser customers will go up as well. If corporations have to offer a higher interest rate to float a bond issue, you can be sure municipalities do, too.

Interest rates, furthermore, sit on top of inflation. If inflation is generally expected to run at 6% a year, lenders are going to feel awfully foolish lending their money at 5%—so they don't. As a general rule of thumb, long-term interest rates on high-quality bonds run around 3% above lenders' expectations of long-term inflation rates.

For a bit of perspective, let alone nostalgia, see page 87 on how interest rates have fluctuated since 1920.

You will notice that someone who bought a 20-year 3% bond at face value ($1,000) when it was issued in 1955, entitling him to $30-a-year interest until 1975, probably began to feel regretful not long after, as similar bonds were soon being issued at more than 4%—$40 a year.

Had one, on the other hand, bought 6% General Motors Acceptance Corp. bonds at $430 each in July 1982—bonds that promised to pay what then seemed to be a paltry $60 a year until 2011 and thus sold for less than half their $1,000 face value—one could have turned around and sold them in January 1983 for $560 apiece, as that $60 a year began to seem a little less paltry. A 30% gain in six months.

Clearly, if you knew which way interest rates were headed,

you could profit handily. Many people therefore try to guess, and some, in any given year, guess right. Few, however, can guess right consistently, least of all you or I or the folks on CNBC. Experts disagree, and the majority view at any given time is about as likely to be wrong as the minority view. The one thing on which there is nearly unanimous agreement is the difficulty of predicting interest rates.

Certainly rates in the 1950s seemed very high by comparison to those in the forties—yet in the sixties they climbed higher still. Almost no one in the world would have believed, in 1965, that a mere 15 years later interest rates would top 20% in the United States of America—which is why they were willing to buy long-term bonds that yielded less than 5%. I like to think we may not see such lofty rates again in our lifetimes. Interest rates as I write this are back down to *Ozzie and Harriet* levels. (Too young ever to have heard of *Ozzie and Harriet*? Well, that's my point.) But by the time you read this—or by the next time you do—rates could be sky-high. Or spiraling inflation could shatter the value of the currency altogether, as it did in Germany after World War I, in which case any long-term fixed-income security becomes worthless. On the other hand, imagine how great you'd feel if you had bought 30-year 15% Treasury bonds in 1981, as many brave souls did. In 2010, you would *still* have been getting $150 a year from each bond for one more year, even as the Treasury was paying others just $2 or $3 to lend it $1,000 for a year. And then in 2011, the 30 years having finally passed, you would have gotten your $1,000 principal back at maturity —and faced the quandary of where to invest it next.

There is general agreement that inflation of much more than 2% or 3% is murderous. It drives up interest rates, eats away at profits, lowers living standards, stifles the incentive to invest, worsens unemployment. Runaway "double-digit" inflation is the economic equivalent of nuclear disaster, a thing that must be avoided at all costs—or so most economists and politicians believe—if the economic order is to survive. As a result, one expects a great deal of effort and energy to be applied at the highest levels to keep interest rates from reaching new peaks.

This was not nearly so much the case in the fifties and early sixties, when the rise in inflation and interest rates, though unwelcome, was not widely perceived to threaten the foundation of society. It was thought, in fact, that a bit of inflation was a good thing. It made everyone feel prosperous—wages and profits and real estate values kept edging up—and the confidence *that* inspired helped to keep the economy bubbling along. But if inflation of 2% and long-term interest rates of 5% are "just about right," double-digit inflation is something else entirely. In 30 years, $1 shrinks in buying power to 54 cents at 2% inflation —but to *3* cents at 12% inflation.

The prospect of $1 shrinking in value to 3 cents in 30 years so threatens prosperity that central bankers and even politicians are likely to try hard to keep inflation in check. Even so, as a general rule, **never buy long-term bonds unless they are "noncallable" and you have good reason to think the general direction of long-term interest rates is down.** That is most decidedly not the case as I write this, with the 30-year Treasury rate under 3%.

So much for background. What sorts of long-term chicken-hearted investments should you consider?

Treasury Notes

These are "intermediate-term" bonds, issued with lives between two and ten years. They compare nicely with CDs you'd get at your bank, especially because the interest they pay is exempt from state and local income taxes. Like Treasury bills, they can be bought through Treasury Direct with a minimum purchase of just $100.

Once issued, Treasury notes trade actively, so you can easily

A Table That Looks Boring but Is Actually Most Revealing

Year	Prime Rate	Triple-A Bonds	Municipal Bonds	Savings Accounts	Home Mortgages	Inflation
1920	6.58%	6.12%	4.98%	4½%	5.75%	2.3%
1925	4.98	4.88	4.09	4½	5.90	3.8
1929	6.02	4.73	4.27	4½	5.92	0.8
1930	3.50	4.55	4.07	4½	5.95	-6.0
1935	1.50	3.60	2.40	2½	5.26	3.0
1940	1.50	2.84	2.50	2½	5.40	0.1
1945	1.50	2.62	1.67	1½	4.70	2.3
1950	2.07	2.62	1.98	2½	4.95	5.8
1955	3.16	3.06	2.53	2¾	5.18	4.8
1960	4.82	4.41	3.73	3½	5.85	1.5
1965	4.54	4.49	3.27	4½	5.74	1.9
1966	5.62	5.13	3.82	4½	6.14	3.4
1967	5.63	5.51	3.98	4½	6.33	3.0
1968	6.28	6.18	4.51	4½	6.83	4.7
1969	7.95	7.03	5.81	4½	7.66	6.1
1970	7.91	8.04	6.50	4¼	8.27	5.5
1971	5.70	7.39	5.70	4¼	7.59	3.4
1972	5.25	7.21	5.27	4¼	7.45	3.4
1973	8.02	7.44	5.18	5½	7.95	8.8
1974	10.80	8.57	6.09	5¼	8.92	12.2
1975	7.86	8.83	6.89	5¼	8.75	7.0
1976	6.83	8.44	6.64	5¼	8.90	4.8
1977	6.82	8.20	5.68	5¼	8.68	6.5
1978	9.06	8.99	6.03	5¼	7.92	9.3
1979	12.67	10.05	6.52	5½	10.94	13.0
1980	15.27	12.77	8.60	5½	13.50	11.9
1981	18.87	14.17	11.23	5½	14.70	8.9
1982	14.86	13.79	11.57	5½	15.14	3.9
1983	10.79	12.04	9.47	5½	12.57	3.8
1984	12.04	12.71	10.15	5½	12.38	4.0
1985	9.93	11.37	9.18	5½	11.55	3.8
1986	8.33	9.02	7.38	5½	10.17	1.1
1987	8.21	9.38	7.73	5½	9.31	4.4
1988	9.32	9.71	7.76	5½	9.19	4.4
1989	10.87	9.26	7.24	5½	10.13	4.7
1990	10.01	9.32	7.25	5½	10.05	6.1
1991	8.46	8.77	6.89	4½	9.32	3.1
1992	6.25	8.14	6.41	2½	8.24	2.9
1993	6.00	7.22	5.63	2½	7.20	2.8
1994	7.15	7.97	6.19	2½	7.49	2.7
1995	8.83	7.59	5.95	2½	7.87	2.5
1996	8.27	7.37	6.75	2½	7.80	3.3
1997	8.44	7.27	5.55	2½	7.71	1.7
1998	8.35	6.53	5.12	2	7.07	1.6
1999	8.00	7.04	5.43	2	7.04	2.7
2000	9.23	7.62	5.77	1¾	7.52	3.4
2001	6.91	7.08	5.19	1½	7.00	1.6
2002	4.67	6.49	5.05	1	6.43	2.4
2003	4.12	5.67	4.73	½	5.80	1.9
2004	4.34	5.63	4.68	1½	5.84	3.3
2005	6.19	5.23	4.40	3.3	5.86	3.4
2006	7.96	5.59	4.40	5.1	6.41	2.5
2007	8.05	5.56	4.40	5.2	6.34	4.1
2008	5.09	5.63	4.86	2.7	6.04	0.1
2009	3.25	5.31	4.62	0.3	5.04	2.7
2010	3.25	5.17	4.35	0.2	4.96	2.0
2015	3.25	2.86	3.60	0.2	3.90	0.5

buy or sell them any time. Unlike bank CDs, there's no penalty for selling early, other than the commission you pay your bank or broker. Because of the interest-rate seesaw, you'll make a profit if interest rates have declined since you bought them, or suffer a loss if rates have risen. (A nice twist here, often overlooked, is that Treasury notes tend to rise in value slightly as time goes by; so if you do sell early, you're less likely to suffer a loss. This is because the market generally demands a higher rate of return to make a long-term loan than a short-term loan. And as time passes, the Treasury note you bought has a shorter and shorter remaining term. Someone thinking of buying your note doesn't think of it as the five-year note you originally bought; she thinks of it as a two-year note, if that's how long it has left to run. When she sees that your "two-year" note yields 5%, that may be enough to entice her to pay you full price, even though the rate on newly issued five-year notes might now be 6%.)

Treasury Bonds

Treasury bonds are the same as Treasury notes, only with maturities in excess of ten years. Generally speaking you shouldn't buy them, because over such long periods you'll nearly always do better to invest in stocks.

True, if interest rates are high and you lock them in for 30 years, you could make a killing when rates fell back down. (That seesaw again.) But falling rates could make stocks go up even more. Only in a Depression-type deflationary situation would Treasury bonds reliably outperform the stock market.

Like 2008. Everything collapsed that year—stocks, real estate, commodities, art—while the price of long-term Treasury bonds rose 26%.

But such times are rare. In the long run, even the U.S. Treasury depends on the productivity of society (the unemployed and profitless can't pay much in taxes), so betting on government bonds to do well while the rest of society fails can only work short-term.

At best, long-term bonds are a short-term hedge against deflation. They might play a part in a rich man's mix (see Chapter 11 on how to use them after you've made your fortune), but they certainly aren't a place for any of your first dollars.

(One way to hedge against both inflation *and* deflation is to buy recently issued TIPS—Treasury Inflation-Protected Securities—which I'll come to in a minute.)

Stocks are perceived to be riskier than bonds—and over relatively short periods of time (and especially if you don't spread your risk by diversifying) they certainly are. But **after inflation, someone who remained continually invested in long-term Treasury bonds from 1946 to 1981 would have had an overall loss of 70%, even before considering taxes.** After taxes, the loss would have been closer to 80%. It's true that after 1981 bonds then turned around, finally, to score a huge gain. But they still didn't equal the performance of the stock market, up more than 20-fold since then (not even counting dividends!).

Today, long-term interest rates would seem to have more room to rise over the next couple of decades than to fall. And —remember the seesaw—higher rates equal lower bond prices.

Inflation-Adjusted Bonds: World's Safest Investment

TIPS. The Treasury began offering Treasury Inflation-Protected Securities (TIPS) in 1997. They pay a low fixed rate for a period of years—but their $1,000 face value actually rises with inflation (and falls with deflation—but not below $1,000). So virtually all major long-term risk is eliminated. There's essentially no risk the U.S. Treasury will default. Deflation is not a problem —your $1,000 at maturity will buy even more. And there is no inflation risk.

Where else can you get a deal like that?

The drawback: Uncle Sam treats the semiannual inflation adjustments as taxable income, even though you don't actually *get* them until you sell the bonds or cash them in at maturity. Yikes!

One way around this is to buy shares of a *mutual fund* that invests in TIPS, like the Vanguard Inflation-Protected Securities Fund . . . or to buy shares of an *exchange-traded fund,* like the iShares Barclay's TIPS Bond Fund, which trades like a stock with the ticker symbol TIP. Both the interest *and* the inflation adjustments are distributed. All taxable, but at least you're getting what you're being taxed on.

Or you could buy TIPS in a tax-deferred retirement account. They're a good alternative for some of your money as you get older — or, for that matter, at times when you think (or someone like Warren Buffett thinks) the stock market has lost its mind.

Caution #1: The inflation protection that TIPS offer is based on *Uncle Sam's* calculation of inflation. Uncle Sam has an incentive to keep that calculation low. (It saves taxpayers money but is not so great for Social Security recipients — or TIPS owners.) The cost of living you personally experience might rise faster than the value of your TIPS.

Caution #2: Even though long-term TIPS will hold their value in the face of inflation far better than any other long-term bond — and even though they will pay off 100 cents on the dollar when they mature — they can still fall in value in the meantime. Let's say you bought a 20-year TIPS issue with a 1% coupon. If sometime in the future Uncle Sam had to offer 3% in order to sell TIPS of a similar maturity, your 1% bonds would be worth less in the open market. Who would pay full price for 1% when they could get 3%? If you wanted to sell, you'd have to knock something off the price.

In this respect, long-term TIPS are similar to any other long-term bond. The big difference is that, because the TIPS yield sits on *top* of inflation, it's unlikely Uncle Sam would ever have to pay dramatically higher rates to sell them. (Higher, like 4%? Maybe. Dramatically higher, like 8%, let alone 15%? No.) Indeed, you can imagine a situation where, with inflation raging, the demand for inflation-protected securities would soar, allowing Uncle Sam to sell them successfully at *lower* yields.

Caution #3: If you buy TIPS when they are first issued, through your stockbroker or through Treasury Direct, you're starting with a clean slate and it's simple. Each bond costs $1,000. It pays, say, 2% interest on that $1,000. A six-year-old could do the math. (And a nine-year-old could grasp that, as inflation over the years boosted the face value of the bond to, say, $1,600, that 2% interest payment would now be *$32* a year, not just $20, with a nice $600 "profit," to boot, if you went to sell.) But if you buy an existing issue in the open market from someone who *has* decided to sell, it's more complicated. Your cost will include the "accreted inflation" from the time the bonds were issued. The price you are *quoted* might be "ninety-three" or "one-oh-one-fifty" — meaning you are paying 93 cents on the dollar or 101.5 cents on the dollar — $930 or $1,015 for each $1,000 bond. But when your brokerage statement arrives, it could be a lot higher. For one thing, there will be a small "accrued interest" charge for the interest the bond has earned since its last payment. No big deal. That, bond buyers are accustomed to. But there will also be what could be a huge charge for all the accreted inflation built into the bond since it was first issued (e.g., that $600 profit your nine-year-old calculated, above). And that's OK, and entirely fair; but it also subjects you to the risks of *de*flation, which is one of the two risks we were trying to avoid. Yes, the bond will ultimately pay off a minimum of $1,000. But if you paid $1,600 for it, there's the risk of loss.

Not that long-term deflation is in any way likely; and not that, if we had it, even $1,000 wouldn't then buy a heck of a lot. But it may still make more sense for most people to buy newly or recently issued TIPS (which would have little or no inflation yet built into them), so they don't even have to think about this added wrinkle.

Series I Savings Bonds. Like TIPS, they guarantee a small fixed return on top of the inflation rate for up to 30 years. Interest is credited monthly, but not paid in cash, and federal income tax doesn't have to be paid until the bonds are redeemed—and perhaps not even then if they are used to pay college expenses for the taxpayer or a dependent. Like all Uncle Sam's bonds, they are never subject to state or local income tax.

You can't trade savings bonds on the open market, but they can be redeemed any time after a year—forfeiting three months' interest if held less than five years.

You are limited to purchasing a maximum of $10,000 worth per owner per year; minimum purchase is $25.

All Treasury bills, notes, and bonds (including savings bonds) bought through **treasurydirect.gov** exist only in electronic form. If you want something to help your heirs remember that you owned them, or something to put into the envelope when you give your daughter I-bonds for her birthday—"Oh, Daddy, it's just what I wanted!"—you can get a printable confirmation. One nice feature of the electronic bonds is that Treasury Direct will *automatically* redeem them (even if you forgot you owned them) and transfer the money to your linked bank account (if you still have it or have linked to the new one). You can also schedule an earlier redemption, if you prefer—just name the date.

These bonds are a slow but steady way to build assets, designed to meet the needs of the smallest saver. How many banks will let you start a savings account with only $25—and with no maintenance fee? Using Treasury Direct, you can arrange for single or periodic purchases by direct debit from your bank account. Easier still, many employers offer payroll-savings plans that deduct your purchase straight from your paycheck.

Series EE Savings Bonds

Series EE savings bonds pay a *fixed* rate of interest — and it's low. If you like savings bonds, stick with the aforementioned inflation-indexed Series I bonds.

Municipal Bonds

There are two kinds of bonds: most of them, which are taxable; and municipals, which are not. Interest on bonds issued by state and local governments or agencies (county sewage authorities and the like) is usually exempt from federal income tax — and from that state's local income taxes as well. Interest on New York City bonds, for example, is exempt from federal, state, and city income tax (but not from California or Illinois income tax). The higher your marginal tax bracket, the more sense it makes for you to favor tax-free bonds.* If you are in the 30% or 40% tax bracket and have taxable bonds in your closet, it's very hard to see why you shouldn't sell them and buy municipals instead. If you have to sell at a loss to do this, all the better. The loss will lower your taxes.

Municipal bonds are not as safe as Treasuries, but "general obligation" bonds — those backed by the full faith and credit of a state or local government, not just the revenues from a hospital or a toll road — are, generally, *individually* safe. Even if a town gets in trouble, the state is likely to find a way to help keep it afloat, because if bondholders lost money it would raise the borrowing costs for all the *other* towns in the state (as bond buyers became warier) and perhaps for the state itself. You might be inconvenienced for a while — some New Yorkers in 1975 were forced to wait an extra year before their "one-year" notes paid off, though they got interest for that extra year — but

---

* You may see ads saying that, to a guy or gal in the 40% marginal tax bracket, a 4% tax-free bond "is the equivalent of earning 6.67%." Nonsense. A 4% tax-free bond is the equivalent of earning 4% — and getting to keep it.

even in a rare disaster, like Orange County's 1995 bankruptcy, you would likely recoup all, or nearly all, your investment. (Likely, but not definitely: Detroit bondholders in 2013 fared worse, as holders of Puerto Rico's bonds seem almost sure to do, as well.)

Just how safe general obligation bonds are *as a class* depends on whether, in a really bad situation, the federal government will step in and prevent defaults. That's highly likely—and arguably what was done as part of the stimulus package to stanch the 2008 financial meltdown and Great Recession that ensued—but, given how deeply and structurally in the red a lot of local governments are, not completely guaranteed. One can imagine some sort of grand plan where it's not just labor contracts and pensions that are forced to take a haircut, but bondholders as well. (That's what happened in Detroit.) More likely, the grand plan will be less dramatic: a period of inflation. That would raise local sales tax and property tax revenues with which to service bond debt, while shrinking the buying power of your bonds without the issuer's having to default on them.

Another risk to consider is the possibility that someday the tax-free status of municipals will be revoked. But even if municipals did lose their exemption—unlikely!—that would almost surely affect only newly issued bonds. In which case old municipals would likely *rise* in value, because there would be a limited and gradually shrinking supply.

A final risk: that income taxes will one day be abandoned for other forms of taxation, rendering the exemption worthless. Fat chance.

If you're buying or selling municipal bonds, always get at least two prices—one from your regular broker, if you have one, and one from a firm like Stoever Glass (800-223-3881 or **stoeverglass.com**) or Lebenthal (877-425-6006 or **lebenthal .com**) that specializes in municipals. You can see recent prices for many bonds online at **investinginbonds.com**.

Especially for smaller and more obscure issues, it may be wise to buy planning to hold on until maturity. That way, even if you are overcharged for the bonds when you buy (how would you know?), at least you won't be underpaid for them when you sell. And it's in the selling that they've really got you, because the broker knows you're unlikely to go to the trouble of setting up an account with some *other* broker just to sell these bonds—so he may make you an offer that's more advantageous to him than to you.

Caution: Avoid "private activity bonds," which governments issue to help finance private projects. They pay better yields than other munis but may subject you to the Alternative Minimum Tax—and thus not be tax-free after all.

Caution: Avoid municipal-bond *funds*—sales and management fees cut deep. If munis are yielding 4% and you give up 3% in a sales fee, that's nine months' interest! Give up a further half-percent annual management fee, and you give up 12.5% of your income! So either buy munis directly, or else use a fund like Vanguard's that charges no sales fee and annual expenses under two-tenths of 1%.

Note: Gains you might make selling tax-free bonds at a profit (if the interest-rate seesaw has lifted their price since you bought them) are subject to capital-gains taxes like any other gains.

Corporate Bonds

Don't buy them. The safest ones, sometimes called investment-grade bonds, pay only a bit more interest than Treasury securities but are subject to state and local taxes. So it's a wash. What's more:

- You can buy Treasuries with no commission, through Treasury Direct.
- If you decide to sell, Treasuries are more liquid than corporate bonds, which means you'll take less of a haircut.

- If you decide *not* to sell, you won't have to worry about having your bonds called in early. Treasuries are noncallable.

- You won't have to worry about default. Treasuries are *completely* safe.

Of course, you can find corporate bonds that pay much higher interest than Treasuries. The riskier the bond, the higher the interest you stand to earn. But ordinarily, if you believe in the issuing company, you might as well buy its stock and *really* profit from its success (and at lower capital-gains tax rates, to boot).

Junk Bonds

Bonds issued with particularly high yields are called "junk" (though not by the companies that issue them). Never buy them when first issued because, as I've said, if they actually turn out to be OK, the underlying stocks will probably turn out even better. Why speculate when the most you can earn is 9% a year (if that's what the bond is issued to yield when safer bonds are yielding 5%)?

But sometimes junk bonds can be an interesting speculation. They promised to pay 9% interest when they were issued, but now times are tough, the interest payments have been suspended, and sellers are dumping them in a panic. The sellers could be right, of course: the bonds could prove totally worthless. But say you buy them at 50 cents on the dollar and worse does *not* come to worst. Now at least there's some real upside. That 9% coupon, if interest payments resume, means $90 a year on each bond you just snagged for $500—an *18%* annual return. And if the interest payments do begin to look secure, the price of the bond will head back up toward $1,000, so you could make another fast profit that way. But as lucrative as this can occasionally be, it's clearly not the stuff of chickenhearted investing. It's much more like buying a speculative stock—to which all the caveats in the following chapters apply.

Bond Funds

Nah. You get diversification and professional management—but why pay for something you don't need? Treasuries are *already* safe; you don't need to diversify. And, especially being free of local income taxes, their yield is already pretty good even without professional management.

The problem is that all the people involved in a fund, not unreasonably, want to be paid for their work, and the brokers executing all the buys and sells want to be paid, too. When you buy a Treasury security direct from the Federal Reserve, with nobody else taking a cut, you are starting with an advantage that turns out to be hard for most funds to overcome.

Unit Trusts

Unit trusts are mutual funds that are not managed. Whatever corporate or municipal bonds (or stocks) they start out with are the ones they keep. As a result, there is ordinarily no management fee to speak of. There is generally a sales commission, however—typically 4%. Imagine a savings bank that charged you a 4% fee to accept your money and only then began giving you interest on the $96 of each $100 that remained. Worse, the fella who assembles the package of bonds is more concerned that the yield look attractive now, so it sells, than that 12 years from now, when he is in his hot tub on Maui, the bonds remain safe.

Ick. If your broker tries to sell one of these to your aging parents, get them a new broker.

Convertible Bonds

These pay interest but also give you the right to trade your bonds for a given number of shares of common stock. That's what's known as an "equity kicker." With a convertible bond, you have a chance to both sleep well *and* eat well. In tough times, unless the company goes bankrupt, you get your interest; but should the company strike it rich, you could profit along with the common shareholders.

Convertible bonds can be fine. But why are you suddenly giving up your other hobbies, or quality time with the kids, to become a convertible bond expert? As I have already argued, corporate bonds don't make a lot of sense—buy TIPS if you want real safety. (Convertible bond issuers sometimes *do* go bankrupt.) And as I will shortly argue, picking individual stocks doesn't make sense for most people, either.

Zero-Coupon Bonds

Zero-coupon bonds pay no interest. Instead, they're sold cheap and rise gradually to $1,000 at maturity. The longer the maturity, the lower their price. Back when interest rates were sky-high, I bought one that sold for barely 5 cents on the dollar. What fun to see the $100,000 face value show up on my brokerage statement each month! Over the next 30 years, the market value of the bonds would rise from the $5,125 I paid for them to . . . $100,000! That's a little better than 10% compounded.

Purchasers of *ordinary* long-term bonds may lock in high interest—but what will they earn in interest *on that*? That's the beauty of a long-term *zero-coupon* bond: assuming the issuer doesn't go broke, the compounded annual return is locked in from the start.

Zeros are far riskier than regular bonds, if you don't intend to hold them to maturity, because small swings in the prevailing long-term interest rate produce huge swings in the market value of the bonds. Think of that seesaw again. With zeros, it's a huge one: 30 feet tall, say, and 30 feet from your seat to the fulcrum. At first, you (and your partner at the opposite end, 60 feet away) go way up and down. But if you both inch toward the center, a foot a year, then by the 29th year, almost nose to nose, neither one of you is going up or down very much. At its exact center, the seesaw doesn't rise or fall at all. To a 30-year zero-coupon bond, "the exact center" is the day of maturity, when — assuming the issuer can pay off (the seesaw hasn't been torn down to build a body-piercing salon) — it's worth exactly $1,000.

So you'd only want to consider a zero-coupon bond when interest rates are very high, and from an issuer you consider impregnable (if you're in this for safety).

Actually (even though this is the wrong chapter for it), it might be more interesting to speculate in zeros of companies in precarious shape — but at such low prices that if they pulled through, you'd reap it. In an earlier revision of this book, I bragged about owning some Revlon Worldwide zeros purchased in mid-1994 at 43 cents on the dollar and promising 100 cents on March 15, 1998. "If they pay off," wrote I — this was an anecdote without an ending at the time — "I will have reaped a compounded annual 25% return. If they don't, I'll get somewhere between zero (if the issuer goes bankrupt and there are not enough assets to pay the bondholders anything) and more than that (if there are)." I took this gamble knowing nothing about Revlon Worldwide except that the guy who controls it, Ron Perelman, is a billionaire who'd be embarrassed if the bonds defaulted. (So it was a no-lose situation. Either I'd make a lot of money, or I'd get to feel superior to a billionaire.) As it turned out, they paid off. And yet, when — emboldened by this success — I tried to repeat it with Perelman-associated Marvel Toy bonds at 20 cents on the dollar, I lost every penny. And I don't even feel all that superior.

The four other big caveats with zeros (the first being that you could lose money): you're taxed on the "imputed" interest each year even though you don't actually receive it; many are callable based on an "accretion schedule" that will limit your profit if the interest-rate seesaw goes your way; many are illiquid, so you could have trouble selling them at a fair price; they complicate your tax preparation.

Preferred Stocks

Preferred stocks are like bonds. You get a fixed payout each year but no piece of the action. They are "preferred" only in that their dividend must be paid in full before any dividend on common stock may be paid; and should the company fail, preferred shareholders come ahead of common shareholders—but behind an awful lot of others, such as bondholders—if anything remains to be split up. What preferreds do not provide is an opportunity to participate in the company's good fortune, should it have any. The dividend never goes up.

A "convertible preferred" does give you some of that upside —but with the same caveats as convertible bonds, above.

A "cumulative preferred"—whether convertible or not—is one that promises to pay its dividend no matter what, even if it can't be paid on time. No common-stock dividends may be paid until all the preferred dividends are brought current.

Who cares?

Unless you think you have a special talent for discerning which desperately ill companies will somehow return to health and pay out all their accumulated dividends, why are we discussing this?

Loans to Friends

"It is better to give than to lend," said British war correspondent Philip Gibbs, "and it costs about the same." Truer words were never spoken. A better solution may be to offer to guarantee a bank loan. You are still on the hook if your friend or relative defaults, but in the meantime the bank sends the nasty letters. What's more, the fear of a bad credit rating might actually do more to get the loan repaid than the fear of losing your friendship.

Sometimes, of course, the "loan" is quite intentionally just a face-saving way to help a friend too proud to ask for a gift but too poor to pay you back. Good for you for being such a nice guy.

Two Final Words to the Chickenhearted

1. *Getting a high rate of interest doesn't help if you don't save money in the first place.* Many people won't save unless "forced" to. For this reason, a payroll-savings plan or some other form of modest-return saving (for years, savings bank Christmas Clubs paid no interest at all!) is better than *planning* to invest in something with a higher return and never getting around to it.

2. *It's important for us chickenhearted souls to understand true risk.* The biggest financial risk you face is not that you will suffer occasional losses on your investments. It is that you will not accumulate enough money to pay the important expenses that must come out of savings: unexpected emergencies, house down payments, college, retirement. Saving more money is the surest way to reduce this risk. But, especially for retirement, it probably isn't enough.

Even if you sock away 20% of every paycheck your entire adult life, you will only have enough to live for eight or nine years past retirement unless you get some growth. After taxes and inflation, it is virtually impossible to get it from "safe" investments. Long-term growth will almost certainly have to come from exposing some of your money to risk in stocks, real estate, or your own business (or perhaps all three).

It is unlikely that you will be able to accept the uncertainty of these investments without having a base of savings that feels truly *safe.* Common sense tells you that trying to squeeze extra interest out of *safe* money is a sure way to expose it to risk. So don't feel dumb keeping your short-term money someplace truly safe and convenient, and exposing your long-term money to prudent risk.

Tax Strategies

A taxpayer is someone who doesn't have to take a
civil service examination to work for the government.

— STOCK TRADER'S ALMANAC

TAXES DRAG DOWN your investment results.

Up until 1986, when the top federal tax bracket was 50%, people would, understandably, do almost anything to try to beat taxes. The world was awash with tax-shelter salespeople. But tax shelters, as it turned out, were generally a way to spend $20,000 to avoid $10,000 in taxes. Oil and gas deals, railcar deals, bull-semen deals—I lost so much money! I never did a bull-semen deal, but boy, did I do oil and gas. In Ohio, mostly, which may have been my first mistake.

Now much of that nonsense is gone—partly because the top tax brackets have come down, partly because people have learned from their mistakes, and partly because, along with lowering the top tax brackets, Congress closed a lot of loopholes.

Good. Most of them just led to stupid behavior anyway.

In this chapter: a few basic notions that can significantly reduce the drag of taxes on the growth of your assets.

(Note: Many of the numbers in this chapter will rise a bit with inflation. A good source for the current numbers is **fair mark.com/reference/index.htm**.)

Kids

The best advice, of course, financially, is not to have any. But if you've already ignored that—and I hope you have—one way to have some of your savings compound tax-free is to save money in *their* names, with *their* Social Security numbers on the savings or brokerage accounts, and let *them* pay taxes on the interest or dividends that accrue. As the tax code currently stands, there will be no tax due on the first $1,050 that a dependent child under 24 earns and only 10% due on the next $1,050, for a total of $105 in tax, versus perhaps $600 you might have had to pay yourself. (Beyond $2,100, the investment income a dependent child under 24 earns is taxed at the parents' rate. From age 24, or when the child ceases to be a dependent, if sooner, it's all taxed at the child's rate.) With two kids each earning $2,100 a year, you'd save twice as much.

Each parent can give each child up to $14,000 each year without having to pay gift tax. As custodian of a child's savings or brokerage account, you have the right to withdraw funds at any time to spend on the child's behalf (except that if you use the income from the account for basic child support, the IRS may tax you as if you, not the child, had earned it). The child may not touch the money before turning 18 or 21, depending on your state, though you can relinquish custodianship sooner.

Say you had twins tomorrow and saved $1,000 a year for 18 years for each of them. Say, further, that you could grow their money at 5% after tax in your tax bracket, but at 7% after tax in theirs. After 18 years, you'd have cleared an extra $11,700 by saving it in their names.

There are drawbacks:

- It complicates your life, having to file a tax return for each child each year.

- The money you save this way *belongs to your child*. She or he might decide to spend it on pernition* rather than tuition when the time comes.

---

* *Pernition:* not a word, but should be.

• When the time does come, financial aid officers will be less generous to a child with $40,000 in blue chips than to a pauper whose parents have that same $40,000 augmenting their retirement fund. This is a moot point if you are fairly well off, since your child will not likely get outright scholarship money either way. Loans are the aid that will be available, and their availability should not be jeopardized by your child's nest egg.

Perhaps the best reason to save some money in your children's names is to get them interested. You might even choose to set up some sort of "matching" program where for every dollar your son or daughter saves from her baby-sitting or computer-consulting fees—or even just from her allowance—you'll kick in an extra buck or two. Not that you want to turn your 13-year-old into a middle-aged Midas, complaining about the double taxation of dividends while her classmates are complaining about homework. But instilling good money habits—like smart shopping and steady saving—is one of the best things you can do for your kids.

Education Savings Accounts

If you qualify—which you do unless your income is well into six figures*—these make great sense for the first $2,000 a year being saved for your child's or grandchild's education.

Coverdell Education Savings Accounts, as they are known —ESAs—may be established in the name of any child, and anyone can make nondeductible contributions to them (not just the child or parents) until the beneficiary reaches 18. After that, all the money may be withdrawn tax-free to pay for higher education costs.

---

* A taxpayer who exceeds the income limit can simply give the money to the child, perhaps in a custodial account controlled by the taxpayer . . . then make the same contribution from the custodial account, which will be considered a contribution by the child, who presumably does not exceed the income limit. Ah, the lunacy of the tax code.

If little Sally should decide to join the circus instead of the Class of '28, the money can be rolled into the plan of her baby brother, or else just sit there growing, in case she tires of trapeze and opts for college after all.

Any money that remains in the account when the beneficiary reaches 30 is then distributed to her, with its growth subject to income tax and a 10% penalty.

Money drawn from an ESA can also be used for private elementary or secondary school tuition or to buy Conner a computer, but don't do it: tax-free income doesn't grow on trees, so you want to keep your earnings compounding as long as possible before you cash in.

Note: The tax credit (or deduction) you are normally allowed for paying tuition expenses does not apply to dollars paid out of an education savings account, as they have already been tax-blessed.

You can set up an ESA at a bank or mutual fund or brokerage house, as you would an IRA.

Qualified Tuition Programs — 529s

A terrific alternative or supplement to the education savings account is the Qualified Tuition Program, known as a 529 plan.

All states have these plans; a consortium of private colleges has created one as well. As with education savings accounts, they allow your savings to compound tax-free. Unlike ESAs, contributions don't necessarily have to stop when the child reaches 18, nor need all the money be distributed by age 30, and the limit on contributions isn't reached, in most cases, until the value of the plan equals the cost of four years at the most expensive private college in the state.

You can spend 529 money at any college, even if it is NOT in the state that is holding your money. And most states open their plans to out-of-state residents, so even though you live in Ohio, you have close to 100 state plans to choose from (several states offer multiple plans).

Most plans let you reallocate your investments twice each year. And by law, you can also roll all or part of the account to another state's plan every 12 months (you can enroll in plans in more than one state). Which is great, because with so many state plans to choose from—and the constant improvements being adopted by each in competition with the others—the best one today might be just average by the time you read this.

Fortunately, a fellow named Joe Hurley seems eager to devote his entire life to evaluating the various 529 plans. You need only visit **savingforcollege.com** for his latest thinking.

Last I looked, Nevada's plan offered Vanguard domestic and international index funds and a fund that invests in TIPS. Nevada's average 0.5% annual total expense ratio wasn't the best, but through an arrangement with Upromise (which administers the plan), you could register your credit and debit cards to have cash added to the account automatically when you bought gas, groceries, books, and hundreds of other items at qualifying businesses. Even Priceline purchases racked up 2% cash back to your child's Nevada 529 plan.

(Just don't let the Upromise tail wag your smart-shopping dog. You don't want to spend 10% more to patronize a merchant enrolled in Upromise in order to save 2% for your child's 529.)

If Nevada's $3,000 minimum is beyond your means, consider Iowa's plan, which also uses Vanguard funds and can be started with as little as $25.

Most people should probably contribute their first $2,000 of college savings each year to an education savings account, which allows total flexibility in the choice of investments, then use a 529 plan for any amounts above that. If you live in a state that allows a tax deduction for contributions to its plan, you might reverse this—use the 529 plan up to the limit allowed for the tax deduction; contribute any excess to an education savings account.

One advantage of both ESAs and 529 plans over saving in your child's name is that these accounts are considered assets of the contributor, not the child, so they have less effect on available student aid.

Retirement Plans

As you doubtless know, the money you've been paying in Social Security taxes, lo these many years, has not been set aside for your retirement. Most of it has been paid out to people already *in* retirement. It's gone. Social Security will always provide at least bare subsistence for those in need (see page 263 for details). But if we want to retire in comfort, we will have to provide, in large measure, for ourselves. Fortunately, there are a variety of tax-deferred retirement plans to help.

401(k) and 403(b)

The best retirement plans are the 401(k) and 403(b) "salary reduction plans" that tens of millions of employees contribute to. What makes them so good is that many employers add 25 cents or 50 cents or even more to each dollar you choose to save this way. *This is free money.* If your employer offers a deal like this and you're not taking full advantage of it, you're an idiot. (Well, I'm sorry, but c'mon: if your local bank decided to give out free money to attract deposits—say, $500 for each new $1,000— there would be riots in the streets, so eager would people be to get in on it.)

Even if your employer doesn't augment your own contribution, you should fund your 401(k) to the limit, because:

- It is a relatively painless way to save.
- You avoid taxes on the money you contribute until, many years later, you withdraw it.
- In the meantime, no tax is due as it grows.

You get Uncle Sam's share of your income working for you all those years as well as your own. The tax drag is lessened considerably.

In 2016, employees could contribute as much as $18,000 to a 401(k) if their income was high enough (the contribution limit is based on a percentage of salary), plus as much as $6,000 more if they were at least 50 years old.

And how to deploy the assets in your 401(k)? Well, this is long-term money, so you should lean heavily on the alternative that does best over the long term: stocks. There will be years when the value of your 401(k) drops sharply. But over the long run, the odds are in your favor. Unless you think you can outsmart the market (hint: you can't), the simplest and most sensible thing to do is just keep building your assets in the fund without trying to switch them in and out of the stock market.

That said, if your plan offers an "international" stock-market fund as well as a U.S. fund, you might split your money over both. We are by no means the only game in town anymore.

The most common mistake 401(k) participants make is to deploy their 401(k) assets too conservatively—although this certainly will not seem like a mistake in years when the stock market plunges. Even as you near retirement, you shouldn't switch all your money out of stocks and into short-term or guaranteed safe stuff. *Some* of it—especially if the stock market is high—but the thing to remember is that the onset of retirement is not the end of the game. A 60-year-old married nonsmoker in decent health has a life expectancy of 26 more years if he's a guy, 31 more years if she's a gal. So even though he or she is contemplating retirement, it's not as if all the 401(k) money will suddenly be withdrawn, spent on canes the first year, walkers the second, and bang—you're gone. With any luck, you still have the long term to provide for. And that means a good chunk of your money, as you near retirement, should stay in stocks.

(Even after you leave your employer, there will be ways to roll your retirement money into other tax-deferred retirement accounts. If the market takes a dive just before you retire, you could roll your stock-market retirement money into other stock-market funds and wait for it to recover.)

The second-most-common mistake 401(k) participants make —out of loyalty, often—is to allocate much of it to their own company's stock. You already have a lot riding on your company . . . your job, perhaps some stock options. To put your retirement eggs in this one basket, too, is not prudent.

Note to 403(b) participants: Nonprofit organizations often offer a variant of the 401(k) called a 403(b) plan. Some of these offer investment choices that include only variable annuities and funds charging high expenses. A little-known loophole, however, lets you assign your contributions to virtually any custodian that handles retirement accounts—mutual funds, for example—if the custodian is willing to establish a 403(b)-7 account. Before your eyes glaze over, just call the mutual fund you'd like to use and ask them to help with the details. It is in their interest to make it easy for you to switch your money to them. Your employer's benefits department may tell you this isn't possible, but unless the law changes, if you persist you will eventually convince them that they're wrong (unless the plan documents explicitly prohibit such transfers, which few plans do). Refer them to IRS Revenue Ruling 90-24 and let their eyes glaze over. The mutual fund trying to get your money will be your ally in providing proof that Congress permits this for all such plans. Don't overlook fees you may be charged for transferring existing retirement savings out of variable annuities or funds with back-end loads; but keep in mind that those with the highest penalties are usually the worst investments, so the penalty may hurt less in the long run than staying put. A book and website—**403bwise.com**—were put together by a couple of educators, Dan Otter and John Moore, who became disgusted with their own 403(b) plans and decided to do better. You can also e-mail TIAA-CREF at **serviceplus1 @tiaa-cref.org** to see if they can help you arrange a 90-24 transfer to them. TIAA-CREF has a long and distinguished history of offering retirement services to teachers and other employees of nonprofit organizations.

IRAs, SEPs, and SIMPLEs

If your employer doesn't offer a 401(k) or 403(b)—or even if it does—you can set up your own retirement account: an IRA (Individual Retirement Account) if you work for somebody; a SEP (Simplified Employee Pension) if you have income from self-employment.* You can do this at just about any bank, brokerage firm, or mutual fund. I recommend the mutual fund route for most people. But the main thing is to *do* it, if you haven't already. Just pick up the phone and call one of the toll-free numbers on pages 275–277 ("Selected Mutual Funds"). They will send you the materials you need to start.

Don't put money in these plans that you might have to withdraw in a year or two, because you will suffer a 10% nondeductible penalty on any money withdrawn before age 59½ (*and* have to pay tax on the full withdrawal). But for money you can set aside for the last 40% of your life (age 60 through 100), these retirement accounts are great.

You could contribute up to $5,500 a year in an IRA as of 2015 ($6,500 if 50 or older), with those limits set to be indexed for inflation.

---

* A SEP is like the old Keogh Plan many of us established, only much simpler. The advantage of either is that you can contribute way more than you can to an IRA—up to 20% of your earnings from self-employment or around $53,000, whichever is less. Or, especially if you have employees, but even if you don't, you might want to establish a SIMPLE (Savings Incentive Match Plan for Employees), a form of 401(k) for small businesses that requires virtually no paperwork or government filings—hence the acronym —yet allows up to $12,500 in pretax dollars to be set aside by each employee (in 2016, rising with inflation)—$15,500 if you're 50 or older—plus an employer match of up to 3% of each employee's wages. Call your mutual fund family for details. Many are not keen on small-business retirement plans. One fund family that welcomes the business is Fidelity (fidelity.com).

Also, **low-income taxpayers get a credit of up to 50% for retirement-plan contributions** (unless they are dependents on someone else's tax return) — including contributions they make to employer plans. So your contribution winds up being half paid by Uncle Sam! **Free money!** (Be sure to put it into a *Roth* IRA — read on — so even the *growth* of this free money will be forever tax-free.) The higher your income, the less the credit; but some credit is available to single individuals with income up to $30,000 and married couples up to $60,000.

Even if you don't qualify for free money, why are these plans so good? (The Roth IRA is a little different and for many people even better — see the next section.)

Let's say you are 29½ and you contribute $5,500 to an IRA next week. At 10% — no slam dunk, but nice to think about — it would compound to $95,972 by the time you were 59½ (when you can begin withdrawing it without penalty) and to $273,819 by age 70½ (when you *have to* start withdrawing it). Let's say you choose at that point to withdraw it all in a lump rather than extend the tax shelter by withdrawing just a little at a time. So at 70½ you'd withdraw $273,819, pay perhaps a third of it in taxes, and have $182,546 left.

Now look at that same $5,500 without the benefit of an IRA. If you had not contributed it to an IRA, at 29½, the first thing that would have happened is that it would have been taxed. Again, say a third of it would have been lopped off in federal and local income taxes, leaving you with $3,667. If you had then invested that $3,667 at the same 10% a year, it would have grown — after paying a third in taxes — at just 6.7%. Thirty years later, at 59½ — assuming you had resisted the temptation to blow the money on lawn furniture — it would have grown to $25,418; by age 70½, to $51,696.

The first way, you are left with $182,546; the second, $51,696. The IRA leaves you with more than three times as much money, even though it requires absolutely no more to start with, no more risk or effort, and less self-discipline (because once it's locked up in the plan, you will not constantly be tempted to do something different with it).

And that's just $5,500, one year.

Which is good, because in 41 years $182,546 isn't going to buy nearly as much as it does today, and you golfers are going to need a lot more than that to live comfortably within driving range of a driving range. **But no matter how much or little $182,546 buys 41 years from now, it will buy a heck of a lot more than $51,696.**

The prime thing to note is the importance of starting early. Indeed, the contributions in your later years will add relatively little to the value of your fund. It is the early contributions that, compounded over time, grow enormously.

You could, for example, contribute just $1,000 a year from age 20 to 35 and then nothing. If you then withdrew the money between the ages of 65 and 80, your initial $15,000 would have grown (at 8%) to provide you well over $400,000!

What's that? You just got out of school and you earn $19,000 and you can't possibly scrape together the money for this even with the low-income tax credit? How about getting your parents or grandparents to give you the cash to do it? When you get your tax credit, you could even pay part of it back. I just hate leaving **free money** on the table.

So why doesn't everyone who qualifies for such a plan set one up and contribute all he can? The primary objection comes from people who don't want to tie up their money for so long.

Yet there are two very strong arguments against that objection. In the first place, you *can* withdraw money from these plans. Yes, you have to pay taxes and a penalty. But you would have had to pay taxes on that income, anyway, if you hadn't put it into the plan—so that part isn't so terrible. And the 10% penalty, while indeed stiff—and nondeductible—may not be much to pay for having been allowed to compound your savings—as well as the portion the government would have taken—tax-deferred for several years.

Second and most important: Do you plan to have *any* money saved up by the time you're 59½? *Any* net worth? *Anything* to supplement your Social Security and the generosity of your children? If so—and for most people the answer is an emphatic *yes*—it may as well be in the form of a tax-free retirement fund. What can you lose by not paying taxes?

The Roth IRA

This is a good one. So long as your adjusted gross income is less than $116,000, you can contribute up to $5,500 a year to a Roth IRA. (If you file jointly with an AGI under $183,000, you can *each* have a Roth IRA and *each* contribute $5,500.) Plus another $1,000 if you're 50 or over. This is permitted even if you are actively participating in other pension or profit-sharing arrangements, like a 401(k), SEP, or SIMPLE.

Much has been made of the difficulty of deciding between the Roth IRA and the traditional IRA (since the $5,500 limit applies to the total placed in both), but it's really very simple. **Especially if you're young and/or in a low tax bracket, but even if you're not, you should probably open a Roth IRA and fund it to the maximum every year.**

The basic difference between the Roth IRA and the traditional IRA is that with the traditional one you get your tax break on the way *in*—your contribution is deductible—whereas with the Roth IRA you get your break on the way *out*. Every penny you withdraw from the Roth IRA is tax-free. (Another advantage of the Roth IRA: you're not *required* to withdraw the money at all, let alone on a rigid IRS-dictated schedule. If you don't need it when you're 70½, you can let it keep growing until you do . . . or your beneficiary does. A Roth IRA contribution at age 25 might compound tax-free for 60 years—and then for yet another 50 or 60 while your granddaughter, named as beneficiary, slowly removes the funds.)

Theoretically, if your tax bracket will be the same at withdrawal as at the time of contribution, it makes no difference which you choose. To keep the math simple, say you're in the 50% bracket. One way, your full $5,500 grows for you but gets chopped in half by taxes when you withdraw it. The other way, only half, $2,750, is left to invest after tax, but is untaxed when withdrawn. Six of one, half a dozen of another.

Theoretically, you'd want to choose a Roth IRA if you're in a low bracket now and expect it might be higher when you retire; a traditional IRA if you're in a high bracket now and expect it to be lower when you retire.

The flaw in all this theorizing is that it assumes you'd put $5,500 in a traditional IRA versus just $2,750 (after paying tax) in the Roth. But why not put the *full* $5,500 in the Roth, if you can afford to?

By allowing you to stash away $5,500 in after-tax dollars, the Roth IRA in effect allows you to save more. **And a person who saves more virtually always ends up with more.** The Roth IRA effectively tricks taxpayers into saving more for retirement (because they have to come up with 5,500 real dollars, not 5,500 tax-deductible dollars) — and that's not a bad thing. Indeed, because the savings grow in this highly tax-advantaged way, it's a great thing.

It's always possible that Congress will do something that could negate the advantages of the Roth IRA — like replace the income tax with a sales tax. There you'd be, having forgone a nice tax deduction year after year, all to avoid what turned out to be *no income tax after all!* Or perhaps one's Roth IRA withdrawals will be taken into consideration when deciding whether you actually "need" Social Security benefits. But that's unlikely, too. Do you know how many elderly voters there will *be* by the time your Roth IRA has a bunch of money in it? Do you know how testy they will get if Congress tries to enact backdoor taxation of the Roth IRA withdrawal?

So anything is possible, but to me the Roth IRA means more saving, more certainty (what you've saved is what you keep), more flexibility at withdrawal—and less *complexity* at withdrawal, as anyone who has tried to figure out the annual withdrawal requirements from a traditional IRA will be quick to affirm.

Save yourself the trouble of agonizing over the choice and go with the Roth IRA. (Or the "Roth 401(k)" if your employer is one of the few that offer them.)

A Few IRA Fine Points

Naturally there are lots of details. Here are just a few:

- **What if I die or become disabled?** The entire fund may be withdrawn without penalty. If you've named your spouse as beneficiary and you die, it may all be rolled over into an IRA for him or her. (Non-spousal beneficiaries can do this but must begin withdrawal at once.)

- **What if I'm *already* over 59½?** It's not too late to set up one of these retirement plans—and the tax savings can still be substantial.

- **What if I'm in a very low tax bracket?** Then you should definitely choose a Roth IRA. Otherwise, you could be sheltering money from, say, a 10% tax rate today and shifting it into the future when you might be in the 40% marginal bracket, between federal and state tax, either because your fortunes had improved or tax rates had risen.

- **Can I set up a Roth IRA *and* a traditional IRA?** Yes, but the annual limit of contributions, however you split it, is $5,500 ($6,500 if over 50) to both.

- **Can I set up my own 401(k)?** Yes. If you have no employees (or employ only your spouse), you can set up an individual 401(k) plan and make both employee and employer contributions to the same plan. With $50,000 of self-employment income (actually self-employment income minus the employer's share of Social Security taxes, but let's not quibble) you can make the employer's 20% contribution and the $18,000 employee's contribution, and another $6,000 if over 50, for a total of $34,000.

- **Isn't the employer contribution limit 25% not 20%?** Technically. But if you're self-employed the contribution *itself* reduces the income on which the calculation is based, so it's simpler to say you're limited to 20% of your self-employment income before deducting the contribution.

- **What if I have a 401(k) or Keogh Plan or SEP or SIMPLE?** You may contribute to a Roth IRA in addition to any of these. Indeed, someone who is married, over 50, with $46,500 of income from self-employment could put all of it into tax-sheltered savings: $18,000 into a 401(k) (plus $6,000 more for being 50 or older, the so-called catchup contribution designed to help folks who got a late start saving for their retirement) . . . plus the 20% ($9,300) *employer* contribution into the 401(k) . . . plus $5,500 in a Roth IRA for each spouse . . . plus the $1,000 catchup contribution allowed for each spouse's Roth IRA. Total: $46,300. Then he or she could figure out how to pay for things like food.

- **What's my deadline for setting up one of these and making contributions?** That's the wrong question. It assumes you want to wait till the last possible minute. In fact, you want to do it right away, if you can. Even if you just missed the "deadline" for this tax year, that just means you're getting the earliest possible start for *next* year. Interestingly, if two people each contributed $5,000 a year to an IRA for 25 years, earning 7% . . . but one contributed on January 2 each tax year (the earliest possible moment) and the other waited until April 15 of the following year (the last possible moment) . . . each would have contributed $125,000 in total over those 25 years. But the one who got the early start would have seen his or her money grow by an extra $30,000 or so, because it would have had longer to compound.

- **What about "nondeductible" retirement-plan contributions?** Many people have the opportunity to put "extra," non-deductible money into their employer's retirement plan, or to put money into an IRA even though they won't qualify for the tax deduction. When you do this, you shelter the growth of the money from taxes until withdrawn; and then only that growth is taxed when it *is* withdrawn. Not bad. But a Roth IRA is better, if you qualify. What's more, see the section on stocks, at the end of this chapter.

- **What about early withdrawals?** Among the other advantages of a Roth IRA is the ability to withdraw contributions—not appreciation, but the money you actually contributed—free of tax or penalty at any time. But this is a weak advantage at best, since the whole point is to keep as much money growing tax-free as you can. Think hard before withdrawing money from a Roth IRA (or from a traditional IRA for the down payment on a first home, or to pay catastrophic medical expenses or college costs). It should be done only as a last resort, since money withdrawn for these purposes cannot later be returned to the tax shelter. Better to borrow from your retirement plan at work, if possible—and then repay the loan as quickly as you can.

- **What about converting my existing IRA to a Roth?** It's as simple as filling out a little paperwork with the custodian of your current IRA. You will have to pay tax on every penny you convert (except pennies that were contributed nondeductibly), but for someone with just a little saved up in an IRA, conversion is all but irresistible. She'd pay just a little tax, and from then on all growth would be tax-exempt forever. On the other hand, someone with a large IRA would have to think twice. Making such a big conversion would put her in a high tax bracket (if she were not already in one). And using some of the money *in* the IRA to pay the large tax bill would be a bad idea, because she'd be reducing the size of her tax-sheltered fund. (One possibility: set up a Roth IRA and convert just a manageable portion each year—particularly in years when, for whatever reason, your taxable income is low. Traditional IRAs are great. But where you can afford it, paying the tax to convert to a Roth is like kicking in more money for your old age.)

+ **Further questions?** Visit **irs.gov/publications/p590a** and struggle through it, or ask the retirement expert at your bank, brokerage firm, mutual fund, or employer.

Kids and Retirement Plans

One last note to tie these two together—your kids (or grand-kids) and retirement. Silly as it sounds at first, you might actually want to encourage your 12-year-old to set up a Roth IRA. Not because he will have the vaguest interest in saving for his retirement, but because the power of compound interest is so amazing (and, again, because of the saving habit it might help to form). Up to $5,000 a year in wages your child earns may be contributed to an IRA, so long as it's legitimate income, earned either from a family business (he stocks the shelves in your store) or from outside sources like baby-sitting or lawn-mowing (but not sitting *your* baby or mowing *your* lawn). It's also legal for you then to give your child enough to replace what she or he has squirreled away in the IRA.

Say your 12-year-old earns $20 a week—$1,000—which she puts in an IRA. Say, further, that you *give* her an extra $20 a week spending money to make up for what she puts away. That way, she won't mind.

What's the point? Well, if she does this for ten years, through age 22 . . . and if she invests it in an IRA account with a mutual fund that manages to earn 10% a year . . . then at age 70 (don't laugh!) that $10,000 you helped her put away would be worth $1.5 million—enough to throw off $180,000 a year for 20 years, to age 90.

There's no magic to this (just the magic of *doing it*—how many readers of the previous paragraph do you think actually will?). And inflation will surely erode the value of that $180,000. But if we average 3% inflation over all those years, it would still be the equivalent of $25,000 or $30,000 a year for 20 years in today's buying power—not bad for ten annual contributions of $1,000. How many old folks do you know today who couldn't use a $25,000-a-year income boost? My dream (well, one of my dreams) is that long after you and I are gone, there will be comfortably retired 80-year-old guys playing poker saying, "Well, and so my Pappy read this little *book* when I was 12, and . . . eh? . . . have I told you this one already?"

Don't worry about terrible inflation unraveling this strategy, either. If we have an inflationary tidal wave at some point, your child or grandchild would likely do fine. The buying power of *bonds* would get creamed, but equity mutual funds, with time, would likely bob up on top of the inflation. Why? Because they would own shares in the companies that are raising the prices!

Annuities

Annuities are hot because they grow tax-deferred and pay a fat commission to the folks who sell them—which leads to a lot of enthusiastic selling. **Don't buy them!**

Basically, annuities are like giant IRAs with no limit on how much you can contribute—but no tax deduction for making that contribution, either.

Some annuities promise a fixed return. Increasingly, people are buying *variable* annuities, where your return depends on how well the insurance company invests your money. It's like investing your IRA in a stock-market mutual fund.

Since you're likely to hear a lot of reasons why you should buy annuities, here are a few why you should not:

+ Annuity income is fully taxed as you withdraw it. If you're mainly looking for a tax shelter, why not buy tax-free bonds instead? (See Chapter 5.) Their interest is *never* taxed.

- The alluring rate some annuities promise is generally guaranteed for only one year. The projections used to sell them are typically illustrations of what *might* happen, not what's guaranteed.

- Once you buy an annuity, your funds are pretty well locked in to age 59½. There's the 10% penalty, as with an IRA (but not the initial tax deduction that makes IRAs attractive); and many annuities impose hefty surrender charges of their own.

- Since annuities are typically bought for the *long term,* why not buy stocks instead? Over long periods of time, stocks are almost sure to beat fixed-rate investments.

- Variable annuities do invest in stocks—but how well? What if the insurance company hires below-average managers? After all, not all money managers are above average. Or what if you want to switch to some other investment manager? At the very least, you would have to hassle with a "1035 Exchange," and you might face surrender charges.

- Even if their investment managers are just as good as anybody else's, most variable annuities will significantly underperform because they are dragged down by heavy sales and overhead costs, and by an insurance component that does you little good.

- In any event, if you're going to invest in stocks, *why do it through an annuity?* Any gains and dividends you withdraw from an annuity are fully taxed as ordinary income, even if they would have qualified as lightly taxed long-term capital gains and dividends outside the "shelter" of the annuity. (This is true of traditional IRAs, SEPs, and Keogh Plans, too; but with those you get that initial tax deduction.) **You are paying big fees to convert low-taxed capital gains and dividends into high-taxed ordinary income!**

- Appreciation within an annuity must eventually be distributed and subjected to income tax—when you die, if not before. Under current law, gains *outside* an annuity escape income tax altogether when you die. Good news for your loved ones.

In short: If you were thinking of a *fixed-rate annuity,* consider tax-free bonds instead. If you were thinking of a *variable annuity,* buy a stock-market index fund. You'll save sales fees and insurance charges; you'll suffer no penalty for early withdrawal; you'll enjoy considerable, albeit different, tax advantages.

If you've already *bought* an annuity: good. It's great that you've put money aside and that it's growing tax-deferred. But with the next chunk of cash you're able to squirrel away, you might be able to do even better.

Two Exceptions

- Teachers at tuition-based institutions have a pretty good deal with TIAA-CREF. If you're one of them, you know what I mean.

- If you're actually interested in buying an annuity—a real one—then go ahead. Long before annuities became highly promoted tax-deferral schemes, they were something almost entirely different—an insurance company's promise to pay you a set amount as long as you lived. For an 80-year-old not sure whether he or she will live another three years or another 30, it's a way to shift the "risk" of exceptionally long life onto an insurance company. The insurer can handle this risk because (a) it will assume, in setting its price, that you're likely to live a long time (cancer patients do not buy annuities); and (b) even if *you* live to 105, enough other annuitants won't. On average, the insurer makes out fine. Annuities are the opposite of life insurance, where insurers suspect all applicants of having hereditary heart disease and the customer "wins" by dying young. Just be sure, before you plunk down $300,000 for an annuity, that you've shopped aggressively for the best deal (**immediateannuities.com** is a good place to start)—and that you really want to do this. Once you've bought an annuity, there are no refunds.

And be sure to remember that most annuities have no "cost of living" clause. The $2,000 a month you get may seem sweet indeed for the first few years, but a bad run of inflation could drastically pinch your standard of living. So it could make sense to put a *portion* of your dough, or your grandmother's dough, into one of these, but retain flexibility with the rest.

Real Estate

Real estate you invest in on your own—where you know the area personally, search for your own opportunity, and are intimately involved in structuring the deal and overseeing the property—is far different from the kind of nutty tax shelters referred to at the beginning of this chapter.

The tax twist is that you get to depreciate your property even as—in real life—it may be *ap*preciating. Say you buy an eight-unit apartment building down the street in a bank foreclosure for $350,000, of which $275,000 is depreciable, and manage to clear $10,000 a year after all expenses. Because residential property is currently depreciated over 27.5 years, you get to deduct $10,000 a year in depreciation from your rental income—so in this example it's all tax-deferred until you sell. Meanwhile, say the property appreciates at 4% a year. That gain is also shielded from taxes until you sell. When you do sell, you have to pay capital-gains tax not only on the 4% annual appreciation but also (currently, at a special 25% rate) on all the accumulated depreciation the IRS "recaptures." *But no one says you have to sell.* You could just keep collecting more and more rent—and perhaps one day borrow more against your now-more-valuable property to enjoy some of the gain without paying tax on it.

These are the basic tax advantages real estate offers. And there is also the amazing leverage it affords. If you can buy a rental property with "20% down," borrowing 80% from someone else . . . and if you can manage to cover the mortgage and all your expenses out of the rent (way harder than many people imagine, especially if the roof one day needs to be replaced) . . . and if, what with inflation and all, you can someday sell it for twice what you paid . . . you have *not* doubled your money—

you have multiplied it *sixfold*. Before tax, anyway. (And if it was your own home, there could well be *no* tax.) Right? You put down $40,000 on a $200,000 property, broke even on expenses (or paid no more to own your home than you would have paid in rent, in this example), and sold for $400,000, leaving you with $240,000 after paying off the mortgage, six times what you started with.

I'm oversimplifying, but you see the point. Many of the greatest fortunes, and millions of small ones, have been built on real estate.

But leverage works both ways, as many investors and speculators — and home buyers — discovered when they got caught up in the real estate bubble. The very modest home next to mine that sold for $105,000 in 1998 fetched *$765,000* in 2005 — can you imagine? — then traded hands in 2010, in foreclosure, at $265,000.

So buy only when the numbers really work.

And recognize that owning rental properties isn't an investment, it's a *business*. That's fine if you have the time, talent, and temperament. But it's sure a lot easier to pick up the phone and buy 1,000 shares of a company that *invests* in real estate (such as a "real estate investment trust" listed on the New York Stock Exchange) than to fix a tenant's toilet on a Sunday morning. Easier still to pick up the phone and *sell* those 1,000 shares than to sell your building.

Real estate, indeed, can be as much a part-time *job* — scouting for properties, arranging their purchase, fixing them up, interviewing tenants, keeping them happy, negotiating the bureaucratic maze, cajoling plumbers in emergencies — as an investment. Some people see only headaches and risks. Others see a chance to be creative, to build sizable equity (and even more sizable bank debt), and to run their own show. If you are one of the latter, there are a great many primers available, not to mention eager real estate brokers who may go so far as to offer to manage your properties for you for a percentage of the rent.

By all means buy that seaside motel as your semiretirement home and business. But recognize that that's what it is: a business . . . and that running a business is a job . . . and that not all real estate *does* appreciate. Don't expect a four-bedroom house to grow to make you rich. At the end of the day, it hasn't grown at all: it's still a four-bedroom house.

Your Own Business

There are thousands of businesses besides real estate to go into. Among the potential tax advantages: you could get rich! But it's a huge undertaking—and another book. This book is about your money, not about switching careers.

Your Own Home

You can't depreciate it. You don't even get any tax benefit if you wind up selling it at a loss, as you do with investments. But the higher your tax bracket, the more of the cost Uncle Sam shoulders by virtue of the tax deductions home ownership provides for mortgage interest and property tax. Meanwhile, paying off the mortgage provides a good method of "forced saving," as your equity builds month by month (albeit imperceptibly at first). Perhaps best of all, any gain when you sell your primary residence is tax-free up to $250,000 ($500,000 for a married couple) as long as you lived there for at least two of the previous five years before the sale.

Stocks

Growing companies pay out little or nothing in the way of taxable dividends. Most of their profits are reinvested, and most of your return, it is hoped, will come in the form of long-term appreciation. The first advantage: tax on your gains is deferred until you actually choose to sell and take your profit. In the meantime, Uncle Sam's share of your capital is working for you alongside your own. The second advantage: long-term capital gains and qualifying dividends—those paid by corporations subject to corporate income tax—are taxed less heavily than ordinary income.

Timber!

Not, "Tim . . . BER!" as the loggers warn at the top of their lungs. But, rather, "timber" in vaguely the same way Dustin Hoffman encountered "plastics" in that famous scene in *The Graduate*—but with a tax advantage.

I claim no expertise in timber, yet feel comfortable suggesting that you consider putting 5% or 10% of your long-term funds in it if the price is right.

I arrive at this conclusion because people who actually do know something about timber think this makes some sense.

Timber, for starters, grows. Gold doesn't. Copper doesn't. Pork bellies and sorghum do, but you have to feed the pork and fertilize the sorghum. (I think. I'm actually not sure what sorghum is.) Trees are fed by God.

And as they grow, they not only become bigger (that much you knew) . . . they become more valuable. Skinny trees may be suitable for conversion to paper or wood chips or something. But as they grow thicker, they gradually become more highly prized for their usefulness in building things.

So, the first thing is that where most inventory actually shrinks—either because it spoils or because some of it walks out the door with the occasional larcenous employee—timber just sits there and grows more valuable. Don't ask me how fast, but you might imagine 5% a year, between actual growth and the growth in value as it becomes suitable for boardroom tabletops.

Then you have what I've been told is perhaps a 2% annual "unpopularity" bonus. That is to say, the market allows you a higher return on your money than it should because people are quite skittish about investing in trees. Leave aside the sheer boredom of it; I'm talking here of the obvious negatives: Fire! Blight! The increasing irrelevance of paper in a world of pixels!

It turns out, these fears may be overdone. The wise forest manager diversifies geographically and by species, so that the risks from fire and disease are mitigated. And while wood is undoubtedly the most substituted-for material on Earth—we are constantly finding other materials to replace it—it seems to grow ever more valuable. With ups and downs, to be sure, but on a general 2% annual long-term trend line.

That long trend could always end or go into reverse. But it might not. Think, for example, of a billion or more Chinese and Indians who don't now have decent houses but might someday be ready to build. That's a lotta wood.

So you get the growth of the inventory and its gradual "seasoning" to more valuable uses. You get what may be a slow but very long-term increase in the value of wood products, generally. *And* you get the same sort of unpopularity premium you might have gotten investing in Philip Morris all these years—without having to feel in any way responsible for helping to addict young children to the world's leading cause of preventable death. There is a large anti-tobacco contingent. Few people are anti-tree.

Yes, there could be times when timber prices fall sharply and remain depressed. But you don't have to sell until you want to. While you wait for the price to recover, your timber just keeps growing. (Contrast that with an airline seat or hotel room that, if unsold tomorrow, is gone forever.)

And there's more!

For one thing, timber should be a good inflation hedge, over the long run. For another, properly managed, income from timber should be lightly taxed. If you cut and sell some trees, Uncle

Sam generally views the revenue not as a taxable dividend, but as a "return of capital" . . . or at least he does until you've sold off most of the trees you started with. At that point, you can sell your forest for a lightly taxed capital gain.

But how are you, who not that many years ago paid off your last student loan, going to buy a forest?

One way, if you have a great deal of money, is to lock up a small fortune in a timber partnership. But an equally good way, accessible to more or less anyone, may be to buy shares in companies like Weyerhaeuser (WY), most recently at around $32 a share. These days, it yields nearly 4%. That ain't hay. (Hay rots when it gets wet.) And over time, the dividend, and with it the stock price, could rise to match, or even outpace, inflation.

Two similar stocks to consider: Potlatch (PCH) and Rayonier (RYN).

Until this edition, I was using Plum Creek Lumber (PCL) as my suggestion. But guess what? After decades of decent payouts —and after "trading around $35" for quite a while, as I noted in the 2010 edition—Weyerhaeuser is in the process of acquiring it, as I write, for about $50 a share.

(You could also buy either of two exchange-traded funds (see page 245), with the clever symbols CUT and WOOD, giving you broad diversification. But you pay an annual management fee. Perhaps check to see which stocks *they* own, and each year diversify—over different timber stocks but also over *time*, by not investing all at once—directly buying shares in a new stock each year.)

You're 24 and have $3,800 to invest? Forget timber—you'll die of boredom. But if you're 50 and have accumulated $700,000 to help hold you from age 70 on through 95, gradually accumulating a timber portfolio this way with 5% or 10% of your assets could make sense.

One caveat: there are no sure things. Anything can blow up somehow. Don't put *more* than 5% or 10% into timber.

Charity

If you write large checks to charity each year, you can save a lot of money in taxes by giving appreciated securities instead. Not only do you get the tax deduction for the gift, you avoid the capital-gains tax that otherwise would have been due upon sale of the securities. In the case of a stock you bought for $4,000 that's now worth $13,500, you could save upward of $1,500 in federal and state capital-gains tax. But be careful:

◆ Be certain to have your broker transfer the stock to the charity *before* she sells it and sends the charity the proceeds. If the stock is held in your name when it's sold, you pay the tax.

◆ Be certain you've held the shares (or the building, or the van Gogh) *at least a year and a day,* or the IRS will allow you to deduct only your original cost.

Of course, this doesn't make sense for small gifts. Too much hassle for both you and the charity to arrange for the transfer of, say, $250 or $500 worth of Apple. But if you're someone who likes to give $100 or $250 a year to a dozen different charities, there's a solution. Open an account with the Fidelity Investments Charitable Gift Fund (**fidelitycharitable.org**). Transfer your $13,500 worth of stock to that account, for which you get an immediate charitable deduction, just as if you'd given it to the Red Cross. Then, from time to time, visit Fidelity's website to issue your instructions. If it's a charity you've given to before, it takes just a few clicks. Fidelity will send checks on your behalf as small as $50, investing the balance in the meantime in your choice of funds—so you may have even more to give away, if those funds grow, than you planned.

This is the poor man's way to set up a charitable foundation —the Ford Foundation, the Rockefeller Foundation, and now *Your* Foundation.

Fidelity's Gift Fund is also handy if you should get a windfall. Say you exercised the last of your Google stock options this year and reaped $400,000, of which you'd like to give $100,000 to charity. The Charitable Gift Fund could be perfect. After all, there you are, a 42-year-old receptionist who just happened to be with Google from the beginning. If you gave all $100,000 to your favorite charities this year, you'd be showered with love and appreciation—and *deluged* with requests next year. But what could you give next year? You're still a receptionist, albeit a darned good one, and you make $46,000 a year. But suddenly the people you gave $5,000 to last year are expecting $6,000 this year . . . and you were thinking more along the lines of $50, which for a guy or gal making $46,000 is a very nice gift. They'll hate you!

With $100,000 in the Gift Fund, you might decide to distribute $5,000 a year—out of the growth in the fund itself, with any luck, perhaps never dipping into the $100,000 at all. That way, you are perceived as a very generous person indeed—how many receptionists give away $5,000 a year?—and can enjoy and refine your giving over the years without undue stress.

Vanguard (**vanguardcharitable.org**) and Schwab (**schwab charitable.org**) have charitable gift funds that work the same way.

Charitable Fine Points

- If you've given $250 or more to a charity, you'll need a receipt —not just your canceled check. Most charities send them automatically, since they are well aware of the regulation, but it's your responsibility to get them and keep them if you're ever audited. It's not good enough to get them a year or two later, when the audit notice comes. The receipts must be dated no later than the date you file the tax return claiming them as deductions. (One more reason to use the Charitable Gift Fund instead: they keep all the paperwork for you, basically, except for the occasional receipt you'll get for the bulk amount you give *them*.)

- Receipts are supposed to make clear that you received nothing of significant value in return for your contribution, or else disclose the fair value of what you did receive—e.g., $40 of your $150 benefit ticket went for food and entertainment. You only get to deduct $110 even if you have witnesses who will swear you ate just *one dinner roll.*

- If you give something other than cash, the charity is expected to provide only a description of the goods, not an estimate of their fair market (read: flea market) value. That's your job.

- If you're giving something (other than marketable securities) valued above $5,000, an appraisal is usually required. Testimony from your aunt who knows antiques ("GAWgeous!") will not do it.

- If you go to a charity auction and buy a Warhol print, or the actual Bic used by Paul Simon to pen "Bridge over Troubled Water," you are entitled to deduct only that portion of your check, if any, that exceeds the fair market value of what you purchased. So if the estimate in the auction catalog is $1,500 and you snag it for $900, you get no charitable deduction. A lot of people take the full amount of the check as a deduction anyway, which is probably one of the reasons the IRS now requires receipts of the type mentioned above. Fifty-some years ago, my mother organized a very successful art auction in our barn. (I know you wouldn't expect this from a city boy like me, but we had a barn.) It raised a few thousand dollars for some worthy cause, and my father, knowing that most of the successful bidders were likely to write off 100% of their expenditures as charitable deductions, dubbed the event *Le Grande Tax Dodgerie.* I think he dubbed it in French so as not to corrupt "the children," much as we used to talk about feeding the D-O-G, so as not to excite "the dog."

- Just as it's rarely wise to invest in something brought to your attention by bulk mail, so is it risky to give money to a charity based on a slick or plaintive solicitation—let alone to a telemarketer calling on behalf of some charity over the phone (and keeping, often, 50% or more of your donation). One of the more remarkable examples was a group that granted the wishes of dying children. According to the *New York Times,* the group raised $237,000 in 1984. Of that, $10,000 went to grant wishes; the rest was spent on "professional fund-raising organizations, salaries, car rentals, jewelry, rent, unsecured personal loans, a VCR, and a videotape entitled *Sex Games.*" Such things resurface frequently. Visit **give.org** to check out your investment in a charity much as you would check out your investment in a stock.

Charity and Your IRA

If you're planning to leave some money to charity when you die and you have a traditional IRA (or Keogh Plan), consider naming the charities as the plan's beneficiaries. That will save the income tax your heirs would otherwise have had to pay on it. Give your heirs "regular" money from outside your IRA instead —money on which income tax has *already* been paid. To the charities it won't make any difference (charities don't pay taxes), but to your heirs it will.

Charity and Your Fortune

If you have no heirs that you're dying to leave money to, check out Fidelity Investment's Pooled Income Fund (**fidelitycharitable.org**). You get a tax deduction for the "present value" of your contribution . . . and you get an income for life. When you die, what's left goes to the charities of your choice.

Something's "present value" depends on how long you have to wait for it. (If I offered you $1,000 tomorrow in return for $900 today, and you trusted me, I'll bet you'd give me the $900. But for that same $1,000 six years from now? You'd likely offer less. The further off the payout, the lower its *present* value.) The amount of the tax deduction you get from a gift like this depends on your age. If you're 85, the present value the IRS assigns your gift is nearly as high as the gift itself because the IRS doesn't realize you're one of those phenomena who are going to be playing tennis at 102. If you're 50, there's no point bothering with this, because the present value of your gift will be tiny.

If you have a ton of dough, you might not want to pool your money with others' money (theirs might be *new* money, entirely unsuitable to socialize with yours). You would set up your own charitable remainder trust. Almost any large charity will eagerly walk you through the basics of that, after which you might discuss it with your accountant and the attorney who prepared your will.

Alternative Minimum Tax (and Stock Options)

This tax was created to keep crafty rich folks from slipping by unscathed. It now often hits middle-class families doing little or nothing out of the ordinary—especially those living in high-tax states, because state and local income taxes, though deductible against ordinary income tax, are among the items *not* deductible in figuring the Alternative Minimum Tax.

Beyond Advil, there's not much defense against the AMT.

If you invest in tax-free municipal bonds, make sure they aren't "private activity bonds," which are included in income for AMT purposes.

If you are going to have a single year of very large income (perhaps from exercising employee stock options), prepay your state and local taxes before the end of the year, so they count as deductions against that high income. Otherwise, they'll count against next year's not-so-high income, only to be knocked out by the AMT.

Speaking of employee stock options . . . when you exercise them, sell the stock immediately. Some people hold on to stock they receive from exercising "incentive stock options," because they were told they could postpone tax until the shares were sold. But for AMT purposes, the excess of the fair market value of the stock over the exercise price is included in income immediately—and you will owe these taxes even if the stock you hold collapses. That's what happened to a horde of Silicon Valley "option millionaires" who exercised incentive stock options in early 2000, planning to hold the stock a year and a day to get long-term gains treatment, only to see their holdings vaporize — but their Alternative Minimum Tax bills remain huge.

Tax Books and Software

Whatever the shape of the tax code by the time you read this, there will almost surely be a current edition of J. K. Lasser's *Your Income Tax* to guide you through it. Just look in the index for what you need.

Online, visit **fairmark.com** to get tax answers.

But if you're an ordinary person, you won't need any of that — just buy H&R Block's Tax Software (formerly TaxCut, the one I've long used, not least because my face used to be on the box) or TurboTax or TaxACT to prepare your taxes. For simple returns, their free online versions may suffice. It's easy, and you can always go to your accountant the first time to have her check over what you've done. Or, if your tax situation is complex, let the accountant keep doing your taxes, but use these programs to check her work. I once found a $2,000 error my mom's excellent accountant made in the IRS's favor. Nobody's perfect.

PART TWO

THE STOCK MARKET

The problem with trying to beat the market is that professional investors are so talented, so numerous, and so dedicated to their work that as a group they make it very difficult for any one of their number to do significantly better than the others, particularly in the long run . . . [It is] so easy, while trying to do better, to do worse.

— CHARLES D. ELLIS,
Investment Policy: How to Win the Loser's Game

7

Meanwhile, Down at the Track

*October. This is one of the particularly dangerous
months to speculate in stocks. Others are November,
December, January, February, March, April, May,
June, July, August, and September.*

— MARK TWAIN

OK. YOU HAVE some money in a savings bank; you are
contributing to your company's 401(k) at the maximum rate allowed; you have equity in a home, if you want it; you've tied up
$1,000 in bulk purchases of tuna fish and shaving cream; you
have lowered your auto and homeowner's insurance premiums
by increasing your deductibles; you have adequate term life insurance; you've paid off all your 18% installment loans and in-
sulated your attic—you have done, in short, all the things that
scream to be done.

Now what?

There are three compelling reasons to invest a large portion
of your remaining funds in stocks:

1.   **Unlike bonds, stocks offer at least the potential of keeping up with inflation,** even if that potential is by no means
always realized. Once the interest rate on a bond is set, it's set.
(Well, leaving aside the special inflation-protected Treasury securities described in Chapter 5.) Bread could go to $20 a loaf,
and the bond wouldn't pay a nickel more in interest. But the
company that bakes the bread might—*might*—be able to keep
its profits, and its dividend, rising in step with inflation.

2. **Over the long run—and it may be a very long run— stocks will outperform "safer" investments.** The reason is that stock and bond prices are set in the open market—and the market, over the long run, rewards risk. From 1926 to 2015, according to Ibbotson Associates, who track these sorts of things, the total compounded annual rate of return you would have had from buying risk-free United States Treasury bills was 3.7%; the return from slightly riskier corporate bonds would have been 5.9%; the return from blue-chip stocks would have been 9.8%; and the return from the stocks of small companies would have been even higher, although there is some controversy over the way the small-stock figures are arrived at. The compounded annual rate of inflation during the same period was 3.0%. Ignoring taxes, $1,000 invested in Treasury bills over that time span would have grown to $20,530—but to $118,630 in corporate bonds, $2,591,820 in large stocks, and even more in small stocks.*

Of course, you can play with numbers like these, depending on the time periods you choose. There were some pretty dreadful five- and ten-year stretches nestled in among those 90 years (in case you hadn't noticed), during which you would have been much better off in bonds or even a savings account.

There was, for example, the period from September 1929 to June 1932, during which the U.S. stock market dropped 83%. Smaller stocks fared even worse, losing 92% of their value. If that seems like ancient history, large stocks lost 43% between January 1973 and September 1974, and small stocks were clobbered by more than 70% in the six years from late 1968 to late

---

* Stock returns include dividends. When you read that the market historically averages a gain of 9% or 10% a year, that's 6% or 7% appreciation, on average, and 3% or 4% from dividends. Lately, average dividends have been very low—under 2%. This is partly because stock prices have been high (a $1 dividend on a $20 stock is 5% but falls to 1% as the stock rises to $100) and partly because CEOs have taken to using profits to buy back shares of the company stock rather than pay dividends. This may be related to the fact that the bulk of CEO compensation comes from stock options—so they have little interest in paying out cash that could be used, instead, to boost the price of the stock.

1974—the first six years of my own investing career, which has made me rather cautious ever since. More recently, you may have noticed slippage in the NASDAQ index, from 5,049 in March of 2000 to 1,114 in October of 2002, a stumble of nearly 78%. In part that was because the NASDAQ was dominated by a relative handful of high-tech bubble stocks. But even the more representative Standard & Poor's 500 index was down 50%. Between October 2007 and March 2009, the most recent period when the world was about to come to an end, the global stock market pretty much collapsed. The S&P 500 dropped 55%.

But time heals all wounds. When the New York Stock Exchange celebrated its 200th birthday in May 1992, it could report that a person who bought shares in all of the companies on the exchange on *any* day in its history would have made a profit over *any* 15-year stretch and would have beaten bonds and savings accounts over virtually any period exceeding 20 years.

Wharton finance professor Jeremy Siegel actually managed to come up with data for stock and bond performance stretching all the way back to 1802. A single dollar invested in stocks would have grown to $12.7 million or so by 2006, he concluded —8.3% a year compounded. After inflation: a "mere" $755,000. After taxes (at the maximum rate) *and* inflation: an almost pathetic $30,000. (In truth, the tax hit would have been much smaller, since he assumed annual taxation, while a buy-and-hold investor would only have paid annual taxes on the dividend distributions.) The same dollar invested in safer long-term government bonds, after taxes and inflation, would have been worth $97. (And the interest on the bonds *would* have been taxed each year.) An investor in the maximum tax bracket might have invested in municipal bonds instead and wound up with $577— but that's still a far cry from $30,000. Obviously, for the long run it is no contest between stocks and bonds. (Not surprisingly, Jeremy Siegel is the author of *Stocks for the Long Run*.)

Will the American economy be as dynamic over the *next* couple of centuries? It could be. (Remember Ray Kurzweil's "dazzling" technological progress from page xx*). So now the only problems are (a) to be sure to set aside that dollar; and (b) somehow to remain spry long enough to enjoy it.

When this book was revised in 1983, things had recently been dismal: inflation nearing 20%, unemployment topping 10%, and the widespread conviction that every car on the road would soon be made in Japan. Yet it seemed, as I wrote then, that "it just might be that we have been going through a toughening-up process over the last several years, and that our sensational technological prowess has been paving the way for enormous strides forward."

The stock market quadrupled in the 12 years that followed. Here's what I wrote in the 1995 revision following that rise:

Technology races ahead faster than ever, a tremendous force for productivity and prosperity. And where for decades the defense budget siphoned off around 6% of our gross domestic output (compared with 1% for the Japanese—a huge competitive disadvantage), today that largely nonproductive spending has dropped to more like 3.5%. At the same time, there's been a sweeping worldwide movement toward free trade and capitalism. Considering these broad forces, the heights to which the U.S. stock market had risen by 1995, while scary, were not totally unfounded. It was not, by and large, a "bubble." Specific stocks may collapse (I can think of a few candidates), but the overall market, no matter where it goes from here, will, over the long run, go much higher.

"All that remains true," I subsequently wrote in the 1998 edition, "(and defense spending is now under 3% of our Gross Domestic Product). Stocks have *soared* since 1995, leaving me all the more nervous for the short run. But the future holds great promise. The eternal question when times are good and hopes

---

* For a bit more on who Kurzweil is, what he thinks, and why you might believe him, see, for starters, the archived December 14, 2007, column at **andrewtobias.com**.

bright: how much of that promise is already reflected in stock prices? And what if things go wrong? When the next real bear market comes, it's likely to be a killer, because so few investors or money managers today have ever really lived through one. But guess what. If you hang in there, and invest more as the fainter-hearted panic, and prices grind steadily lower month after excruciating month, in the long run you'll do just fine."

In the next revision (this is the only investment guide you will ever need so long as the world never changes), in 2002, I noted, "We seem to have entered that killer bear market (what else would you call a 70% drop in the NASDAQ?). By the time you read this, the pain may be over—or not. But the greater the pain, the greater the ultimate opportunity."

In the 2005 revision, I added . . .

The bear market finally ended about a year later, and the broad market soared around 50% over the next 15 months (and the NASDAQ was up 94%) . . . and so I am nervous again.

I am dismayed by the reelection of George Bush. Yes, my taxes are likely to stay low, but I don't see how we become more prosperous if much of the world hates us . . . if we are adding to our National Debt at a tremendous rate . . . if we are investing in missile systems instead of education . . . if we are giving tax incentives to encourage the purchase of Hummers rather than fuel efficiency. And that just begins the list.

. . . As I write this, stock and real estate prices do not seem to me to reflect all the challenges.

As it happened, the market crashed in 2008, from a high of 14,165 on the Dow to a low, in March 2009, of 6,500.

With its having recovered to 10,000 by the time of the last edition, in 2010, I wrote that "by staying cautious, you might sidestep the next 40% drop in the market. But you could also miss the next impressive gains. If you're able to take the long view, a program of steady investments in the stock market is wise indeed, no matter where the market is when you start."

And that's still true.

"If you're looking out 40 years," famed investor John Marks Templeton told *Mutual Funds* magazine in early 1995, "I think you can probably do 15% a year. [The short-term outlook is not as rosy, he said, because we're coming off such a rapid run-up already—and that was 1995, when the Dow was at 4,000!] A strong reason is that progress is speeding up. The improvements in most companies and industries are coming faster and faster. It's been an absolutely marvelous time to live. Just in my [82-year] lifetime, the world standard of living has quadrupled, and that's amazing. Through history, it took 1,000 years to double the standard of living. The reasons why it is speeding up have not stopped; in fact *they've* speeded up. Take the amount of money spent on scientific research. Eighty-two years ago, the world spent about $1 billion every three months. Now the world is spending $2 billion a day."

I buy that—and I don't. It's one thing for stocks to grow spectacularly from 1982, when the Dow was wildly undervalued —if the world didn't end—at 777 and long-term interest rates, anticipating terrible inflation, were 15%. But with the Dow having topped 18,000 in 2015 and long-term rates more like 3%, the pendulum had swung. As noted in the first pages of this book, it was the spectacular decline in interest rates that powered much of the spectacular rise in stock and bond values. Where will interest rates go now?

With luck, we've learned enough lessons about inflation (and the way budget deficits stoke it and free trade restrains it) to avoid driving interest rates back up *too* far. And have enough lingering memory of the Depression to avoid something catastrophic that would drive them down much further.

The market won't go to zero. But investors need to understand that in a really, really bad economy, which I do not expect, share prices of many businesses *can* go essentially to zero without those businesses closing their doors. They just get new owners. Unable to make good on their bond payments, the current owners (shareholders) basically have to hand ownership over *to* the bondholders.

So — especially if you have a *lot* of eggs — think twice before putting them *all* in the stock-market basket.

One final thought is that the "new economy" is great for consumers, but not necessarily for investors. I am *thrilled* by what I can do on the Internet, and the way I can use it to find the best prices. But price competition, while great for consumers, is murder on investors.

So you know what? It may turn out to be a brave new world, yet the same very tough, challenging stock market it always was. Rewarding, over time, but no pushover. The rewards remain real, but so do the risks.

3. **If all goes well, stocks can act as a tax shelter.** Long-term capital gains are generally taxed less heavily than ordinary income. And *no* tax is due on your gains until you choose to take them. Only the dividends face immediate taxation.

Because many companies pay out relatively little of their profits in dividends, you pay relatively little tax on your share of those profits. Instead, the company retains and reinvests them for you. If they do a good job, future profits, and your share of them, will be even larger. This is the bird-in-the-bush strategy of investing. With it, you can ultimately profit two ways. First, after a period of years the company may decide to pay out a greater portion of its (by-then-fatter) profits as dividends. Second, you can sell your stock. If the company has invested your profits wisely, there is a reasonable chance you will get more for it than you paid — perhaps even several times as much.

It thus becomes a matter of some interest just how well a company is likely to reinvest all those profits they don't pay you as dividends. Unfortunately, there is no way to know for sure. However, you can determine how well they've done — or, because accounting is open to so much qualification and interpretation, how well they seem to have done — in the past. The number you are looking for is "return on equity," and it is, simply, the company's profits expressed as a percentage of all the money shareholders have dumped in over the years, much of it by forgoing dividends.

There are companies that have been able to reinvest those accumulated unpaid dividends at returns well above 15% a year. Others have earned less than half as much. And then there are those that have diddled it away altogether.

Investors would naturally prefer stock in companies more like the former than the latter, all other things being equal. So all other things are *not* equal. You have to pay more for stock in companies that are known to reinvest profits at a high rate of return. Indeed, there was a time (1973) when you had to pay $60 or more to get a $1 slice of Avon's profit pie, so excited were investors by Avon's ability to earn 25% on that dollar. At the same time it cost only $8 to buy a $1 slice of Goodrich's slower-growing profit pie. What investors failed to note was that, although 25% was a boffo return on that one reinvested Avon dollar, a dollar—no matter how well it was reinvested—was a pretty lousy return on a $60 investment! Subsequently Avon stock fell about 85% even though profits kept growing.

So there's more to choosing the right stock than finding the company with the highest "return on equity." But I'm getting ahead of myself. I should not talk like this until you know as much about the essentials of the stock market—the forest—as the professionals do. This will take up most of the rest of the chapter. (Getting to know as much about the trees could take up most of the rest of your life.)

The stock market could hardly be simpler. There are just two ways a stock can go: up or down. There are just two emotions that tug in those opposite directions: greed and fear. There are just two ways to make money on a stock: dividends and capital gains. And there are just two kinds of investors in the market: the "public," like you or me; and the "institutions," like mutual funds and pension funds and (cue the scary music) hedge funds. It's the amateurs against the professionals, and it's not all that clear who has the advantage. Often, both lose.

The bottom line, if you want to cut straight to the chase, is that most people should do their stock-market investing through no-load index funds—mutual funds that don't attempt to actively pick the best stocks, but just passively invest in *all* the stocks in the index they are designed to match—or else through the index funds I describe on page 162 or possibly even the funds on page 164. If you do, you will outperform at least 90% of all your friends and neighbors—including many who work much harder at this than you. But if you do decide to go it alone, either because you believe you can beat the pros or because it's fun to try, read on.

What is a stock worth? Market veterans will tell you that a stock is worth whatever people are willing to pay for it. Price is determined by supply and demand. If lots of people want it, it will be worth a lot. If everyone ignores it, it won't be worth spit.

But it is too simple to say that a stock is worth whatever people will pay for it, because what people are willing to pay for it depends on what they think it is worth. It is a circular definition, used as a rationalization of financial foolishness rather than as a rational way to appraise value.

The value of a stock should not be nearly so subjective as, say, the value of a Picasso sketch. A share of stock merely entitles the owner to a share of present and future profits (or, in the event of bankruptcy or acquisition by another company, assets). Where two paintings of equal size may reasonably command vastly different values, two companies of equal profits, assets, and prospects should not. Yet do.*

---

* I'm going to give you AN AMAZING EXAMPLE OF THAT TO PROVE THE POINT, but you're just going to have to wait and let the suspense build.

The market veteran will readily agree that this is irrational, but he will ask you, with a laugh, "Who ever said the stock market was rational?"

That gets the market veteran off the hook and may eliminate in his mind the need to search for value. But there are other market veterans, perhaps even a majority by now, who believe that rationality does pay off in the market over the long run. Sooner or later, they say, bubbles burst; sooner or later, bargains are recognized. A company cannot prosper forever without its shareholders at some point benefiting.

Indeed, if the market is driven by irrational greed and fear to excesses of over- and undervaluation, as it surely is, then it is the rational man, they say, seeing these excesses for what they are, who will be buying the excessively undervalued stock, particularly when the market as a whole is depressed; and selling the excessively overvalued stock, particularly when the market as a whole is flying high. Thus may he profit from the swings in between.

All of this assumes that a rational man can determine what a stock is "really" worth.

Rational men differ. A company's future prospects—and even its current profits—are open to widely differing assessments. Obviously, no one can answer precisely what a stock is worth. But that doesn't eliminate the need to arrive at some rational valuation, or the possibility of setting some reasonable guidelines for doing so.

What a stock is worth depends at any given time on the alternative investments that are then available. It is a question of relative value. Think of investments as wallets. A 2% savings account is a wallet you can buy for $50 that miraculously fills up with $1 (2%) by the end of every year. It is safe and convenient —you can "sell" it whenever you want and be sure of getting back your full $50—but it's not necessarily a great investment if, when savings accounts are paying 2%, you can buy other "wallets" that fill up with the same $1 just as fast—not for $50 but for a mere $20. For example, high-grade corporate bonds that pay 5% interest.

You can say that the first wallet sells for "50 times earnings" and the second for "20 times earnings." This is the famous "price/earnings ratio," or "multiple," you have heard so much about, although it's generally applied to stocks, not bonds or wallets.*

Now, if a nearly risk-free investment like a high-grade bond sells for 20 times earnings, what should a stock sell for?

On the one hand, a stock should sell for *less*, because it involves more risk. There is no guarantee that the $1 will show up in the wallet by the end of the year—or even that the wallet itself will be in any shape to be sold to someone else, should you want to do so. What's more, only a portion of your $1 is actually paid out to you as a cash dividend. Much, most, or all of it may be retained by the company. So, really, stocks should sell for way below 20 times earnings.

On the other hand, a stock should perhaps sell for *more*, because of its greater potential for gain (the earnings and/or stock price could go up) and because of the tax advantages referred to earlier. So, really, stocks should sell for way *over* 20 times earnings.

In deciding how much more or less to pay for a stock than the 20 times earnings you might pay for a high-grade bond—or whatever the going rate is at the time you read this—one weighs the extra risk against the potential for extra return.†

---

* To find basic data on any stock, such as its "p/e ratio," visit **finance.yahoo.com**.

† Up until 1958, stocks consistently yielded more in dividends than bonds yielded in interest. And "for a simple reason," writes Morgan Stanley's Byron Wien: "Stocks were known to be riskier than bonds, and therefore should provide a higher current reward." For that to be true again as I write this today, the Dow Jones Industrial Average would have to fall back to around 10,000. But stock buybacks, which were insignificant in 1958, now exceed dividend distributions. So, based on the *effective* dividend yield, the Dow may actually be outyielding bonds by even more than in 1958. A stock buyback puts no cash directly in your pocket each quarter; but by reducing the number of shares outstanding, it makes each one more valuable. Each slice of a pie cut into four pieces is larger than if it were cut into five. So too with slices of a company cut into 95 million slices, say, instead of 97 million before the buyback.

For shares of a dull company whose earnings over the long run seem about as likely to increase as to fall—where risk and reward about cancel one another out—you might expect to pay 20 times earnings. So if you find such a stock selling for 10 or 12 times earnings, it could look pretty good.

For stock in a company whose earnings seem likely to be able to keep pace with inflation—no "real" growth, that is, but growth in earnings all the same—you might expect to pay more than the 20 times earnings you would pay for a high-grade bond, the earnings of which do not rise with inflation. In fact, some such companies sold at five or six times earnings back in 1974 and 1982. A bargain? You bet.

Finally, for stock in a company whose prospects are really bright, with the possibility of real growth, above inflation, of 5% or 10% or even 20% a year for the foreseeable future, you might expect to pay a lot more than 20 times earnings.

All other things being equal—that is, if all stocks were selling at 20 times earnings—you would choose only those companies whose earnings were expected to grow the fastest. But the question is not whether a fast-growing company is better than a slow-growing one. Any fool knows that. The question is whether you should pay 35 times earnings for the one or 12 times earnings for the other. Which stock, at any given time, is a better relative value? The real trick—and payoff—is to find a company selling for 12 times earnings that you think will grow as fast as the one selling for 35 times earnings. Then you know for sure which to buy.

Admittedly, it's not quite this simple. For one thing, it makes sense to look not just at what a company may earn but also at what it owns. A company whose business is lousy, but which happens to be conducted on 50,000 acres of wholly owned real estate between Dallas and Fort Worth, might have a liquidation value—if you closed down the business and paid off all the creditors—of $25 a share. Yet such land, if it had been acquired early in the last century, might be valued on the company's books at next to nothing—so it might not even show up in quick calculations of the company's "book value." It could be what's known as a hidden asset, and well worth buying shares in, regardless of the company's dismal earnings.

I should also stress that the 20 times earnings I've been using as a benchmark is by no means eternal. It all depends on what wallets are going for at any given time. If you can get 15% from a high-grade bond, as you could in 1982, then you have a low-risk wallet that produces $1 for every $6.67 you put up—6.7 times earnings. The higher the prevailing long-term interest rate, the less you should be willing to pay for stocks. And vice versa. That old seesaw again.

Now it happens that far from looking at assets or relative value, the professional money managers of the late sixties and early seventies, when I was getting my first exposure to all this, concentrated their attention and their megabucks on a relative handful of fast-growing companies, bidding their prices up to truly remarkable heights. The "Nifty Fifty," these stocks were called — "glamour" stocks, "one-decision" stocks (you just had to decide to buy them; you would never sell them, no matter what price you could get). The group included such indisputably fine companies as Polaroid, Disney, Avon, Merrill Lynch, Xerox, and Coca-Cola.

Barron's first issue of 1973 bore this headline: "Not a Bear Among Them. Our Panel Is Bullish on Wall Street." Uh-oh. When everyone is bullish—meaning, they think the market will rise—watch out: they've done their buying and now are waiting for others to bid the stocks up even higher. But the "others" have already done *their* buying, too. There's no one left to buy! It's vaguely like your basic cartoon where the rabbit races out past the edge of a cliff, looks backward and forward to see where everybody is, and then plunges. Only with bulls, not rabbits.

Here's how some of the best-known stocks of that period fared, from their highs of 1972 to their lows of 1974:

What a Real Bear Market Looks Like

	1972	1974	Change
Avon	$140.00	$18.62	-87%
Coca-Cola	149.75	44.63	-70
IBM	341.38	150.50	-56
Intel	56.00	10.25	-82
Johnson & Johnson	133.00	73.13	-45
Kodak	151.75	57.63	-62
McDonald's	77.38	21.25	-73
Merrill Lynch	46.00	6.25	-86
Polaroid	149.50	14.13	-91
Procter & Gamble	112.75	67.00	-41
Walt Disney	211.63	30.75	-86
Xerox	171.88	49.00	-71

Prices unadjusted for subsequent stock splits.

Most stocks the pros ignored altogether. Not because they lacked merit, although some did, but because it's a lot less trouble to put $100 million into Johnson & Johnson than to stay late at the office each night hunting for 50 less-visible companies — perhaps better values — in which to invest $2 million each. The first rule of fiduciary bureaucracy was (and is): You can't be criticized for losing money in IBM. Corollary: He who does what everyone else does will not do appreciably worse. In other words, it was *unfortunate* to lose money in IBM, Avon, Polaroid, or Xerox; but it would have been *imprudent* to lose (somewhat less) money in stocks no one ever heard of.

In talking with people who managed billions of pension-fund dollars at some of the nation's largest banks during this period, I got the distinct impression that it would have been *un-*

dignified for top-drawer financial institutions like theirs to invest in anything but large, top-drawer American corporations.

That posture has a fiduciary ring to it, until you consider how much extra they were paying to invest in such firms, and how much they ultimately lost for their clients by doing so.

One major money manager told me that it was his bank's policy to invest only in companies whose earnings they expected to grow at an above-average rate. What about companies they expected to grow at only an average or sub-average rate? No, he said, they did not buy stock in such companies. Regardless of price? Regardless of price. Was there *any* price at which the bank would buy stock in an average company?

This question made the money manager uncomfortable. He clearly wanted to answer no, because he clearly would be damned before he would buy stock in such a company. But he couldn't come right out and say that, because he knew that, theoretically, there must be *some* price at which he should choose the stock of the mediocre company over the stocks of his Nifty Fifty.

On Wall Street, this sort of irrationality happens all the time. It's not impossible to profit from it, if you have an eye for value, nerves of steel, and a level head—but only with hindsight is it easy.

Subject to the caveats and additional suggestions in the next chapters, here's the most sensible way for most people to invest in stocks:

1. **Only invest money you won't have to touch for many years.** If you don't have money like that, don't buy stocks. People who buy stocks when they get bonuses and sell them when the roof starts to leak are entrusting their investment decisions to their roofs.

2. **Buy low and sell high.** You laugh. Yet most people, particularly small investors, shun the market when it's getting drubbed and venture back only after it has recovered and appears, once

again, to be "healthy." **It is precisely when the market looks worst that the opportunities are best; precisely when things are good again that the opportunities are slimmest and the risks greatest.**

Item: At what was probably the most opportune time to buy stocks since the Great Depression, December of 1974, with the Dow Jones Industrial Average struggling to break above 600 and countless lesser stocks selling for a half or a third or even a quarter of their book values, financial columnist Eliot Janeway was advising small investors to stay away. "No investment market in the coming year," he said with his customary self-assurance, "is going to be safe for civilians." In point of fact, the Dow climbed 40% in 1975, and many of the stocks that had been battered far worse than the Dow "blue chips" doubled and tripled.

Item: A Washington, D.C., investment club purchased 200 shares of a stock at 18. "Club sold all holdings at 12½," it reported to *Black Enterprise* magazine, "due *to decline in price;* intends to reinvest *when price moves up.*" (Italics mine.) What kind of strategy is *that*?

Item: In September 2002, with the Dow hovering around 8,000 (off from a peak of nearly 12,000 in early 2000), all of the financial publications were reporting the advice of Bill Gross, who manages nearly $1 trillion in bonds and is considered (by me along with everyone else) the smartest bond investor in the history of the planet. Within a month of his warning—that the Dow could plunge a further 3,000 points—it began a long climb.

Item: On March 3, 2009, three days before the Dow's 6,595 bottom, President Obama suggested it could be a good time to buy stocks. "What you're now seeing is profit and earnings ratios are starting to get to the point where buying stocks is a potentially good deal if you've got a long-term perspective on it." That call, unlike the others, turned out pretty well.

Torn as we all are between greed and fear, we tend to do just the wrong thing. When the economy is sinking fast and stocks faster, we get more and more scared. Finally, we quit in disgust. Better to get out with the big loss, we say to ourselves, than to watch our holdings disappear altogether. In fact, of course, this is just the time to be getting into the market, not out.

By the same token, avoid getting carried away with enthusiasm when the market is generally judged to be healthy, when you are becoming excited by the gains in some of the stocks you already own, when prospects for the economy are generally conceded to be bright, and when people are talking about the real possibility that the Dow Jones Industrial Average will finally break through to new ground. In such a climate people are *expecting* good news. If it comes, it won't move the market much because it has been so widely anticipated. If, by chance, bad news should come instead, that *will* move the market—down.

Whether concerning an individual stock, or the market as a whole, always ask yourself which would be more of a surprise: good news or bad news. News that is expected never has as much impact—if any at all—as news that is not.

Market analyst Dr. Martin Zweig has written:

> The truth is, that the stock market does its best when earnings and dividends are getting drubbed, and worst when [they] are zooming. For example: In the fourth quarter of 1972 and the first quarter of 1973 . . . earnings of the Dow Industrials soared upward by 35% over year-earlier periods. The market responded by crashing more violently than at any time since the thirties. Then, amid the depths of pessimism, first- and second-quarter 1975 Dow profits collapsed an average of 31%; yet the stock market simultaneously vaulted 43%, one of the best six-month surges in history.

Another of the very best six-month surges was the explosion that began in August 1982. Unemployment was higher than at any time since the Depression, business leaders had finally lost confidence, the international banks were widely believed to be all but officially bankrupt, the federal deficit was exploding—and the market soared.

It works the same way, only in reverse, when the market is peaking. Zweig continues,

One reason that so many investors get overloaded with stocks at market tops, is their ill-founded reasoning: "Business looks good." It always looks good at the peaks. With prospects ripe for continued gains in earnings and dividends, investors optimistically lick their chops in anticipation of further market appreciation. But something goes astray. Business gets too overheated; the scramble for borrowed money to keep the boom rolling grows more intense, pressuring interest rates upward. The Federal Reserve, spotting increasing inflation, begins to tighten monetary growth, further exacerbating the surge in interest rates. Then, as short-term money instruments such as Treasury bills become more yield-attractive, the stock market begins to groan as the switching away from stocks accelerates, aided in no small part by the illiquidity in overly optimistic investors' portfolios [investors, that is, who have spent all their money on stocks already and now have no more cash with which to buy any more]. Yet, most folks just continue holding their stocks —or worse, buying more—because "Business looks good." Finally, many months later it becomes apparent that business has slowed down . . . but it's too late for most investors. They've already been trapped by a crumbling stock market. "Optimism" gives way to "hope" that the business slowdown won't become a recession. But the drop in stock prices rocks consumer confidence, business dips some more and recession is reality. The stock market slump becomes a rout and investors' "hopes" are finally dashed. Seeing that a recession is in progress, investors "know" that earnings will slump; in "panic" they sell their stock, absorbing huge losses. Finally, all that selling, amid tons of pessimism, improves stock market liquidity [people once again have some cash], building a base for a new boom in the market . . . one which *always* begins before business turns up.

That's the cycle, all right, but it's a lot easier to identify in hindsight than on any given Tuesday afternoon. If in the early sixties you had held off investing while you waited for the next recession, you would have had to sit on the sidelines for six or eight years. "Business looked good"—and was good—for nearly a decade.

Similarly, if you had gotten into the market after its 508-point October 19, 1987, crash, you would have done great . . . but had you gotten out when profits were soaring a few years later and the market had left its old highs in the dust, you would have missed a spectacular gain.

So for most people, the most practical, prudent way to avoid buying at market tops and selling at bottoms is to:

3. **Diversify over time by not investing all at once.** Spread your investments out to smooth the peaks and valleys of the market. **A lifetime of periodic investments—adding to your investment fund $100 a month or $750 a month or whatever you can comfortably afford—is *the* ticket to financial security.**

Steady periodic investing also gives you the benefits of *dollar-cost averaging.* Part of the theory here is that if you are in a terrible rush to buy the 300 shares, convinced the stock is about to take off and there's not a minute to lose, you are very likely reacting to some hot news. And believe me, unless you are trading (illegally) on inside information, chances are you are one of the last to hear this hot news. Nine times out of ten you will be buying your shares from someone who heard it first. In which case, when the dust settles you may not regret having snagged only 100 shares instead of 300. If, on the other hand, you are not reacting to any particular news when you decide to purchase the stock, it is simply unlikely that the stock would go straight up without any dips from the day you buy it. And dips allow you to average down your cost.

Attracted by its 9% yield and hopelessly ignorant of its problems, I once bought 50 shares of Con Edison, New York City's power company—Rock of Gibraltar—at 20. Shortly thereafter, Con Ed omitted its quarterly dividend for the first time in ten thousand years and, to my dismay, I found myself buying 100 more shares at 12. Then 100 more at 8½. Then, even, 100 more at 6. I kept buying because I just could not believe that the State of New York—which needed only to grant Con Ed's rate requests to solve all its problems—would prefer to have the company go bankrupt, and thus have to take on the burden of power generation itself. (Especially considering New York's own financial position at the time.) Sure enough, the state began cooperating, the dividend gradually was restored (even raised a notch), and the stock recovered to 20. (It would later go on to double and split.) I would be lying if I told you I was smart enough to hold all 350 shares, or even most of them, all the way back to 20 and beyond. But at least I held some. And I made sure that the first 50 shares I sold were the 50 I had purchased at 20, thus giving me a nice loss to help out with my taxes. The last shares I sold I had held long enough to qualify as a long-term capital gain.

Strictly speaking, dollar-cost averaging is a little fancier than what I've described here. Strictly speaking, the idea is to invest in a stock, or in the market, in equal dollar amounts on a regular basis—say, $3,000 mailed to a mutual fund faithfully at the end of each year. By doing so, you will buy more shares when the fund is low and fewer when it is high. And look what happens. Say the price of shares in the Sakoff Illustration Fund (and hence the number you can buy) fluctuates as follows: $25 (so your first $3,000 buys 120 shares), $45 (so your next $3,000 buys only 67 shares), $25 (120 shares again), $5 (600 shares), $25 (120). The shares went up $20, came back, went down $20, and came back again. (This is, remember, the Sakoff Illustration

Fund.) Yet even though the shares are no higher than when you started — $25 — and even though they went down as much as they went up and averaged $25, do you think you wind up with only the $15,000 you put in? No, you wind up with — *ta-da!* — $25,675. That's dollar-cost averaging. It forces you to buy more shares when they're low, fewer when they're high.

The problem with what I did with Con Ed and what you just did so nicely with the Sakoff Illustration Fund is that *some stocks don't recover.* Con Ed made it, but many don't. You can lose a fortune buying more and more as a stock gets cheaper and cheaper. Trust me — I know. The stock *market,* on the other hand, "always" recovers.* And so will most broad-based stock-market mutual funds.

In truth, your fondest wish should be for a long and devastating bear market to begin right after you start your periodic investments. If you are a systematic investor, you should welcome declines with open arms and a checkbook. At the end of the day, when the market recovers, you'll be sitting pretty.

Diverting a portion of your paycheck to the market each month is a discipline that actually makes it easier to handle market declines, because you can focus on the bargain prices you are getting for your newly invested money rather than your shrinking fortune. But until you've been through a major bear market in stocks, you won't know for sure that you have the emotional stability to stay with your investments when they suffer a substantial, prolonged decline in price, as periodically they surely will.

4. **And then — for the most part — just stick with it.** As your periodic investments mount, hold on.

Sure, it could make sense to sell a few shares if you come to think the market is hugely overvalued and you just happen to be looking for $20,000 to back a friend's new software start-up

---

* Barring a 1917-style Soviet revolution.

(kiss *that* cash goodbye) or $50,000 to build an addition to your house.

Sure, it could make sense (because of taxes) to keep your *regular* money fully invested but shift some of your *tax-sheltered* retirement money out of stocks and into a money-market fund for a year or two, until the values appear more reasonable.

Sure, it could make sense to take money out of stocks and shift it into something that's gone through a terrible bear market of its own—as farmland did in the mid-eighties, while stocks were zooming, or as junk bonds did when the government forced banks to sell them.

But by and large, for your long-term money, "buy and hold" is the way to go.

Had you bought all the stocks in the table on page 150 and just stuck with them as they dove lower and lower from their all-time highs in 1972 and 1973, an original investment of $12,000 —$1,000 in each stock—would 40-odd years later have been worth more like $400,000. (Then again, had you somehow had the brilliance to invest that $12,000 at the bottom instead of the top, it would now be worth three times as much.) Yet if you had needed the money in "just" *20* years, you would still have taken a hefty loss.

Part of the problem is knowing when the market is wildly overvalued. With hindsight, it was obvious in 1929 and 1987 and 2000—and in Japan in 1990 (when the Nikkei index was 40,000; 20 years later under 10,000). But at the time? Well, if you read *Forbes* or *Barron's* you may get some clue. But there's a risk in that, too. You'll get interested! You'll start playing the market! You'll forget that you're just trying to spot those thrice-in-a-lifetime bubbles and start trying to spot subtler over- and undervaluations instead.

And there's this problem: it's not as if the Nikkei—wildly overvalued at 40,000 yen—was not also wildly overvalued at 25,000 yen. It was! Yet imagine you, the young Japanese with his or her money in the market, bailing out at 25,000 and watching all your friends reap it month after month as the market steadily climbed and climbed and climbed and . . . at some point you might have jumped back in, having missed much of the gain but fully exposed to the upcoming loss.

Worse, imagine that you had held on as it climbed to 40,000 and *still* held on. You had read the Japanese version of this same "buy and hold" advice. And for a couple of years—which is a long, depressing length of time when you are losing money every day—you watch your portfolio fall. And then for three more long years you watch it sit around 16,000, barely 40% of its former glory. And *still* Japanese stocks are, by some measures, badly overvalued! So do you sell then? Buy more after such a steep drop? Only to see the index drop below 10,000? This "buy and hold" stuff is fine if you're Rip Van Winkle, but not so easy if you're human.

So like any rule, this one is meant to be applied with common sense. "The U.S. stock market is not Japan in 1990," I wrote in the 2005 edition, "but with the Dow around 10,000 and the NASDAQ around 2,000 as I write this, it remains high by many historical measures. Just as a Japanese investor in 1990 would have been smart to put some of his buy-and-hold money into American stocks, so an American investor in 2005 might be smart to put a little money in Japan, a little money in Europe, and a little money someplace really safe. Keeping some of that tax-deferred retirement plan cash invested in TIPS, staying a little ahead of inflation, and waiting for a market that *does* feel like 1974 all over again"—hello, 2008–2009!—"might make it easier to ride out an extended decline—and even benefit from it by having some money to add near the bottom. The higher the market climbs since the last really bad scare, the more cash you might hold someplace safe."

Still true.

But except with the funds you have stashed under the umbrella of a tax-deferred account, any skill you might have "timing the market"—knowing when to get in and out—will be more than wiped out by the cost of paying capital-gains taxes along the way. Warren Buffett is America's most successful investor and perhaps its leading capital-gains tax avoider. He's held his stock in GEICO since the 1950s. Consider this: if he had turned over his portfolio once a year while getting the same astonishing pretax investment returns, he'd have been worth not $40 billion, last time I calculated this, but barely $4 billion. You can't even build a decent *aircraft carrier* for $4 billion.

Impossible? Well, look at it this way: as of the time of my calculation, Buffett had managed to compound his money at roughly 23% a year for 46 years. At that rate, $1 grows to $13,700. But chop taxes out of that 23% annual return (using a 28% tax rate, which cuts the return to a "mere" 16.6%), and that same $1 grows to $1,150, less than a tenth as much.

5. **Diversify over several stocks in different industries.** If all your money is riding on two or three stocks, you are exposed to far more risk than if you've diversified over 20 or 30. And, because stocks of companies within the same industry tend to move together, you will only be truly diversified if you choose from among different sectors of the economy—and the globe.

What's more, a huge proportion of the market's gain has come from a small number of big winners—Microsoft and Intel, for example. (The main reason the Nifty Fifty ultimately worked out all right is that Philip Morris alone multiplied more than 100 times.) So you *could* attempt to find these stocks to the exclusion of the rest of the market (and, if you succeed, make us all look poor by comparison) . . . but probably miss them. Or you could be content to buy very broad index funds that, while they'll perform only "average," will almost surely *include* these great stocks in their average.

A program of periodic investments in no-load mutual funds is for many people the easiest, most practical way to achieve diversification—and the most prudent.

But if you do throw the darts yourself . . .

6. **Ignore the noise.** If there's anything that makes it difficult to succeed in stocks, it's that investors can see how they're doing throughout the day. Stocks move up and down all the time, but that doesn't mean there is significance to every move. John Maynard Keynes, who was not only an economist but also an enormously successful stock market investor, suggested that "one must not allow one's attitude to securities which have a daily market quotation to be disturbed by this fact. Some Bursars will buy without a tremor unquoted and unmarketable investments in real estate which, if they had a selling quotation [regularly available], would turn their hair grey." Just because it's easy to buy and sell stocks on a moment's notice, or get instant quotes, doesn't mean you should. Your time would be better spent trying to figure out what the heck a Bursar was.

7. **Or maybe you can take advantage of the noise.** As much as I believe the market is generally smarter than I am (and have the results to prove it), I don't buy the idea that there is no way to benefit from its occasional insanities.* There is, in fact, a theory known as the "noisy market hypothesis" that suggests you can. The traditional indexes that index funds follow are usually "market-weighted," meaning that the mutual fund doesn't put an equal amount of money into each stock that is in the index but instead allocates the money based on the total market value (stock price multiplied by shares outstanding) of each company. So, through the index fund, you'll be betting twice as much on a company with a $10 billion market value as on one with $5 billion.

So what? Well, here's where the "noise" comes in. We know that some of the companies are going to turn out to be better investments than others; we just don't know which. But market-weighted index funds are going to automatically overinvest in the stocks that are overpriced and underinvest in stocks that are

---

* And don't worry: I still plan to give you AN AMAZING EXAMPLE OF THAT TO PROVE THE POINT — the suspense keeps building.

underpriced, because *that's what market-weighting does.* So what would happen if a fund weighted its investment in each stock based on some factor other than market price, such as total income? Or what if the fund just mindlessly put an *equal* amount into each stock in the index? Well, as it turns out, they would have done much better, in both cases. They'd still have stakes in overvalued companies, but those stakes would be smaller. And their stakes in undervalued companies would be larger.

The Standard & Poor's 500 Market Index was first published in 1957 (actually, it held only 425 stocks until 1972). If you had invested in it at the start, making changes only when stocks were added to the index or removed from it, you would have earned a return slightly better than 7% over all those years, assuming you invested as traditional index funds do, weighting each stock by the total stock-market value of the company. If, however, you had invested in the exact same stocks, but did so equally, not proportional to market cap, and adjusted each year to keep the amounts equal, you would have earned a rate of return of almost 10% — more than 2% per year higher. In the exact same stocks.

Needless to say, that 2% is a big deal. Over a lifetime, if your results can outpace inflation by 5% instead of 3%, say, you will have a meaningfully more secure retirement. (A dollar growing at 3% over 50 years grows to $4.38 — but to $11.47 at 5%.) All (potentially) just from choosing an index fund that does its market weighting a little more rationally.

And it turns out that investments allocated based on "fundamentals" (like total income, book value, revenues, and/or cash flow), rather than market capitalization, provided similar results. See the "Selected Mutual Funds" appendix for suggestions.

Of course, easy strategies that would have beaten the market at a time when nobody was actually applying those strategies have a tendency to lose potency once the strategies are advertised and exploited, and the same might apply here. And the fees these index funds charge are a little higher. (I'm not crazy about that part.) But the *risk* in trying to get this extra 2% strikes me as small.

And this leads me to one last question. **What if you could invest in an index fund that somehow skipped all the worst businesses and concentrated instead on only the best? And not just the best, but those of the best that were selling cheapest relative to their bestness?**

Thirty-five years ago, a guy came to talk to me about investing, and ideas for a book he wanted to write . . . I don't remember much about it, except I can picture where we sat and that, well, why *would* I pay much attention—he was 23.*

He went on to become a famous value investor, whose success is rivaled only by his modesty (which is why you may not have heard of him) and his generosity (which is why, if you live in Harlem, you may attend one of the charter schools he's underwritten), but the point is, I was a fool to say no to whatever Joel Greenblatt was pitching me 35 years ago; but now we have another chance.

Ten years ago he published *The Little Book That Beats the Market*. Despite my initial horror at his concept of a "magic formula," I was won over. From my foreword:

> In the beginning, there were mutual funds, and that was good. But their sales fees and expenses were way too high. Then came no-load funds, which were better. They eliminated the sales fee, but were still burdened with management fees and with the tax and transactional burden that comes from active management.

---

* I was 33, and so a world of wisdom his senior. That same year I interviewed an 18-year-old to be one of the programmers on what was then a nascent personal finance software package. The young man was so memorably uncommunicative, sitting there with two other young Yalies in my office—on a chair I still have in the same place—that, whatever genius may have been locked inside, we hired the other two guys but not Rob. Rob went on to found RealNetworks, with a personal net worth before the dot-com crash that *Time* estimated at $2 billion. I am not a great judge of genius.

Then came "index funds," which cut fees, taxes, and transaction costs to the bone. Very, very good.

What Joel would have you consider, in effect, is an index-fund-plus, where the "plus" comes from including in *your* basket of stocks only good businesses selling at low valuations. And he has an easy way for you to find them.

Not everyone can beat the averages, of course—by definition. But my guess is that patient people who follow Joel's advice will beat them over time. And that if millions of people *should* adopt this strategy, two things will happen. First, the advantage of investing this way will diminish but not disappear. Second, stock market valuations will become ever so slightly more rational, making our capital allocation process ever so slightly more efficient.

I still feel that way. His basic notion of "buying good businesses at bargain prices" is hard to argue with. Over the long run, won't that beat overpaying for bad businesses? The question is: how do you do it? Joel's formula looks for businesses that have a high return on capital (that's what *makes* a business good) yet sell at low multiples relative to other such businesses. And it adjusts for things neither you nor I would have the time or sophistication to take into account.

People are always coming up with "back-tested" formulas that *would* have made you rich had you just followed them over the last 40 years yet have no *predictive* value. (If the Super Bowl winner was originally in the NFL, the stock market will be up for the year; if AFL, down. Has worked with 77% accuracy!) I get that, and so does Joel. This may be a little different. (For one thing, Joel wasn't looking for a formula to make him rich—or, for that matter, a formula to sell *you* to make him rich—he already *was* rich.)

Visit **magicformulainvesting.com** to learn more and, perhaps, "do it yourself," buying 20 or more of the formula's top-ranked stocks as described on the site—although this takes some time, exposes you to taxes if done outside of a retirement account, and racks up commissions. An $8 commission on 40 trades a year — $320 — isn't much if you're working with $250,000 but is significant (1.6%) if you're working with $20,000. (If you *are* working with $250,000, consider one of Joel's Gotham Funds instead. Yes, you give up 2% in fees — normally a terrible handicap — but in addition to the funds buying above-average businesses selling at below-average valuations, these funds *short* crappy businesses selling at above-average valuations, which could lower your risk in bear markets.)

8. **Beware high-fliers and stocks that "everyone" likes,** even though they may be the stocks of outstanding companies. Their hefty multiples (price/earnings ratios) discount earnings growth far into the future. Which is to say that even if the growth comes in on schedule, the stocks may not go up. They're already up. Should earnings *not* continue to grow as expected, such stocks can collapse, even though the underlying company may remain sound. What's more, it can hardly be argued that these stocks have been ignored and that they therefore represent hidden value Wall Street has failed to discover.

Forty years ago, I attended an *Institutional Investor* conference — 1,000 money managers representing billions upon billions of dollars. The men and women who really move the market. One of the panel sessions was devoted exclusively to ITT. The seminar organizer hadn't been able to find anyone bearish on the stock, so three of the panelists were bullish and the fourth volunteered to play devil's advocate.

When I heard their discussions, and saw all the heads nodding in the audience — at 1,000 shares a nod, I figured — I got this very guilty rush of adrenaline. What if I ran out of the room, rushed to the pay phone,* and bought ITT? Would that be a misuse of inside information? I decided it would not, and that's exactly what I did. At $44 a share. Any fool could see that

---

* Text your grandmother to explain what those were.

at least a few in the audience would do much the same thing after the meeting, or certainly when they got back to their desks. If they were not interested in ITT stock, why were they sitting through this seminar? And as there was no opposition meeting going on that I knew of persuading an equal number of people to rush to the phones and sell, I figured there would just have to be buying pressure on the stock. How could I miss?

The stock went straight down to 12.

Apparently, they had all put ITT in their portfolios and were now waiting for it to go up. But there was no one left to buy it.

Or how about Yahoo!? YHOO hit $500 a share as 2000 was rung in, which gave it a market cap of around $130 billion, more than 1,000 times earnings. If all the profits were paid out to shareholders each year, it would take them 1,000 years to get their money back — or perhaps 1,500 years after taxes. Of course, the bet was that earnings would zoom. Instead, they fell. The stock slipped nearly 97% from its peak. Today, Yahoo!'s profits are up manyfold from 2000 and the stock is down only 75%.

Well, OK, how about stocks with serious profits, like Dell Computer or Cisco? You *had* to own companies like these.

In March 2000, DELL was selling at about 80 times earnings. A decade later, down 75%, it sold at a more sane 19 times earnings.

And Cisco? If you owned nothing else, you *had* to own CSCO, the backbone of the Internet. Valued by the market at more than $500 billion in April 2000, it was the bluest of chips — and is still a phenomenal company, 70% off its peak 15 years later.

ITT . . . YHOO . . . DELL . . . CSCO — it's hard to buck the crowd.*

---

* And, hey — those are just the *good* stocks. On February 29, 2000, Jim Cramer, whom you may now know from CNBC, made a speech in which he listed his "Winners of the New World." Namely: Mercury Interactive ($96 then, acquired at $56 in 2006) . . . Veritas Software ($198 then, merged into Symantec at $30 in 2005) . . . InfoSpace ($217 then, $2,

One of the rare investors who *was* always able to: the late John Marks Templeton, a deeply religious former Rhodes scholar who managed to beat the Dow by an average of 8% a year for 50 years. A dollar invested in the Templeton Growth Fund at the end of 1954 was worth around $80 when he retired from active management of the fund in 1987. "Because John felt that God was with him," one associate asserts, "he invested with incredible boldness. The results make me think maybe he's right—maybe God is with him." Even more instrumental in his success than the Lord, however, may have been his relentless insistence on value, wherever he had to go to find it. He bought European stocks after World War II, convinced that the Marshall Plan would cause business abroad to boom. At one time fully three-fourths of his fund was invested in Japanese stocks, because stocks there were selling at much lower price/earnings ratios than stocks in the United States. When those p/e's rose dramatically, Templeton shifted his equally dramatic profits to countries offering better values. It takes special initiative and courage to do what no one else is doing. But it can pay off.

9. **Beware the deceptive p/e.** The price/earnings ratio is the guide most investors use to get a quick fix on a stock. The p/e tells you how much *p* (price) you have to pay for $1 of this wallet's *e* (earnings).

However, the best the news services can do is calculate the p/e based on that day's price and last year's earnings. What you are buying is the right to share in *future* years' earnings. It would have done you little good to know, in 1977, that Chrysler, at 16½, was selling at just three times its most recent year's earn-

---

after adjusting for splits, a decade later) . . . VeriSign ($253 then, $67 in 2015) . . . Ariba ($264 then, $5, adjusted for splits, a decade later) . . . Digital Island ($116 then, acquired in 2001 at $3.40) . . . Exodus ($71 then, later bankrupt) . . . Inktomi ($137 then, acquired at $1.65) . . . Sonera ($56 then, acquired at $8) . . . and 724 Solutions ($1,880 then; acquired in 2010 for an undisclosed sum, quite possibly less than $1). Jim doubtless sold before losing much if anything—indeed, nimble trader that he is, he may have made money on these "winners." But the point is that their stories were even more typical of the time than those of YHOO, CSCO, and DELL.

ings, when the following years' earnings turned out to be massive losses. The low p/e was deceptive. It would have done you equally little good, not long after, when Chrysler was 3, to note its astronomical p/e. (A $3 stock earning a penny a share sells at 300 times earnings.) Once the company recovered, it turned out that its $3 price had been less than *one* times its future annual earnings.

Thus it's necessary to keep the p/e figure in perspective, taking an average of the last *several* years' earnings and thinking more in terms of the future than the past. This is particularly true with companies—autos, cement, construction, paper, and many others—whose profits rise and fall in cycles.

10. **Don't waste money subscribing to investment letters or expensive services.** The more-expensive investor newsletters and computer services only make sense for investors with lots of money—if then. Besides their cost, there is the problem that they are liable to tempt you into buying, and scare you into selling, much too often, thereby incurring much higher brokerage fees and capital-gains taxes than you otherwise might. There is the added problem that half the experts, at any given time, are likely to be wrong. Indeed, there is one letter that simply analyzes the sentiment of all the others—and advises you to do the opposite, on the not-unreasonable theory that when most of the services are bullish, it's time to sell, and vice versa.

You want to know my idea of real market brilliance? A well-heeled former associate editor of *Forbes,* now back in the business world, sold all his stocks the day before the market began a rapid 10% slide. It was pure genius. I was green with envy and admiration.

"Peter, how did you know?" I asked him, making a mental note to pay better heed to his opinions in the future.

"I needed the cash to buy my apartment," he said.

You can tell a lot about most publicly traded companies just by going to **finance.yahoo.com.** You can look at annual reports, SEC filings, insider trading information, every financial ratio you can think of, charts of performance, recent news, earnings estimates, and real-time quotes. For mutual funds, your best choice is **morningstar.com,** which also has good stock coverage and excellent educational articles on investing. To research foreign companies, you can head over to **adr.com** and **adrbny .com.** There are also plenty of message boards where people discuss stocks (including self-serving management personnel and investors already long or short trying to manipulate the price without disclosing their interest). Or just Google "best investing websites" and see where that takes you.

But will you ever find your way back? *You could drown in all this information.* Far better, if you ask me, to stick to *Forbes* and *Barron's.* The editors of these magazines have always stressed a levelheaded, value-oriented approach to investing. They frequently run stories on companies, or whole lists of companies, that seem undervalued (or overvalued). Any one of them will give you more good investment ideas than you'll possibly have time or money to pursue. For a few dollars a year, you can get the services of several dozen financially sophisticated editors, writers, and columnists. In fact, if you just bought the first three or four issues of *Barron's* each year—for its annual expert "roundtable"—you'd have spent $15 or so to get more than enough good ideas. (Or visit **forbes.com** and **barrons.com.**)

11. **Invest—don't speculate.** It's one thing to take risks in low-priced stocks you hope, over time, may solve their problems and quintuple in value. That's a kind of speculation I admit to having a weakness for. If you can afford the risk, it may reward you handsomely.*

But it's quite another thing to jump in and out of stocks (or options or futures) hoping to "play the market" successfully. Every time you jump, your broker cuts down your stake. Even if

---

* A stock called Boise Paper dropped from $10 in December 2007 to 30 cents 16 months later, where I simply could not resist the gamble. It bounced back above $6 the following year, a 20-fold gain. I took my profit and bought a Ripley's Believe It or Not pinball machine. God bless America.

you're using a deep discounter, where the commission is trivial, there is also the "spread" to contend with—what costs $12.25 if you're buying often fetches just $12 if you're selling. And for any profits, there is that meat cleaver: taxes.

Buy value and hold it. Don't switch in and out. Don't try to outsmart the market.

12. **Sell only when a stock has gone up so much that you feel it no longer represents a good value.** Don't sell because you think business or the market generally is going to get bad, because:

- if you think so, chances are lots of other people think so, too, and the market may already have discounted this possibility (that is, the stock price may already reflect it);

- you could be wrong;

- even if business does get bad, someday it will get better—and in the meantime you are collecting dividends rather than paying brokerage commissions and capital-gains taxes.

13. **If you have both taxable and tax-sheltered portfolios, keep your riskiest holdings outside your tax-sheltered accounts.**
Risky stocks—and risky mutual funds—can produce losses that, up to $3,000 a year, reduce your taxable income. Those losses are *wasted* inside an IRA or some other tax-deferred account. Conversely, the huge gains you will occasionally reap from your riskiest holdings are favored with long-term capital-gains treatment if held directly by you and for more than a year. Inside a tax-sheltered account, they get no such treatment. They will be taxed as ordinary income when withdrawn. It's the less-speculative securities, for the most part, that you should stick in your tax-sheltered accounts.

8

Choosing (to Ignore) Your Broker

What always impresses me is how much better the relaxed, long-term owners of stocks do with their portfolios than the traders do with their switching of inventory. The relaxed investor is usually better informed and more understanding of essential values; he is more patient and less emotional; he pays smaller annual capital gains taxes; he does not incur unnecessary brokerage commissions; and he avoids behaving like Cassius by "thinking too much."

— LUCIEN O. HOOPER, *FORBES*

WAIT A MINUTE (you say). You've told me all this but you haven't told me the part about choosing a brilliant but level-headed, highly experienced, and highly ethical broker. Where's the part about her? If I can find someone who knows how to make money in the market, and who spends all day at it, why do I have to know about anything except how to retire?

There is a bit in a Woody Allen movie where Woody is standing in line, and a man behind him is lecturing his date, loudly and pretentiously, about Marshall McLuhan. Finally, Woody turns and says (in effect): "I don't know why you're talking so loud, but since you are I have to tell you I think you've got McLuhan all wrong." "Oh, yeah?" says the other man. "Well, I just happen to *teach a course* on McLuhan at Columbia." "Well, that's funny," says Allen, unfazed, "because *I* just happen to have McLuhan right here." Whereupon he goes behind a prop and pulls out Marshall McLuhan. McLuhan looks at the man and says dryly: "You know nothing of my work. How you ever got to teach a course in anything is totally amazing."

Woody Allen looks straight into the camera, at us, and says: "Boy, if life were only like this!"

Indeed, I have terrible news about brokers and money managers generally—news that I expect you've suspected, but couldn't quite believe, all along. There *are* no brokers who can beat the market consistently and by enough of a margin to more than make up for their brokerage fees. Or, if there are a few, they are not going to work for peanuts—and any account under $500,000 is peanuts. Or if they will—because they are just starting out in business or have a soft spot in their heart for you—*there's no way for you to know who they are.* Even if they can prove to you that they have done very well in the past (not just say it—prove it), that doesn't mean they will do well in the future.

If you get 256 people into a room and give them each a coin to flip, the odds are that half of them—128—will flip heads on the first try. That is the object, you tell them: to flip heads. Of those 128 winners, 64 will flip heads on the next go-round as well. Twice running. Not bad. Thirty-two people will flip heads three times in a row, 16 will flip heads four times in a row, eight will flip heads five times in a row, four will succeed six times in a row, two will rack up an incredible seven straight successes, and one—one out of all 256 in the crowd—will flip heads eight times in a row. What talent! What genius!

What nonsense. This man is no more or less likely than anyone else in the room to flip heads the ninth time. His chances are 50–50. He is not a genius, he is a statistic in a probability formula. As is someone else in the crowd of 256 (who may actually *be* a genius) who, odds are, failed eight times running to flip heads.

In any given year, half the stock-market players will beat the averages and half will do worse.* After eight years, one player

---

* Actually, more than half will do worse because players pay brokerage commissions and stock-market averages don't.

out of every 256—be he broker or mutual fund, private investor or bank trust department—is likely to have done better than average every single year. (Except that, since we all want to put our best feat forward, chances are that more than one will say he did.)

That player, naturally, will attract quite a following. What talent! What genius!

What nonsense.

I'm not saying the stock market is all luck. Indeed, I will be providing you with AN AMAZING EXAMPLE TO PROVE THAT IT IS NOT. Nevertheless, it is enough of a crap shoot that luck has a great deal more to do with it than any professional money manager is going to want to admit.

By and large you should manage your *own* money (via no-load mutual funds). No one is going to care about it as much as you. And no one but you is going to manage it for free.

This runs very much against the accepted line. The accepted line is that your money is too important to be managed in your spare time: you should let a full-time professional manage it for you, even though you will have to pay him or her to do so.

Who are these professionals and how well do they do and what do they charge? How do you find one who has been right eight times running—and *are* her chances any better than anyone else's to be right the ninth time?

I am being driven from a Boston TV station to Harvard Business School by a fellow alumnus, an investment counselor with an outstanding firm. He is paid not to manage money or make trades but to advise people on how to invest.

"My biggest pitch," he says, "is so simple, really—it's that clients shouldn't put all their eggs in one basket. I know that sounds like plain common sense you'd learn in the third grade, it's real simple, but that's what I'm paid to advise." He is paid handsomely; his services are billed out to clients at two or three times what he's paid. He advises Big Money. He recommends utilities on TV *after* they've doubled in price (maybe they'll double again?). Welcome to the world of professional money management.

Item: On June 30, 1967, the publisher, editor in chief, and editor of *Forbes* magazine mounted the *New York Times* stock pages on the wall. They threw ten darts apiece, tried again with the darts that missed the pages altogether, and invested a hypothetical $1,000 in each dart-selected stock. Fifteen years later, by 1982, the portfolio had appreciated 239%. Over the same period, the Standard & Poor's 500 rose just 35%, and many money managers hadn't done even that well.

Item: Computer Directions Advisors, Inc., a Maryland financial consulting firm, programmed a computer to choose 100 different portfolios of 15 stocks apiece—*at random*—from the 2,700-odd stocks on the New York and American stock exchanges. *Eighty-two* of the 100 randomly selected portfolios did better than the S&P 500 over the ten years from 1967 to 1976. Ninety-nine of them beat the S&P 500 in 1976. Concluded *Money* magazine: "These results suggest that it pays to look—as the computer did—beyond the large, intensively analyzed companies in the S&P 500." It was, quite simply, a time when smaller-company stocks were outperforming larger ones—as in many time periods they do—and the "darts" hit lots of smaller companies along with the larger ones in the S&P 500.*

Item: On February 28, 1977, the *Wall Street Journal* reported that "judging by the results of the pooled investment funds banks and insurance companies run, more than three-fourths of the professional managers failed to do as well as the market averages over the past two years. In fact, fewer than one-fourth of them have achieved results as good as or better than the averages,

---

* As mentioned in the last chapter, an equally weighted S&P 500 index has routinely outperformed the traditional (market-weighted) S&P 500 over the long term, and the randomly selected portfolios would have reflected this superiority.

whether for the past year, the past two years or the past four or eight years."

You see the same kind of story year after year. It's not that professional money managers are dumber or lazier than average—just that the market averages don't have to pay brokerage commissions or advisory fees and so generally outperform people, or institutions, that do.

What is significant is that among money managers there are exceedingly few who consistently do substantially better than their fellows (or substantially worse). This year's winners may be next year's losers.

In school you can pretty well assume that an "A" student this year is likely to do well next year. Not so among money managers. They will flip heads a few years in a row . . . but they are just about as likely to flip tails the next. On Wall Street, it is not enough to be smart and hard-working. There are a great many smart, hard-working people on Wall Street. Smart is taken for granted.

As for the not-inconsiderable number of dumb people on Wall Street (and in "Wall Street" I include the entire network of electronic tributaries flowing from all over the world into the mighty Manhattan delta), their existence is undeniable. Which naturally gives rise to the question, If They're So Dumb, How Come They're Still in Business? But this just proves my point: investment success has at least as much to do with luck, patience, psychological balance (unconflicted greed, for example, versus unrelenting guilt and masochism), and inside information (you don't have to be a genius to be well connected) as it does with intelligence.

If the professionals do no better than darts—and most do not—then how much is it worth to have them manage your money?

The answer is that you are probably better off minimizing your "overhead"—investing in index funds or, if you choose to buy individual stocks, paying as little as possible in brokerage and advisory fees. But before we get to discount brokers, it's worth spending some time discussing a theory that has caused much wringing of hands on Wall Street. It is called *random walk,* and to the extent that it is valid it helps to explain why professionals are just as apt to blunder as you or I. That is, after all, an intuitively unpalatable notion.

The random walk theory holds that you cannot predict the price of a stock by looking back at charts that show where it has been ("technical analysis") or by studying the business prospects of the underlying company ("fundamental analysis"). On any given day, a stock—or the market as a whole—is as likely to go up as down.

The reason, according to this theory, is that the stock market is "efficient." As soon as a new bit of information becomes known about a company (or the world), it is reflected almost immediately in the price of the stock (or the market). By the time that bit of information filters down to you or me or much of anyone else, it is already reflected in the price of the stock. It has been "discounted."

True, if you happen to be the daughter of the judge who is presiding over a $900 million antitrust suit brought by a tiny computer firm against Microsoft, and if no one on Wall Street is taking the suit at all seriously, but your daddy has just told you he's going to surprise the *pants* off those bastards at Microsoft and award the full $900 million to the little computer company . . . well, you could probably profit quite handsomely by buying stock in the little computer company. (You could also get yourself and your daddy into prison.) You have inside information.

But, inside information apart (and believe me, if you're hearing it from your broker or the company's sales manager's brother-in-law, it's no longer inside information—everyone and his brother has heard it), the market, according to the random walk theory, efficiently digests all the information available to it.

Thus, when a company announces higher earnings, the stock may go up—or it may sit pat or even decline. It depends how those higher earnings compare with what the market was expecting. It's not enough to buy Southwest Airlines thinking that, with an upturn in the economy, airline profits will be good. If *you* think that, chances are lots of other people have already thought so, too, and the possibility is already reflected in the price. Only if the gain proves more than expected will the price rise.

So you not only have to know what profits will be—you also have to try to figure out how that compares with what other people expect. Which gives you not just one but two chances to guess wrong. Between 1967 and 1982, IBM profits sextupled and its dividend grew eightfold. Yet a share of IBM was actually worth less in July 1982 than in December 1967. It finally did move to new highs as the 1982 bull market took hold, but 15 years is a long time to wait.

Choosing a horse, you just have to guess which one will run the fastest. With a stock, you have to guess how well a company will do, whether that will make the stock go up or down, and which way the track itself (the market) is moving. (The advantage in owning a stock is that the race doesn't end. You don't have to sell the stock until you want to . . . you *own* something. If you have chosen a good value, you will receive dividends, share in future growth, and, with any luck, ultimately be vindicated.)

The random walk theory naturally is anathema to the men and women whose livelihoods and self-esteem depend on convincing clients they know which way stock prices will go. Many studies have been undertaken to refute it. It is in connection with these studies that computers are made to simulate dart-throwing monkeys. Yet the evidence is that it is exceptionally rare for anyone regularly to beat the averages to any meaningful degree.

Burton Malkiel, a professor at Princeton drafted by President Gerald Ford to sit on the three-person Council of Economic Advisers, wrote an excellent stock-market guide called *A Random Walk Down Wall Street*. In it he made a tight case for random walk, citing numerous rigorously designed and executed studies. Yet he remained himself "a random walker with a crutch." He argued that random walk theory does not have to be absolutely right or wrong. It is *largely* right. It is *largely* true that you can't outguess the market. And it is particularly difficult to outguess the market by enough to justify the transaction costs you will incur by switching in and out.

David Dreman, author of *The New Contrarian Investment Strategy,* writing in *Barron's,* made a good case against random walk. He pointed out that stock markets have always been irrational and concluded that a rational investor could therefore outdo the herd. "Market history gives cold comfort to the Random Walkers," he wrote. "'Rational' investors in France, back in 1719, valued the Mississippi Company at 80 times all the gold and silver in the country—and, just a few months later, at only a pittance."

It is true, I think, that by keeping one's head and sticking to value, one may do better than average. But it's not easy. Because the real question is not whether the market is rational but whether by being rational we can beat it. Had Dreman been alive in 1719, he might very reasonably have concluded that the Mississippi Company was absurdly overpriced at, say, three times all the gold and silver in France. And he might have shorted some. At six times all the gold and silver in France he might have shorted more. At 20 times all the gold and silver in France he might have been ever so rational—and thoroughly ruined. It would have been cold comfort to hear through the bars of debtors' prison that, some months later, rationality had at last prevailed. A driveling imbecile, on the other hand, caught up in the crowd's madness, might have ridden the stock from three times to 80 times all the gold and silver in France and, quite irrationally, struck it rich.

Fast-forward 281 years to the dot-com bubble. One very smart Wall Street trader I know took a slam-dunk shot writing "naked calls" on Amazon, meaning that he pocketed $50,000 or so for taking a minuscule risk for a week—the stock, already *wildly* overpriced, would have had to rise more than 50 points in that week for him even to *begin* to feel any pain. He was completely right and Amazon stock soon fell precipitously—but not before a final for-the-record-books spurt that totally wiped out every penny he had worked his entire life to earn. In one awful week.

There are rare individuals who can consistently outperform the market. Peter Lynch. Warren Buffett. And they poke big holes in the random walk theory, however valid it may be for most investors buying and selling widely followed stocks. You can read books about Lynch, who ran Fidelity's Magellan Fund with such astonishing success, or about Buffett, who became the richest man in the world. But knowing how they did it is different from being able to do it yourself. Nor is it likely to help you find the *next* Peter Lynch or the *next* Warren Buffett.* Unfortunately, choosing a winning investment advisor, even if you can afford his or her services, is not much easier than choosing a winning stock.

Choosing a winning *broker* is even harder. Unlike investment advisors, brokers spend much of their time on the phone selling to new clients, cajoling old clients, talking sports, talking

---

* Actually, at this writing, the current Warren Buffett is very much alive and well, and you can buy shares in his company—stock symbol BRK.A—just by picking up the phone and calling any broker. But you've missed a lot of the run. When I *first* thought the stock was a little ahead of itself, 35 years ago, it was $300 a share, up from $19. I have long rued my folly in failing to buy—it's now $200,000 a share—and ruminated on possible explanations for his success. How to explain it? The way I see it, Warren Buffett is smarter and wiser than almost anybody . . . completely single-minded in his efforts . . . aided by his equally clear-sighted and extraordinary partner, Charlie Munger . . . boosted by the financial leverage in his shrewd insurance businesses (he gets to invest the premiums until you crash your car or the earthquake hits) . . . and the beneficiary, by now, of three special advantages: people all take his calls; potential acquirees enjoy a certain cachet and accept a lower price in Berkshire stock than they might otherwise; once Buffett invests/anoints, the world follows. So Buffett is clearly real—but an exception. Still, we can all learn a lot from his example. Buffett almost never traded in-and-out, never took imprudent risks. It's been brilliant, patient investing, with a firm insistence on value and a great premium placed on the quality of management.

politics, making excuses for recommendations that have gone sour—or handling paperwork, seeing that trades get made, and straightening out back-office snafus. They have little time to search out exceptional values or to formulate broad economic and financial views, as investment advisors and money managers theoretically do.

And unlike investment advisors, who take a set annual fee for their services, brokers respond to incentives. Eager as a broker may be to see your account prosper, his first interest is to feed his family. And perhaps hitting the bonus level at the end of the month that will pay for a trip to Disney World. He is as anxious as any salesperson that you be pleased with your purchase—more so, because the better you do, the more money you will have to make future purchases—but his first interest is to make the sale. He will never tell you this, but you should never forget it.

("One happy consequence of 'Dodd-Frank,' the financial reform bill of 2010," I wrote in the last edition of this book, "is that—pending SEC rule-making that should be complete in 2011—brokers are now likely to have a personal fiduciary responsibility to act in your best interests—contrary to the way it worked, say, in Venita Van Caspel's day. Also: brokerage firms may no longer be able to force aggrieved clients into binding arbitration when there's a dispute.* You can still *agree* to go to arbitration, but—if the SEC follows through with the authority Congress gave it—it will not be your only recourse." Five years later, all the above remains true; just change "2011" to "2016." Which gives you a sense of how outmanned the SEC is by vested interests on Wall Street.)

Which reminds me:

---

* In those, the brokerage firm has the edge: arbitrators know that to get the assignment, and, thus, paid, they must be approved by both parties . . . and they know that the brokerage firms will have lots of future cases coming to arbitration, whereas for the client this is probably a once-in-a-lifetime thing.

14. **Never buy anything from a broker who calls you up cold.** This is so basic as not to warrant elaboration.

If most brokers are wrong as often as they are right (and they are), if the market is *largely* a random walk, and if *Forbes* and *Barron's* are likely to do as well for you as a team of personal advisors (at a tiny fraction of the price), then why do you need a broker at all?

You need a broker to execute your trades, to give you stock quotes, to allow you to buy stocks on margin, to hold your certificates, to mail your dividend checks and monthly statements and annual reports—*and all these services are available from "discount brokers"* who make trading almost free.*

What discount brokers will not do is hold your hand, give you bad advice (or good), or try to sell you anything.

A discount broker won't call you in the middle of the day—in the middle of a root canal, if you are a dentist—to tell you the bad news that's just come over the tape about one of your stocks.

But that's good.

Had she called, you might have panicked into selling. In so many cases, seemingly dreadful news turns out to be news everyone expected, or news about a Brazilian subsidiary that accounts for just 3% of the company's sales, or news that pales beside the good news that will be announced the following week. If it's really important news, and no one expected it, the stock will be shut down from trading before you can sell, anyway; and when it reopens, sharply lower, the new price will reflect investors' assessment of the news.

With a discount broker, you won't rush into making unnecessary trades. You can finish the root canal in peace.

---

* At Ameritrade or Fidelity, the two I use, I pay $8 a trade. The same trade typically costs $356 at my full-service broker. And with the discounter, it's easier. I can do it all online, any time of day or night, and see the result (if the market is open when I place the trade) all but instantly.

There is an old joke on Wall Street. "Well," the joke goes, "the broker made money and the firm made money—and two out of three ain't bad." I have heard this joke, often, from a broker with an unobstructed view of the Statue of Liberty and a number of important institutional accounts. One of these accounts entrusted his firm with $175,000 for a flier in options. The institution was shrewd in its timing, as it turned out. The stock market rallied dramatically. Never could one have made as much in options as then. Yet in two months, through an elaborate series of computer-assisted ins, outs, and straddles, the firm's options trader managed to turn that $175,000 into $10,000— generating $87,000 in commissions along the way.

Anyway, if you are already "in the market," making occasional trades, my first suggestion—if you can bear to do it—is that you go through last year's confirmation slips to see what you paid in commissions. You may be surprised. I didn't know I churned my own account, either. Next to rent, it turned out that brokerage commissions were my biggest expense in life.

Adding up one's commissions is a calculation rarely performed. Computerized monthly brokerage statements leave the figure tactfully untallied.

If it turns out you didn't spend much on brokerage commissions last year, fine. But if you are unpleasantly surprised, as I was, I have another suggestion. Not a silly suggestion like "stop churning your account"—a practical suggestion that allows you to enjoy your little vice for less. Switch your account to a discount broker.

Depending on your relationship with your current broker, this may be easier said than done. My own full-price broker is probably the best in his mid-Manhattan office. The brightest, the most personable, the busiest. Our typical phone conversation used to go like this:

VOICE: Mr. ——'s office. (*Already this was ridiculous because* he *had neither an office nor a secretary, so this just meant both his hands had phones in them and he couldn't pick up a third.)*

ME *(playing along):* Is Mr. ——— in?

VOICE: One moment, please.

HIM: Hello?

ME: Who was that who answered the ph—

HIM: Can you hold on a minute?

(All I want to know is one stock quote, but I want to know it badly enough to hold on.)

HIM: Hi.

ME: Hi. How am I doing?

HIM: Fine, thanks, how are *you?*

ME: Fine. How's my stock?

HIM: Not very . . . can you hold on a minute?

(Silence)

HIM: Can you believe that guy? He's short 500 Xerox and . . .

Eventually I got my quote, but it took some doing. Getting a whole list of quotes could be like sitting through a soap opera waiting for the plot tidbits. To keep me listening, once in a while he would throw me a quote.

The problem was, we'd become friends. Because we were friends, I'd resent it if he was busy when I called. And because I *worked* for a living, I'd resent it if I was busy when he called. What's ludicrous is that, because we were friends, he'd resent it if *I* was busy when he called.

So it boils down to this: I wouldn't drop my broker any more than I would have dropped any other good friend. And over the years this has cost me a small fortune. Three such friends and I'd have been out on the street.

I paid him to listen to my troubles, and I paid to listen to his troubles. The fact is, I think my troubles were more interesting than his, and I think my investment advice was as good — so why wasn't he paying me? We often discussed that very point, and he couldn't agree with me more, and I kept paying him.

Now, finally, with his kids grown and through school, I do most of my trading elsewhere and don't have to beg for stock quotes — I have an iPhone.

15. **Minimize your transaction costs.** This is the one piece of the investment equation you can control, and it is hugely important.

Picking a mutual fund to outperform the market is even harder than picking a bunch of stocks that will. Why? Because the fund's performance is dragged down by annual expense charges. So when it comes to funds, you know my advice is to stick to *index funds* because they charge no sales fees and their annual expenses are typically very low. **In the investment race, the horse with the lightest jockey — the fund with the lowest expense ratio — wins.** Not every year, certainly, but over the long run. An index fund is a horse with an 18-pound jockey (18 hundredths of 1% annual fee); most *actively* managed funds have 100-pound or even 150-pound jockeys, and that's *before* what may be literally hundreds of pounds more in the commissions and "spreads" they incur trading in and out of stocks (an index fund just sits pat for the most part), let alone the weight of taxes incurred on profitable trades along the way (did I mention that an index fund just sits pat?).

The reason most mutual funds (and bank trust departments and pension funds and individual investors and anyone else) underperform the market is that they struggle under the weight of 200-pound and 400-pound jockeys.

The market itself is a riderless horse — it flies like the wind.

Unless yours has consistently outperformed the market, in which case you won't believe any of this anyway, you should shop around for the cheapest broker. (See page 273.) You will save hundreds or thousands of dollars in commissions and lose little or nothing. I repeat: Most discounters perform all the services of a regular broker, minus the advice and the personality. Full-rate brokers will claim that they provide better executions on trades — that they get you better prices than discount brokers can. But there's no evidence to support this, especially as regards trades of just a few hundred or a few thousand shares.

You can even use a discount broker to buy no-load mutual funds. You won't save money, because no-loads already carry no sales charge. In fact, there can be a small processing fee (though quite a few funds have arranged with the largest discounters to have it waived). But there are advantages. You can buy and sell funds with a simple phone call or a few clicks online (no applications to fill out and mail), switch easily from one fund to another even if they're from different fund "families," avoid worrying about minimum purchases, and get one consolidated statement for tax purposes. Through a discounter you're also able to borrow against the value of your funds or buy them on margin (careful!). And you have access to the cash-management accounts some discounters offer, with check-writing privileges.

16. **Do your homework.** I left this one for last, because it's no fun at all (at least for most of us), and I don't actually expect you to do it — and it will do you no good *to* do it unless you do it very, very, very well.

But the truth is, you CAN beat the market. And here — at last — is what I, at least, consider AN AMAZING EXAMPLE OF THAT TO PROVE THE POINT.

Background: Occasionally companies will have two classes of common stock, the "A" shares and the "B" shares, where the only difference between the two is voting rights. Otherwise, the two shares are treated identically. Their share of profits is the same, any dividends are the same, and if that great day ever comes that the company is acquired by some bigger company at a magnificent price, both classes of stock get it. As a result, the two classes of stock generally trade for about the same price, with minor variations.

And yet . . . a couple of years ago a bright young hedge fund manager, who does his homework very, very, very well, asked me if I knew Blockbuster. Well, of course — we all knew Block-buster. They rented the movies we can now get more easily with Netflix. Blockbuster's "A" shares, he pointed out, far from trad-ing at about the same price as its "B" shares, were trading for about *double*. And so, he said, since he had no idea whether Blockbuster could possibly survive as an ongoing business, why not just short the "A" shares and buy the "B" shares? Oversimpli-fying a bit: you'd get $1 for each "A" share you sold short — call it $10,000 if you shorted 10,000 shares (more on shorting in the next chapter) — but pay just 50 cents to *buy* each of 10,000 shares for $5,000. If Blockbuster eventually went under, you'd have come out $5,000 ahead. And if it ever recovered, surely this crazy spread would narrow. (Indeed, he suggested doing the trade with a "ratio" that was a little more long than short, so you'd still make money if Blockbuster went to zero, but more still if it recovered.)

Being ever skeptical of sure things and free money, I ran through with him some things that could go wrong (especially when shorting stocks, *things can go wrong*), but the first and most obvious point I made was, "Well, there must be a reason for this" — maybe in some kind of battle for control of the company the voting shares will get bid up to crazy prices while the nonvot-ing shares languish, and your broker, alarmed to see you losing a fortune on your short, will call to ruin your life (see "Margin Calls" in the next chapter).

But here, now — and I thank you for your patience — is the AMAZING part. Both classes of Blockbuster stock had voting rights. The only difference between the two classes of stock — and I do mean the *only* difference — was that the bargain-priced "B" shares entitled you to *two* votes, where the much more ex-pensive "A" shares entitled you to only one.

It made no sense, but there it was. And not just for a day or two; the anomaly persisted for a long time, and I did indeed make a little free money.

So don't tell me the market is 100% efficient. Few examples of its inefficiency are so glaring, but that doesn't mean there aren't a multitude of under- and overvaluations to be taken advantage of.

The problem comes in finding them. If you are a genius with one eye and Asperger's syndrome who spends 18 hours a day actually *reading* the unreadable and endlessly long prospectuses for collateralized debt obligations, you can wind up with a fortune and a Michael Lewis profile in *Vanity Fair*.

But if you're just very bright, you need to listen to the words of famed hedge fund manager Michael Steinhardt. Asked once for the single most important thing that an amateur investor could learn from him, he shot back: "That I'm their competition."

The fellow who told me about Blockbuster has two eyes and no named syndromes that I know of, but he spends a great deal more time at this than you or I would, and—I discovered almost by accident, *after* entrusting some of my own retirement money to his care—he is even smarter than I thought. I once shot him a recommendation from another off-the-charts investment guru I know and he e-mailed back asking for more detail on *why* such-and-such stock was a buy. I e-mailed that, well, because my other friend *said* so, and my other friend has an amazing track record and is, like, off-the-charts smart (like Steinhardt: our competition). My Blockbuster friend e-mailed back: "I respect your guru's skills, but math/science guys like him and me do not take large gambles on questions addressable by math/science on the recommendation of some other guy. It requires internal confirmation of the merit of the idea. I had a perfect score on the math, science, and reading comp scores of my ACT, a perfect score on the reading comp score of my MCAT, won the National Beta Club science contest, won the Bio-Process Lab event (basically looking at data and drawing the right conclusion) at the National Science Olympiad, and had the highest score in my only stat class at the University of Chicago by a wide margin. I have the processing power to get to a reasonable answer here on my own if I use the right inputs."

Do you see my point? He is our competition. And even for him, beating the market by a few percent a year, which so far he's done nicely for me, is no walk in the park.*

So Why Not Hire a Monkey?

If it's unlikely you can beat the market picking stocks on your own, does all this mean a monkey could handle your financial planning? No. It takes intelligence to match your financial strategy with your circumstances. It takes intelligence to perceive value. A monkey might buy municipal bonds for an IRA—but that's like throwing money out the window.† A monkey might buy growth stocks for an 80-year-old widow who needs a secure income. A monkey might buy Avon at 60 times earnings as the Morgan Guaranty Trust Company and so many others did.

A monkey does not have what investing well really takes: common sense.

---

* I am not printing his 800-number both because he doesn't have one and because he doesn't think he could do well managing billions of dollars. He mainly trolls for undervalued small to tiny companies Wall Street analysts do not follow.

† Why accept a lower yield for a tax-free bond in an account that isn't subject to current taxation anyway—and in effect turn it into a taxable bond, since the income it produces *will* eventually be taxed when you withdraw it?

9

Hot Tips, Inside Information — and Other Fine Points

If you bet on a horse, that's gambling. If you bet you can make three spades, that's entertainment. If you bet cotton will go up three points, that's business. See the difference?

— BLACKIE SHERROD, as quoted by James Dines in *Technical Analysis*

Hot Tips

Here is what to do with hot tips. If you get a hot tip, make a note of it and pretend to be very interested. But don't buy. If the thing takes off, listen a little more closely the next time this fellow has a tip. If it gets mauled, look bitter the next time you see him. He will assume that you bought the stock; he will feel guilty; and he will buy you a very nice lunch.

Annual Reports

Annual reports are organized very simply. The good news is contained up front in the president's message and ensuing text; the bad news is contained in the footnotes to the financial statement.

You should be aware that for big, widely followed companies, everything of any substance contained in the annual report was known to sophisticated investors months earlier.

Inside Information

It's much easier (although illegal) to make money in the market with inside information than with annual reports.

A Republican I know in the executive suite at a major insurance company called a close friend in a distant city (a Democrat) and told him to buy all he could of a company then selling at $6 a share. Several days later, the insurance giant tendered for the company at $10 a share. The Republican and the Democrat quietly split the profit.

Or say you are a trader with a major firm and you get a call from one of the big banks asking you to buy two million shares of Raytheon, the defense contractor. That's a lot of stock. It will in all likelihood spike the price of Raytheon, at least temporarily. You have this friend somewhere you owe a favor and, when you bump into him, you mention that Raytheon sure looks good for a quick move. He buys options on the stock and doubles his money in two days. Now he owes you a favor.

Unfortunately, very few investors are anywhere near close enough to the center of financial power ever to be tempted by genuine inside information.*

Charts

Charts look like they should work, but don't. Everybody uses them anyway, just as everyone knows his astrological sign. Some people even take them seriously. Much good may it do them. The various precepts, strategies, systems, rules of thumb, and general folklore that chart readers espouse have been rigorously tested. To quote Malkiel: "The results reveal conclusively that past movements in stock prices cannot be used to foretell future movements [any more than past flips of a coin will help determine the next flip]. The stock market has no memory. The cen-

---

* Or perhaps I should say "fortunately." A lot of people who never dreamed they could get caught have been — and some have even gone to jail. What could ImClone CEO Sam Waksal have been *thinking* when he told his daughter to sell stock ahead of bad news from the Food and Drug Administration? Well, for that and a few other things he took up residency at the Schuylkill Federal Correctional Institution in Pennsylvania in 2003, released in 2009.

tral proposition of charting is absolutely false, and investors who follow its precepts will accomplish nothing but increasing substantially the brokerage charges they pay. Yes," Malkiel writes, "history does tend to repeat itself in the stock market, but in an infinitely surprising variety of ways that confound any attempts to profit from a knowledge of past price patterns."

Nonetheless, chartists are likely to be right about as often as they are wrong, and so constantly find new reasons to believe in their craft. The bookshelves bulge.

Don't waste your time.

Splits

Splits are accorded great excitement on Wall Street. Before the split you had just 200 shares of the stock, at $40 each ($8,000). Now—presto!—you have *400* shares of the stock, at *$20* each (still $8,000). Nothing has happened; your share of the pie is exactly what it was. They have exchanged your dollars for twice as many half-dollars or four times as many quarters or ten times as many dimes.

The advantages corporations hope to gain from splits are: to lower the price of the stock to make it look "cheaper"; to create the aforesaid sense of excitement and forward motion; to increase the number of shares outstanding, and hence the trading volume and liquidity of the stock.

Although splits can affect a stock's price temporarily, they in no way change its underlying value (or lack thereof).

Stock Dividends

The only difference between a stock dividend and a stock split is that, being a very *small* split, it is hoped no prospective buyers will even notice it has taken place.

Stock dividends are under no circumstances to be confused with real dividends. Their (dubious) value is entirely psychological—it is hard to believe that it merits the cost of adjusting everyone's records and answering the questions of confused shareholders.

Prior to the dividend, 100% of the company was divided among the shareholders. Then, in an attempt to keep those shareholders happy without having to pay them anything, each one is given 3% more shares. Now they have exactly what they had before—100% of the company. It is just divided into slightly smaller pieces.

You pay no tax on a stock dividend, because it adds no value to your holdings. What you hope, however, is that Wall Street will not notice that your company has made this quiet little "split" and, accordingly, will keep paying what it used to pay for each now-slightly-less-valuable share.

Sometimes it actually works.

Dividend Reinvestment Plans

These are not the same as stock dividends. Many big companies give their shareholders the choice of receiving their (real) dividend either in cash or in stock. Either way you have to declare the full amount as income. But if you choose to take stock instead of cash, the company takes your dividend, along with a lot of others, and either goes into the market and buys its own stock for you with your money or else sells it direct to you from the corporate treasury.

The advantages to you are that you are forced to save money you might otherwise have spent—if you consider that an advantage—and you pay no brokerage commission to buy the stock. Often, you even get a 5% discount.

The advantage to the company is that it helps keep the stock up (if purchased in the open market) or raises new capital without having to pay underwriting fees and going through lengthy SEC prospectus procedures (if sold from the corporate treasury).

Although there is no harm in taking dividends in stock—for small investors it's actually quite a good deal—it makes more sense for substantial investors to take the cash and then decide the optimum place to put it.

Selling Short

When you sell a stock you don't own, you are "selling short." You do this if you think a stock is likely to go down and you wish to profit from its misfortune. To sell a stock short you instruct your broker to (a) "borrow" it from someone who does own it, (b) sell it, and then, eventually, (c) buy it back—ideally at a lower price than you sold it for—so that you can (d) return it. Buying it back to return it is called "covering" your short position.

Selling short is not un-American, as some people seem to feel, but it carries with it three problems. First, a relatively small one, is that instead of *receiving* dividends while you sit with your position, you may actually have to *pay* them. (You borrowed the stock from some nameless, faceless person who does not even know it's been lent; then you sold the stock; now the company pays a 40-cent-a-share dividend, which the lender naturally expects to receive. Your broker deducts that amount from your account and deposits it in his.)

Second, by selling short you are in effect betting against the management of a company, who are doubtless applying their best efforts to making things turn out all right. They could succeed. (Actually, you are betting that others have not fully grasped what a mess the company is really in, or how little value really underlies its inflated stock, and thus are willing to pay you more for it than they should.)

Third and most serious, shorting stocks makes the amateur investor even more nervous than buying them. It is not at all atypical for small investors to spot a stock that is genuinely worth shorting, short it, begin to go crazy as it climbs yet another 20 points, lose their resolve, and bail out at the top—just days before the bottom falls out.

This can even happen to big investors. One man of my acquaintance observed the wild rise in gambling stocks occasioned by the development of Atlantic City and shorted Resorts International, wildest of the bunch. He shorted a lot. And it went up a lot. But this gentleman is nothing if not confident in his acumen, and so he left the country for a six-month round-the-world jaunt, short many thousands of shares of Resorts International, checking in with his brokers every so often by phone. Each time he checked in, from country after country, Resorts was higher. The bubble, against all reason, refused to burst. It is easy to say with hindsight that, had he held on for just a few countries more, the bubble would indeed have burst (all bubbles do) and all his paper losses would soon have been erased. But there in the Australian outback (or wherever) it had begun to look to my friend as though he might actually lose everything. Discretion being the better part of valor, he decided to cut his losses— $19 million—and cover his short position. That was, of course, the top.

It was a rare mistake for this remarkably successful investor, but a useful tale for the rest of us.

With shorts you are swimming against the tide of the brokerage commission you have to pay, the dividends you may have to pay, the market's long-term upward bias, the efforts of management, your own psychological frailties (like getting scared), your own financial limits (like running out of cash to meet your margin calls as the stock rises, so you *have to* take your loss, even though you want to hold on), and—should you actually make a profit—the lack of any long-term capital-gains break for short-sale profits, no matter how long you've held your short.

In sum: don't short stocks. If you do want to bet against a company, buy puts on its stock instead (read on). You will likely lose what you bet—but not *more* than you bet. Not, in the case of my friend, $19 million.

The Counter

If there is really a counter somewhere, I have never seen it. "Over-the-counter" used to be an arena of stocks too small to be traded on a stock exchange. Instead of there being an "auction" market for these stocks, where buyers and sellers meet to do business, there are dealers who keep them in inventory. You want some, we got some.

Over time, this over-the-counter stuff got pretty sophisticated and became the NASDAQ, which is almost like an exchange, and home to such giants as Apple and Google. The really small stocks are now found on the "bulletin board." (I have not seen that, either.) To find quotes on obscure stock symbols, try **otc markets.com.**

The problem with tiny, obscure stocks, particularly if you're not planning to buy and hold for the long haul, is that in addition to brokerage commissions you have the "dealer spread" to contend with. The dealer spread, in percentage terms, can be enormous. A stock may be quoted at $4.50 bid, $5.50 asked. That means you have to pay the dealer $550 for 100 shares, plus a commission to your broker; and then you can turn around and sell the same 100 shares for $450, *minus* a commission for the broker. Although your broker can often do a little better for you than the listed quote, it is very discouraging. In this example the stock has to rise from $4.50 bid to nearly $6 bid—a 33% gain —just for you to break even after commissions.

The SEC under Arthur Levitt in the late 1990s did some excellent work to narrow spreads. We little guys should be grateful. Still, with small, illiquid stocks, you must take their often-enormous spreads fully into account before investing.

Portfolio

You have heard of a pride of lions, a medley of ducks, a hysteria of hyenas? So, too, a portfolio of stocks and bonds.

Beta

Beta is a measure of a stock's volatility. When the market goes up, does this stock tend to go up faster? Or not as fast? When the market is falling, does this stock plunge? Or just slump? The more speculative the stock (or portfolio), the higher its beta. If it moves twice as sharply as the market—a 10% decline in the market produces a 20% decline in the stock—its beta is 2. If it moves only half as forcefully—a 10% market gain produces only a 5% gain in the stock—then its beta is 0.5. Most stocks move about like the market, give or take a little, so most stocks have betas around 1.

It doesn't take calculus to know that utilities are relatively stodgy and that hot technology stocks are more speculative. But beta quantifies it. "What's your portfolio's beta?" you can ask show-off friends to put them in their place. On the off chance they have any idea, you should react this way:

- If beta is under 1: "Playing it safe this year, eh?" (Particularly biting if the market has recently been zooming.)
- If beta is over 1: "Looking for a good run in the market, are you?"

Beta late than never.
You beta believe it.

The Dow Jones Industrial Average

Against all reason, this highly unscientific average of 30 stocks is probably the most widely followed "financial barometer" in the world—and probably always will be, which is why, reluctantly, I have referred to it throughout this book. (To see where it's been over the past century, in broad strokes, see the graph on the facing page, courtesy of **macrotrends.net.** And visit that site to see it adjusted for inflation. Bottoming at 40.56 July 8, 1932 and rising 450-fold *un*adjusted for inflation to 18,351 May 19, 2015, it requires a logarithmic scale to fit it on the page.)

The Only Other Graph in This Book

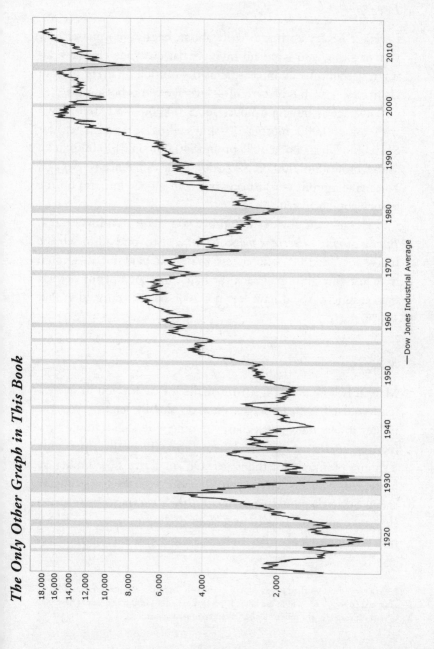

— Dow Jones Industrial Average

Leverage

Leverage is very boring to write about, because no matter how you attack it, you wind up saying what everyone else says, always, without variation, as sure as the caution on every pack of cigarettes: " . . . but be careful — leverage works both ways."

Leverage is buying a house for $100,000 — $20,000 down with an $80,000 mortgage — and selling it, years later, for $140,000. That's not a 40% profit ($40,000 on $100,000); it's a 200% profit ($40,000 on *$20,000*).* The difference is leverage. You make a profit not just on your own money but also on the money you borrowed.

Leverage can obviously improve your return on investment. *But be careful — leverage works both ways.* If you had to sell the house for $80,000 — 20% less than you paid for it — you'd have just enough to pay back the bank, but not a penny of your own cash left. You'd have lost not 20% on the transaction, but 100%.

Margin

Margin is how brokerage firms make it easy for you to overextend yourself with leverage. They do this by lending you the money to buy more stock than you otherwise could. It's not unlike the credit card a department store will gladly issue, only it's more profitable for the issuer. On small sums the brokerage house will typically charge you 5% more than the banks charge them. Since they hold your stock in their computer as security, they take no risk. If your securities decline in value anywhere near enough to jeopardize the loan, either you ante up more se-

---

* Well, except that you had to pay a lot of interest on the loan along the way. But if, all in, after tax, your cost of owning the home happened to be the same as you would have paid to rent — possible — the profit numbers would not need adjustment.

curity, or else your position is sold out, like it or not, before it can deteriorate further. (Of course, it is just when others are having their positions sold out from under them that you should be in there with a wheelbarrow *buying*.)

Never use margin to buy stock. The one time it's handy, when used responsibly, is as a convenient, low-cost way to make yourself a quick loan while you wait for your next paycheck, or your home sale to settle. Better that than a high-interest credit-card loan.

Margin Calls

A margin call is what alerts you to the fact that your life is going to hell and that you never should have gotten into the market when you did, let alone on margin.

Options

One way to get incredible leverage is with options.

As if the stock market weren't already enough like Caesars Palace, someone decided the real action would be in trading not stocks, but options. He was right.

Own a stock and you could wait years before it doubles. Buy an option and it can double overnight.

Own a stock and you own a small portion of a company's assets and earning power. Buy or sell an option and you are placing a bet—nothing more.

Options, therefore, are a great deal more fun than stocks, more potentially lucrative, and much more likely to wipe you out. Brokers love them.

If you know which way a stock is going to go, you can make a fortune with options. But the stocks on which options are traded are the most widely followed and intensively analyzed . . . the ones most likely to conform to the random walk theory of price movement. The hardest ones to outguess. That being the case, the odds in this game are with your broker.

This doesn't mean that I personally have summoned the will-power to abstain, or that I would pass up for any sum the opportunity to tell you about the time I bought Merrill Lynch options at ⅜.

There I was at the old Beverly Hills Hotel, in one of the smaller suites (a converted maid's room), charged with writing a story about the remake of *King Kong* ("the most exciting original motion picture event of all time," as it was billed) but thinking, instead, about Merrill Lynch.

It was the first week of January 1976, and the market had suddenly begun to go wild. Volume on the New York Stock Exchange, which had been running at an unspectacular 15 or 18 million shares a day, was suddenly hitting 30 million shares. Party to each trade, I knew, were a buyer, a seller—and a broker.

Merrill Lynch stock was selling for around 16½. For some reason it had not yet reacted to the surge in volume. It seemed to me that if the volume kept up, Merrill Lynch stock would rise. So I bought "10 Merrill Lynch April 20s," which means I purchased ten options, at 100 shares an option, to buy Merrill Lynch stock at $20 a share (the "strike price"), any time between then and April.

The right to buy a stock for 20 when it is selling at 16½ is not tremendously valuable, so it cost me just ⅜ of a dollar per share—$37.50 per 100-share option—$375 in all. Plus $76.88 in commissions.*

Stock-market volume continued to surge.

Merrill Lynch stock began to move up.

My options began to move up with it.

---

* For centuries, stocks were quoted in fractions. In this century, they have been "decimalized." Decimals are better, because they tighten "the spread" at which stocks can trade. Where once it could generally be no thinner than an eighth or a sixteenth of a dollar, now the spread can be as little as a penny.

God, it was thrilling!

As the stock passed 20 — the "strike price" — the option was being traded at 1½. This was the "premium" people were paying for the chance that Merrill Lynch would go still higher before April (possibly much higher) and that the option would thus actually be *worth* something. (Its "intrinsic" value at 20 was still zero. The right to buy something for 20 that *anybody else* can buy at 20 is worth nothing.)

The price I had paid for this option was ⅜. Now it had quadrupled — 1½.

I sold two of my options for $300 — almost as much as I had paid for all ten. I did this because I am a candy ass.

Stock-market volume continued to set records. Why this was happening I had no idea.

I sold two more options at 1¾.

Another at 2¹⁄₁₆.

Two more at 3⅛. Another at 3⅜ (Merrill Lynch stock was now trading for around 22½).

Another at 5½ — $550 for an option that had cost me $37.50.

And, finally, the last at 6.

Total investment: $375. Time elapsed: one month. Profit after commissions (but before taxes): $2,397.67.

Options have a certain allure.

Indeed, had I held all ten until the April expiration date, instead of selling on the way up, I could have turned my $375 into $15,000!

One thing you have to bear in mind, however, is that somewhere there is a person who sold me those ten Merrill Lynch April 20s at ⅜. I won. He lost. Between the two of us, we generated $500 in brokerage commissions.

(I'd like to have given you a more recent example of a triumph I've had with options, but I don't have any. What usually happens with options is that they expire worthless. I could provide lots of examples of *that*.)

Options are what's known as a zero-sum game — for every winner there is an equal and opposite loser — except it's worse than that, because of the brokerage commissions.

The Merrill Lynch options I have been describing are called *calls*. They give the purchaser a call on someone else's stock. If you think a stock is going to go up, you can buy a call on it. If you think it's headed down, you can buy a *put*.

If you buy a put, you are buying the right to sell a stock at a specified price. That right becomes valuable if the stock goes down. Say you buy a Procter & Gamble April 70 put. You have the right to sell 100 shares of P&G to me (put it to me, as it were) at 70 any time up until April. Say you pay me $50 for this right, and P&G is selling at 73. Then laundry detergent starts exploding in washing machines around the country. (You anticipated this how?) The market panics and the stock falls to 51. You buy it at 51 and put it to me at 70. You have made 19 points a share, or $1,900 — minus commissions and minus the $50 you paid me for the put.

All you stand to lose when you buy a put is the cost of the put. If you had shorted P&G instead, and it had gone to 80, you could have lost a lot more.

We could go on at some length in this vein . . . I have not yet talked of selling puts, just buying them; let alone straddles (buying a put and a call on the same stock at the same time, hoping the stock will make a dramatic move in one direction or another, but not caring which), spreads (buying an option at one strike price and selling another at a higher or lower strike price), or any of a dozen other arcane strategies one might employ. Applying these strategies, a very sharp CPA friend of mine managed to lose, in one day, October 19, 1987, everything he had managed to make through a decade of patient and intelligent investing in stocks.

If you play the options game as a buyer of puts or calls, you will have some terrific gains, lots of little losses, and lots of brokerage fees. Your broker will stress that you are getting to "control" $16,500 worth of stock (in the case of my ten Merrill Lynch calls) for a commission of merely $76.88 — peanuts. But the fact remains that of the $375 you actually bet, little over 20% went to the house. And should you wish to cash in your chips, that's another 20%. The commission rate declines sharply with the size of the trade — and at my deep discounter today would be just $26 — but it's never insignificant.

Just remember this: it is a zero-sum game and the odds are against you. Anything you do win is fully taxed as a short-term capital gain. There are no dividends, lots of commissions. It may be addictive.

Covered Calls

Say you own 100 shares of IBM, which is trading at 90. You think that at 90 the stock is awfully high; but you think, too, that it's a great company. You really don't want to sell it and have to pay capital-gains tax on your enormous profit (you bought the shares not that long ago at 40), so you do the opposite of buying a call on IBM — you *sell* a call. You give some nameless, faceless buyer the right to buy your 100 shares at, say, 95 any time between now and the third Friday in October. In return, you receive $300, say (it all depends on what someone is willing to pay you), less a commission to your broker. This is what's known as "writing a covered call." Should IBM rise above 95 and the call you sold be exercised, you're covered — you have the stock sitting right in your account, waiting to be sent off to its new owner.*

You figure: Hey. I get to keep any appreciation in the stock up to $95. I get to keep the dividend. And now, to light a fire under my rate of return, I get this $300! In fact, I get it maybe four times a year, writing 90-day options each time — an extra

---

* The truly self-destructive write *naked* calls. With naked calls your gain is limited to the premium you receive; your potential loss is unlimited. That's what happened to my friend (see page 178).

$1,100 or so a year (after commissions) on my $9,000 of IBM stock. That adds 12% a year to my return!

Writing covered calls is perceived as the conservative way to play the options game, on the intuitively appealing notion that if option buyers lose money, it must be option sellers who make it. But that notion is wrong. It is option *brokers* who make money. The problem with writing covered calls is that you retain virtually all the risk while eliminating any chance of a really exciting gain. What if IBM drops off a cliff and you're still holding it? What good's a lousy $300 if the value of your shares drops from $9,000 to $5,750? Or what if IBM shoots from $90 a share to $135? You make the first five points of profit but give up everything from $95 to $135 — $4,000 on 100 shares — all in return for that lousy $300 (less commission, less taxes).

Like most low-risk gambling systems, writing covered calls works well under ordinary circumstances but kills you at the extremes. It certainly isn't as dumb as buying puts and calls looking for a big profit. But neither is it as smart as some people think.

LEAPS

LEAPS are long-term puts and calls — "Long-term Equity AnticiPation Securities" — traded on hundreds of stocks and market indexes. They're risky but can be more interesting than regular puts and calls. For starters, if you hold them more than a year, to satisfy the long-term capital-gains requirement, your profits are less heavily taxed. More than that, while it's no more possible to know where a stock is headed in the next few weeks than to predict a breeze, you just *may* be right in your longer-term assessment that a stock is unduly beaten down (or pumped up). Had you bought two-year IBM LEAPS the day Lou Gerstner was announced as CEO, betting he could breathe new life into the company, you would have been richly rewarded. Of course, you could have bought the stock, too, but less of it. LEAPS give you leverage. And because many investors seem to lack patience, preferring to pay for excitement, LEAPS—requiring patience and being relatively unexciting—are often reasonably priced.

Commodities

Again? I thought we'd disposed of commodities in the first chapter.

Well, yes—but there is no end to the persistence of the nation's commodities sales reps. I once wrote a very negative column on commodities for *Esquire.* In the ensuing weeks, I got six different calls from as far off as Arkansas (that one touting coffee)—not with complaints, but to sell me commodity futures! (What do they know about coffee in Arkansas?)

To reinforce your resolve, I quote from investment veteran John Train's *The Money Masters:*

> Stanley Kroll spent 13 years as a commodity broker. He had about 1,000 nondiscretionary customers [customers who made their own decisions with or without his advice] . . . He even wrote a book on commodity trading. Stanley Kroll says that none of his original 1,000 customers made money. Not one . . . Kroll and the other commodity specialists I've talked to agree that the retail commodity speculator will almost always sooner or later lose his money, as infallibly as if he cranked away day and night at a slot machine.

And yet away they crank.

Financial Futures

In the old days, you were limited to speculating in physical commodities like cotton, soybeans, or copper. Today, you can buy Treasury bond futures, to bet on the direction of interest rates, and stock-index futures, to bet on the direction of the market. And that's just scratching the surface. All of this is loads of fun and, if you know which way interest rates or the market averages are headed, highly profitable. Unfortunately, you don't; and neither do I.

Options on Futures

With futures, you put up a tiny down payment to control vastly more of something than you could ever afford to pay for in full. The leverage is enormous. A modest swing in the price of sugar or gold can make you rich or wipe you out. It was to get around this wipe-out aspect of futures trading that Wall Street — Chicago, actually — invented *options* on futures. With these, you will almost surely lose all you invest, but you can't lose more. Now isn't that terrific? Your loss is limited to the size of your bet. They even have options on Treasury bond and stock-market index futures. *Come onnnnnnnn, WILLow!*

Penny Stocks

Commonly defined as those selling for under $3 a share, penny stocks fall into two broad categories: those initially issued for just pennies a share — a marketing ploy — and those that became penny stocks against their will.

The former are typically Canadian gold-mining stocks and other ventures whose principal merit is that even a pauper can afford to buy 1,000 shares and a dream. They are wildly speculative and burdened by backbreaking spreads. You are all but certain to lose money.

The latter are shares in real companies that have fallen close to or into the arms of bankruptcy, their once-lofty shares commanding just pennies, or at most a few dollars. These are highly speculative investments but sometimes not stupid ones. With Chrysler at 2⅝ (pre-split), all you could lose was 2⅝. On the off chance it recovered, you could multiply your money 30-fold. The advantage of these stocks is that, unlike the others, no one is out promoting them. Quite the contrary—everyone is dumping on them. If Wall Street tends to overreact in both directions —and it does—these involuntary penny stocks may sometimes be the object of that overreaction.

Even so, you could lose a lot of money betting on the next Chrysler. The more conservative approach is to invest in a no-load fund like Tweedy, Browne Global Value with a nose for value in the securities of fallen angels.

(It should be noted that a company worth $100 million could just as easily be divided into 1 million $100 shares or 500 million 20-cent shares. By itself, a low share price means nothing. Many British blue chips trade for mere pence. In the United States, however, by convention, few healthy, well-regarded companies sell for less than $20, or certainly $10, a share; and few tiny speculative companies sell for much over $10.)

Strategic Metals

These are metals like chromium, germanium, and niobium that no thriving military-industrial complex should be without. It's just not likely to occur to you to speculate in them—which isn't all that easy, incidentally—when nobody's talking or worrying about them. Only when the world is in an uproar and the prices of these metals are going through the roof, as they occasionally do, are you prey to the pitch. And that, of course, is an even worse time than usual to invest in strategic metals.

Cash

Cash is variously meant to mean *cash,* as in dollar bills, or "cash equivalents"—things like money-market funds or Treasury bills that you could immediately turn into cash, but that pay some interest until you do. To hold cash (of whichever variety) is to sit on the sidelines. This is sometimes the wisest, but most difficult, thing to do.

Tax Timing

It is common advice that you not let tax considerations interfere with investment decisions. Don't hang on to a stock to avoid tax on your gain if, by doing so, your gain will gradually disappear; or wait for a gain to go long term if it's likely to evaporate while you do.

Even so, there are a few things to keep in mind:

+ All your gains and losses for any given tax year get lumped together. Losses wipe out gains. If, as the year draws to a close, you have net gains, you may want to take enough losses to wipe them out and avoid having to pay tax. In fact, you might want to take extra losses, because *up to $3,000 of net losses in any given year can be deducted from ordinary income.* (Anything above $3,000 is carried over to future years.) If you're in the 33% tax bracket (between federal and state income tax), a $3,000 deduction saves you $1,000.

+ Because they are taxed less heavily, long-term gains are more valuable than short-term gains.* Thus—other things being equal—it's better to use losses to cancel out short-term gains (and thus save a heavy tax) than to cancel out long-term gains (and derive a somewhat less impressive tax benefit).

+ If you bought a stock at 20 that's now 15, you might save taxes by selling it for a loss . . . but if it was a good value at 20, might it be an even better value at 15? You don't want to get into the habit of buying high and selling low. There are three ways of dealing with this (if you calculate that your tax savings will justify the extra brokerage commissions): You could sell the stock to establish your loss, then buy it back 31 days later (the IRS disallows

---

* In 2015 those earning less than $37,450 ($74,900 filing jointly) paid *zero* tax on long-term gains. The top rate was only 15% for most people (though 20% on income above $413,200 or $464,850 filing jointly)—plus another 3.8% on the amount by which taxable income exceeds $200,000 ($250,000 filing jointly) to help defray the cost of broader health-care coverage. Then there is the Alternative Minimum Tax, which can effectively raise the rate as well. All part of Congress's commitment to simplify the tax code.

anything less as a "wash sale"). Or, if you have a primal dread that the stock will take off during those intervening 31 days, as it could, you can do it the other way around. Buy a *second* 100 shares, wait 31 days, and then sell the *first* 100 for the loss. The hope is they won't fall farther during the month you've doubled up. Or, if this 31-day notion throws you, sell your shares for a loss right now, but simultaneously buy something you consider similar—swap one timber stock for another, say.

+ Remember that if you make large gifts to charity, the best way to do it is by giving securities in which you have a long-term gain. You avoid paying *any* tax on the gain, yet get a deduction for the full value of the securities as of the date your charity receives them. (This emphatically does *not* work with short-term gains! You only get to deduct the *cost* of the gift, not its appreciated value.)

+ None of this matters inside a tax-sheltered retirement account.

VSP

You own 200 shares of some stock bought piecemeal at different times. You may have a long-term profit on some of the shares and a short-term profit on the rest—or even a gain on some and a loss on others. If you're selling just 50 shares, it becomes important to know which 50 they are. *You* say they're the ones that provide you with a short-term loss, but why should the tax man trust you? Unless you can prove otherwise, he will assume the shares you've sold are the ones you've held longest. But what if that's not your intention? The way to handle this is to tell your broker to sell 50 Intel "VSP ten one fourteen"—namely, the shares you bought October 1, 2014. VSP could be an important brandy but stands for "versus purchase." (Oh? The brandy classification is VSOP? Well then, "Never mind.")

Your broker, of course, doesn't care in the slightest which 50 shares you are selling and is hardly going to go running around for the right stock certificate, in part because no one uses stock certificates anymore. They use electronic ledger entries. But your confirmation will arrive duly noted "VSP 10/1/14," and all will be square between you and the United States of America.

Re-org

I can't imagine you'll run into this. With luck, I'll never run into it again, either. But in the bowels of most brokerage firms dwells a department called "re-org." My conception of "re-org" is that it is made up of plainclothesmen whose extensions at the firm are unlisted.

I know about re-org because I once owned a stock that was converted through some exchange offer for bonds. It was not something I paid close attention to (this is why we have brokers, and why brokers have computers), but every month thereafter an entry appeared in my statement showing that I owned four GEICO bonds. After several months, I disposed of two of them. Several months later, the other two. No problem. More months passed. Then out of the blue came a call from my full-service broker. Re-org, he said, had just notified him they were debiting my account for $1,719. They said I had sold four GEICO bonds when in reality I had only owned two.

"Re-org?" I asked. I couldn't really make out what he was saying.

"Re-org," he said.

"Who the hell is re-org?" I asked.

"Re-org. They're down in the basement or something. I don't know."

"Well, how can they just take money out of my account? Don't I get to argue about it first?" I asked.

"I argued for you," he said. "You lost."

My broker, who as I've explained is by now a close friend, was genuinely upset by re-org's high-handed tactics — but helpless.

"But the four bonds were in my account for more than a year!" I said.

"I know," he said. "Apparently there should only have been two." He recited a litany of conversion ratios and transfers and journal entries that re-org had supplied to substantiate its case. And it seemed clear (in a hazy sort of way) that re-org was right. But a year later?

"You mean, they can make a mistake and confirm it in fourteen monthly statements and then, out of the blue, come and loot my account?" I asked.

"Yes," said my broker, "and they're going to debit you for the interest you were paid on the two extra bonds, plus interest on the proceeds of the second sale. They wanted you to pay the loss they're going to take to buy back the two extra bonds, because they've gone up since you sold them, but I put my foot down."

To date, re-org has not called to correct any year-old errors made accidentally in *its* favor.

Investing Online

In addition to cutting commissions dramatically, the Internet has all but closed the gap between the kind of information small amateur investors can get—and when they get it—versus "the professionals." Thus for the right kind of people—disciplined investors who do their homework—the Internet has been a boon. Why pay some fund 1.5% a year in management fees and expenses when you could just do it yourself? *And* control the tax consequences of your portfolio?*

But for every person you know who is disciplined, financially savvy, and does her or his homework, is it not fair to say you know 50 who aren't or don't? For no small percentage of them, investing online has become just one more way to gamble . . . an addiction.

"My name's Alan," began a TV commercial you may have seen, with the speaker addressing a group of his peers, "and I

---

* See page 247 for more on this.

haven't used . . . [long pause, as you are expecting him to say alcohol or cocaine] . . . E*TRADE . . . since yesterday." "Hi, Alan!" responds the crowd (or maybe I just imagine that part), and the commercial goes on to say that Alan is building up his nest egg via this popular Internet broker. He may indeed be able to build it up a lot faster via an online broker than the old-fashioned, high-commission way. Absolutely. But I also think the Internet has led many a lamb to slaughter. It's so easy to click "OK" and make a $10,000 bet. Look how mesmerized we become on a stool in front of a slot machine. The Internet positively *teases* you to play. It makes you feel powerful — moving thousands of dollars in and out, click, click, click. Talk about computer games!

But click often enough — even just once or twice a week — and four things will surely get you: the commissions (they're low, but imagine a slot machine that charged $8 a crank), the spreads (another $25, typically, on a 200-share trade), the taxes (a big chunk of your winnings, versus a much smaller chunk, deferred, if you buy and hold), and human nature. There are few places where one's self-destructive tendencies are more likely to surface than in an addictive gambling situation.

Thus for many investors, despite the allure of the game, index funds really do remain the smart way to play.

Hedge Funds

These are open only to "accredited investors" who meet certain income requirements and have $1 million or more in assets beyond the value of their homes — and that's not necessarily a bad thing. Some have done very well (I was in one that multiplied my stake four-and-a-half-fold in five years), but some have blown up (including, unfortunately, the same one, totally wiped out), and all charge high fees, typically "two and twenty" — 2% of your assets each year, no matter how well or poorly they fare, plus 20% of the profits.

The original notion of a hedge fund—just so you know—was to do what mutual funds could not. Mutual funds could buy stocks to profit from a rising market but were (and are) prohibited from *shorting* stocks to hedge their bets, in case it fell. And some hedge funds still do some of that. But they basically can do *anything* to try to make money, and they can do it with leverage, which is how some of them manage not just to do poorly, but to "blow up" altogether.

Private Equity/Venture Funds

Here, the "accredited investor" commits to invest, say, $500,000, but on an as-needed basis. The fund managers take 2.5% a year to find and make investments in private companies (generally, though not always, fledgling ones, and generally in the hope they will someday go public as Google did). Typically, the fund will be set up with a proposed ten-year life. In the first two or three years, you are called on for funds as deals get done; in years four and five the remainder of your $500,000 might be called upon for yet more deals or to provide additional financing to companies now in the fund's portfolio that have run short of cash; and at various unpredictable times—sometimes even within months!—you get cash *back* as one or another of the portfolio companies gets acquired or does go public. It sounds like fun, I know, but the first thing to note is that the 2.5% starts immediately and after ten years has become 25%, if I'm doing the math right here—so you're paying $125,000 of your $500,000 in management fees. And, as with hedge funds, you are giving up a portion of the ultimate profits, if any.

If you are hugely rich, you likely already know all this. But rich or not, I wouldn't spend a lot of time bemoaning your lack of participation in private equity funds (or hedge funds). As rewarding as they can sometimes be for their investors, for the most part you want your son or daughter to grow up to be the *manager* of a hedge fund or private equity fund.

Financial R&D

Research and development is a wonderful thing. It develops life-saving drugs, fuel-efficient washing machines, and pocket-size symphony orchestras ready at the tap of your finger to play any of your 10,000 favorite songs. (Remember GE's old slogan? "At GE, Progress Is Our Most Important Product.") Yet the truth is that—for the most part—you can get only so many pennies out of a dollar's investment, given a certain level of risk. And so in the financial industry, for the most part, research and development isn't about how to get you more pennies out of your investment dollar but, rather, how to get more investment dollars out of *you*.

Wrap accounts! For a while, most of the major full-service brokers were touting this wonderful new commission-free product. They would merely charge you 3% of your entire account each year and provide their advice and trading for free! Astonishing numbers of clients accepted this awful deal.

Variable annuities! They have generated billions of dollars in fees but, as argued on page 119, have been a relatively poor choice for most who bought them.

One of my favorite inventions was the Bull & Bear Fund years ago that had two components—a bull fund that invested in stocks it thought would go up and a bear fund that shorted stocks it thought would go down—and a mechanism for allowing you to decide how much of your money you wanted in each. Such a clever concept! Such high annual fees! *Both* funds went down.

And then there are the systems, often discovered by "back-testing" many years of data to find methods of investing that would have worked *brilliantly* if you had thought of them at the beginning of the back-test instead of discovering them at the end. The brochure can fairly state that if you had followed this system over the past 30 years, you would have made a gazillion dollars (and that, of course, past performance—in this case past hypothetical performance—is no guarantee of future success). One such system was the widely circulated idea that the average person could significantly outperform the market just by buying the ten highest-yielding stocks in the Dow each year. Refinements were developed to improve the return even more, and mutual funds sprang up to help the small investor follow the strategy with a single transaction. In reality, this strategy only worked during the time period *before* the book first recommending it was published, and the author himself stopped using it in 1993. But the book continued to sell well for years.

The Only Other Investment Guides You Might Want to Read

As I said in Chapter 1, even if this is the only investment guide you'll ever need, it is hardly the only one that's any good. To get an idea of how difficult it is to beat the market, and for a very readable tour: *A Random Walk Down Wall Street* by Burton Malkiel. For a different slant: *One Up on Wall Street* by Peter Lynch and John Rothchild. My favorite Buffett bio: *The Snowball,* by Alice Schroeder. Charles Ellis's slim *Winning the Loser's Game* does a great job of explaining why the best minds on Wall Street haven't got a chance to beat the averages, the role of time in determining risk, and the importance of being equity minded when you are investing for long-term goals. (It is also a good antidote to any encouragement you may take from the Lynch and Buffett books.)

But remember, the more time you spend reading about the stock market, the more you are likely to want to try your hand. Are you sure you want to begin devoting a good portion of your waking, worrying life in pursuit of this hobby? Have you the temperament to succeed? Can you afford to lose? Are you really that likely to outdo the pros in your spare time? Can you tell the good books from the bad?* Have you made out well with past sorties into the market?

If not, then just buy—and hold—a few no-load mutual funds.

---

* "Robert Kiyosaki has built an empire out of giving financial advice in such bestsellers as *Rich Dad, Poor Dad*," *Smart Money* reported in a biting February 2003 exposé that pressed him to back up his claims. "But look beneath the surface and you may be surprised by how little real advice he has."

PART THREE

FAMILY PLANNING

*We are not inheriting the world from our parents;
we are merely borrowing it from our children.*

— JIM HENSON

10

Kids, Spouse, Heirs, Folks

I've consolidated all our bills into one missed payment.

— TRIUMPHANT WIFE TO DOWN-AND-OUT HUSBAND
Frank Cotham cartoon, October 11, 1999, *The New Yorker*

IT'S ALL ABOUT you. At least until you have a partner or a family. Then, as you may have noticed, it gets more complicated.

Let's start out with your offspring, move on to your spouse, your heirs, and then your folks.

Teaching Your Kids to Save and Invest

I'm keenly aware that they are your kids, not mine, so I offer these suggestions with humility. But they have 70 years of financial security ahead of them if they get this right — perhaps the greatest gift you can give them — or else 70 years of money-worry if they get it wrong . . . so let's try. Not least because if they're financially secure when they're grown, *you'll* feel more secure.

The overall ideas are so simple that any child can easily grasp them. *Spend less than you have. Save the difference. Watch it grow.* How complex is that?

But how to bring these notions to life?

"Your mother and I want to give you some money," you **might begin. (This is likely to capture almost any child's attention.) "But we want to have some fun with it, to let you in on one of the most important secrets in the universe. It's called compound interest, and it determines whether people are rich or poor.**

"Normally, compound interest—though incredibly powerful—is slow. We're going to speed it up. We're going to give you $1 right now, here, in this cookie jar, as if it were a bank. And then every night at dinner we're going to pay you 10% interest. Ten percent is awfully generous, but we love you—and it's easy to calculate. And instead of paying you 10% a year, the way it works in real life, we're going to pay you 10% a day. Not forever—we'd go broke—but as long as we can. At the end, we'll take this money over to a real bank and open up your first savings account."

And off you go.

The first night, there being $1 in the jar, you add a dime—10% interest. The second night, there now being $1.10, you add 11¢. The third night, you teach your child about "rounding." (You'd either round down to 12¢ on $1.21 or—what the heck—up to 13¢.)

Obviously, you would vary the game based on your child's age, math skills, and your own resources.

But after a month, there would be $17.45 in the cookie jar and after another month, if you choose to go that long, $304.48. (After a third month, $5,313. After six, $28 million.)

Of course, you need to put it in perspective: it normally takes a year, not a day, to make your money grow by 10%. And even 10% a year is a lot to expect. You won't get it from a bank, and you can't count on it from the stock market. "And there's that little thing called taxes you hear Mommy and Daddy cussing about when you're supposed to be asleep. You'll understand when you're older." Still, the power of compound interest is very real.

Now, suppose you did this with two kids. A dollar each. But tell them you happen to have something they both like—a bag of Reese's Pieces—and that if one of them doesn't mind waiting three days before starting to earn interest, he/she can have it.

A battle ensues for the Reese's Pieces. If tears are involved, all the better. Only one child gets them, and he/she doesn't have to share.

Two months later, the kid who grabbed the candy has seen his sibling's dollar grow to $304, versus just $228 for him.

The lesson, of course: not only is compound interest incredibly powerful, starting early makes an enormous difference! Forgoing something now pays off handsomely down the road. Even if it's just a little, save something now, to get compound interest working for you!

Given a chance to do it over, would Junior still have fallen for the Reese's Pieces trick? Probably not.

Weeks pass. You announce that you want to try something new.

With luck, they are by now very fond of the cookie jar. (This could be especially true if you let them spend some of the money.)

"This is the last cookie jar game we're ever going to play," you warn them (because you don't want to go broke, and because it bestows even more weight on your announcement), "but it's going to be even faster, and even more important than the last one."

All little eyes are now keenly fixed on you. (Or at least that's the way it would have worked in my family. I got $5 for turning five and waited excitedly all year to get $6 when I turned six.) "This time," you announce, "we are not going to pay 10%, we're going to pay what credit cards typically charge their customers — more like 20%."

You give each kid $1, adding 20¢ the first night, 24¢ the second night (20% of $1.20 is 24¢), and so on.

Indeed, from the outset, why not draw up a 60-day Cookie Jar Calendar for your refrigerator door? In the first box, you could write "$1" in black for one kid and "$1" in red for the second, tracking the progress of each child throughout that first 10% exercise.

Now, for this final cookie jar game, you come back to the

same calendar and, in a different set of colors, start with a fresh $1, adding *20%* each night.

(No Reese's Pieces this time.)

After 19 days, at 20%, each kid has $32—a heck of a lot more than the $6 the refrigerator shows they had on Day #19 at 10%!

After 35 days, if you could afford to keep going that long, the cookie jar would be bulging with $590, while the refrigerator door would show that on the same day at 10%, the kids had only $28. (Even less, if one of them fell for the Reese's Pieces trick.)

At some point in this exercise ask them: "Which would you rather be? Someone who goes through life being careful what you spend and earning 10% on your savings—eventually living a very comfortable life? Or someone who goes through life buying things on credit, *paying* 20% to the credit-card companies, and crying the way Mommy does each month when the bills come? It's fun getting 20% interest. But imagine how hard it must be to have to pay it!"

"Don't say anything to embarrass anyone," you might whisper in your child's ear next time you're at the mall, "but about half the people you see in this mall are smart with their money and half are . . . not so smart. Your daddy and I try very hard to be in that first half, even if it means not buying you all the Reese's Pieces we'd like, because we know that if we're careful, we'll never have to worry about money."

On your way back from the mall, detour through a low-income neighborhood, to let your kids see that not everyone lives the way you do. Or, if you *live* in a low-income neighborhood, drive through a really nice one, for the same reason. Kids need to understand that choices about spending and money will affect the way they live. ("The easiest way for your children to learn about money," writes Katherine Whitehorn, in her book *How to Survive Children,* "is for you not to have any.")

Another time, you might pull your child close—don't delay, because most smokers start between the ages of eight and 14—and say, "See that nice young man over there with his collar up in the wind, smoking outside that building? They won't let him smoke inside, because a lot of people don't like smoke, and his family is probably worried that he might get sick someday—but forget all that. Here's his real problem. Those cigarettes he's become addicted to cost him $6 a day. By now, he'd probably like to quit smoking, but it's very, very hard to quit once you start. So he gives the tobacco companies $6 a day and probably will for the rest of his life. But if he hadn't gotten hooked, or could somehow quit now and put that $6 a day into a mutual fund at 7% instead, he'd have an extra $2 million by the time he's Grandpa's age."

A few other ideas for teaching your kids about money:

- **By example:** "The best thing my parents ever 'taught' me about money," writes one of my website readers, Marian Calabro, "was by this example: They never spent a dime they didn't have. So I've never spent a dime I didn't have, unless you count the mortgage (paid off last August, hooray)."

- **By allowance:** "Allowance isn't pay," suggests Dan Nachbar, a reader who actually *has* kids. "Don't link allowance to specific tasks. Work around the house is a responsibility. An allowance is a privilege. Give an allowance once a month rather than once a week. The dollar amounts will be higher, and lessons on managing your cash more real." (A month between paydays? Yeah, right—like the kids' union will ever accept that. But in whatever installments you pay it, see if you can inspire your child to save some of it in that bank or mutual fund account you just opened.)

- **Buy stock:** Although it makes little financial sense, a lot of people like to give kids a single, framed share of some cool stock—Disney, Apple, Harley-Davidson—as a learning tool. Visit **giveashare.com** for ideas. Otherwise, skip the frame and go directly to the company's website to see what sort of direct-purchase program it may offer, as many of them do.

- **Buy more stock:** "When I was 16," writes Henry Scheck, 36, of Bethel, Pennsylvania, "my dad gave me $1,000 from a small inheritance. He suggested the stock market, and I bought 20 shares in the company that ran the place we spent a lot of time in after school: McDonald's. I watched as it split again and again, and sold the stock when I was ready to make the down payment on my first house. My dad and McDonald's had made it possible for me to buy my first home years before I otherwise could have. This simple act by my dad started me on a lifelong interest in saving my money and investing it. Which is a pretty neat legacy."

- **Drip by drip:** Or visit **dripcentral.com** to learn everything you'll need to know about starting out very small but growing through dividend reinvestment plans — DRIPs.

- **By bike:** "The best 'money' training I obtained was from having a paper route," Ted Strange of Kelowna, British Columbia, wrote me.* "You have to be reliable. You have to collect. You have to make change. You have to get new customers." And then you have to sock away some of that dough in a Roth IRA.

Tips for Married Couples

Is it too late to suggest a prenup? (See, for example, **nolo.com**'s *Prenuptial Agreements: How to Write a Fair & Lasting Contract.*)

It is?

Well, then, you're just going to have to make this thing work. And with two such fundamentally wonderful people as yourselves, how could it not?

---

* Yes! Paper routes! Warren Buffett had one at 13, oil magnate T. Boone Pickens and Vanguard founder John Bogle had them at 12, Walt Disney had one at 9! Get to work, kid!

Because the last thing you ever want to have to buy is **nolo .com**'s *Divorce Bundle* (though it sure beats paying for a couple of real, live, out-for-bear divorce attorneys).

Here—and oh, *boy,* am I ever stepping out of my lane in offering you this advice—is "the only relationship guide" you'll ever need: **Be nice to each other (as I'm sure you already are) . . . and find humor in the compromises (as I'm sure you already do)**—*they're worth it.* That's it.

Tips for Unmarried Couples

There are more than 1,100 legal benefits and protections couples receive when they wed. Unmarried couples need to take special steps to protect their relationship.

- Each of you must have a will. For less than $50, Quicken Will-Maker Plus (also from **nolo.com**) is available to prepare one —and most of the other documents you might need. Without a will, an unmarried partner will generally get nothing beyond life insurance policies and retirement-plan proceeds in which she or he is the named beneficiary. (So check to be sure you have designated her or him as your beneficiary, if that's what you want.)

- A living trust may also be a good idea—see the next section, "You're Dead," for that and other ideas.

- Prepare a health-care proxy to empower your partner to make medical decisions you can't.

- Prepare a "living will" to express your preferences as to how heroic you want your care to be when things look bleak. If you plan to be frozen, pending further medical breakthroughs— I have one smart, wealthy friend who is fully paid up for just such a program—be sure to let people know while you're still warm.

- Consider a durable power of attorney for financial decisions. Be extremely careful, though, when a relationship is new or if you have even the slightest concern about the integrity or levelhead-edness of the person in whom you are vesting this power.

• If you are in a lifetime relationship and think of your partner's family as part of your own—and want them to, also—think about having each of your wills name family members on the other side as co-beneficiaries or "contingent beneficiaries"* along with your own.

• Similarly, if you and your partner are well off and sometimes help out your respective families with a check, consider having the *other* partner sign that check from time to time, again to communicate that you both care.

• If you have unequal wealth, remember that there may be serious gift tax consequences to transferring assets between you. There are several ways around this, involving trusts and other methods, but for this, you need to speak to an expert planner or attorney.

YOU'RE DEAD—Why Didn't You Read This First?!

"There are no luggage racks on a hearse," as the old saying goes—so where does all that junk of yours *go* when you die? Well, it will normally go to a legal entity known as "the estate of the decedent"—you are the decedent, less tastefully known as the corpse (not to be confused with the corpus, another legal term)—and it will stay there for several months or even years before finally ending up in the hands of the people you hoped would get it. If you're lucky. (Well, you're dead, so I guess you weren't that lucky.) And/or in the hands of people whom you had *not* been eager to enrich, including attorneys, court-appointed administrators, and relatives to whom you haven't spoken for years.

The process of settling your estate is known as probate (after the Latin, "to prove" that this is really what you, the dead per-

---

* In the event you were skydiving in tandem and your partner does not outlive you.

son, intended), and it has a justifiable reputation for being an expensive and emotionally draining exercise in even the best of circumstances. And in the worst? Well, Marilyn Monroe died in 1962 and her estate wasn't settled until 1980, with probate fees consuming more than ten times the $100,000 that the inheritors finally got. Famed blues guitarist Robert Johnson, meanwhile, lived just 27 years — 1911 to 1938 — but his $1.2 million estate lived 62 years, being finally settled by the Mississippi Supreme Court in 2000.

If you truly care about your loved ones, especially those to whom you're not married, you will not put them through probate if you can avoid it. And you CAN avoid it, quite easily, by taking some inexpensive steps that don't require a lawyer (though a lawyer might offer useful assistance if your estate is large). Here are seven:

- Bank accounts can have a "pay on death" designation that gives you exclusive control of the account during your lifetime but only requires presentation of a death certificate to be transferred to your intended without probate. Just ask the bank for the proper form: it normally costs nothing to make this designation (the bank may refer to the pay-on-death designation as a Totten Trust).

- Brokerage and mutual fund accounts can, in most states, have a "transfer on death" designation that has a similar effect (at this writing, only Louisiana and Texas fail to allow it). Though many brokers charge a nominal fee to add this designation, some will waive the fee if you ask — so ask.

- Automobiles in Arkansas, Arizona, California, Connecticut, Delaware, Illinois, Indiana, Kansas, Missouri, Nebraska, Nevada, Ohio, Vermont, and Virginia can be registered with a designated "transfer on death" beneficiary. One hopes more states will adopt this procedure; perhaps yours already has.

- Your IRA, 401(k), and other retirement accounts should, of course, have designated primary and contingent beneficiaries.

Otherwise, the proceeds will not only be taxed—something you can only avoid if you designate a charity as the beneficiary —they'll be haggled over.

- Same for life insurance. Do you recall that first day at work, 18 years ago, when you filled out some forms for the company life insurance plan? The one that provides a life insurance benefit equal to twice your salary? And do you remember (is it coming back to you now?) how—as a kick—you named that waitress from the college pub? (What was her name?) Well, now your salary is $65,000 a year, not $16,500, that waitress is who knows where, and, more to the point, you've got *dependents*. Be sure you still like the beneficiary you named when you first took out the policy!

- You may want your life insurance beneficiary to *own* the policy and to pay the premiums with money you give him or her each year, since a policy *you* own will be subject to estate taxes when you die, while a policy he or she owns will not. (Happily, for most people this won't be an issue if the estate-tax threshold —already over $5.3 million for each spouse—continues to rise, as seems likely.)

- For real estate and other major assets (including cars and bank and brokerage accounts if your state doesn't allow the suggested alternatives), you can bypass probate by establishing and transferring your assets to a living trust. Most people who do this use a lawyer (and that's fine); but you can actually establish a valid living trust using Quicken Living Trust Maker. Don't forget, though, that the trust is useless until you actually transfer the assets *into* it, and that the trust does nothing to avoid estate taxes, as many mistakenly believe. Assets in a living trust are as easy to manage as your personal assets during your lifetime, and all income is reported on your individual tax return (no trust return is needed).

• • •

Another way to bypass probate often recommended: registering ownership in a "joint tenancy with right of survivorship." *But beware the potential dangers:*

- If you add Biff as a joint tenant, Biff has immediate rights to it. In the case of a bank account, he can withdraw funds as easily as you can. Are you sure you're comfortable with that?

- The transfer of assets without payment is considered a gift: if you establish a joint tenancy for any significant asset, you may have to file a gift tax return and could owe gift taxes.

- When you die, the IRS assumes that property you held in joint tenancy with anyone other than your spouse belonged entirely to you (now, the estate of the decedent), unless the other joint tenant or tenants can prove they paid part or all of the costs of acquiring and maintaining the property. So if you and your partner each put up 50% to buy a house, and establish a joint tenancy, the IRS will consider 100% of it to be part of your taxable estate when you die unless your partner can prove she or he paid 50%. So keep checks and other records permanently if you use joint tenancy and be prepared to present them to the IRS.

- Joint property can be accessed by the personal creditors of either person. Especially if one of the partners is in a high-risk profession, it is best to have the other own significant assets separately, so that a lawsuit won't take everything.

- Similarly, the owner of property is always responsible if the property causes harm to others. This makes it especially dangerous to register an automobile jointly. Regardless of who is driving, both of you can be sued for all your assets in the event the car hurts someone. So keep each of your cars in the name of the primary driver (but do inform your insurance company if the other occasionally drives it). Or if you have just one car, keep it in the name of the partner with the least to lose.

Now let's talk taxes.

Your estate passes tax-free to your spouse, even if you just met and married in Las Vegas a week before you died. If unmarried, it *is* taxed . . . but only to the extent its value exceeds the aforementioned $5.3 million or so.

Given the exclusion, almost no one need worry about estate tax! Still, just as you showed uncommon wisdom by purchasing this book, so may you amass an uncommonly large estate. So let's assume it *is* a concern.

You can't get out of the tax by giving it all away while you're alive (unless you give it to charity) — gifts during your lifetime count against the exclusion total. But there's a happy exclusion to that, too: you can give up to $14,000 a year (indexed to inflation) to as many individuals as you like (not just family members) and your spouse can, too. So a couple with two kids and three grandkids could send $140,000 per year down the family tree with no reportable gifts at all (and could pay all the tuition and medical bills of the clan gift-tax-free on top of that). Once you get all this money out of your estate, there's that much less to be taxed on when you die.

In addition, there are trusts.

- A *bypass* trust. If you're married, you and your spouse *each* get the exclusion — but only if the first spouse to die hasn't wasted his or hers by leaving everything to the surviving spouse (who would *already* have gotten everything tax-free). The way around this is to arrange for the exclusion to bypass each spouse. Instead, that excluded money goes into a "bypass trust" that pays *income* to the surviving spouse for life, but that, upon his or her death, gives the remainder to the children, free of estate tax, so that *both* exclusions can eventually pass tax-free to the kids.

- A *qualified personal residence* trust. You give the kids your house but retain the right to live there for a few years. The value of the gift is reduced because they have to wait, and because you might die before the few years are up. So you might give them a $2 million house and use only $600,000 of the $5.3 million exclusion. (An accountant or trust and estates lawyer will help you figure this out.) After the trust expires, you'll have to pay your kids rent if you stay in the house, but that lets you transfer even more wealth to them free of estate tax (namely, the cash you pay them as rent). If you die before the term is up, the trust is useless. The house goes back into your estate. So if you set up a QPRT, don't die before it does.

- A *life insurance* trust. If you don't want to own the policy directly (lest the proceeds become part of your taxable estate)—yet you don't trust the beneficiary to own it and pay the premiums on time—you can set up an irrevocable life insurance trust and have an objective third party make the premium payments with money you gift to the trust each year (which is still treated as a gift to the beneficiaries of the policy).

- A *charitable remainder* trust. You can give property to a trust that pays you (and even a second beneficiary) a lifetime annuity, and then gives the remainder to your favorite charities after your (or the second beneficiary's) demise. You get an immediate income tax deduction for establishing the trust (the older you are, the more the IRS allows); the charities get whatever is left after you (and the second beneficiary, if any) are gone.

Talk to an estate planner before attempting any of this. Unless you are rich, it should all be unnecessary. That tens of thousands of bright minds have, for more than half a century, been engaged in arranging such things instead of, say, teaching kids math and English is one reason we are not an even more prosperous nation. But such is the nature of modern life.

Helping Your Parents

You laughed when they came back from the Grand Canyon with that new bumper sticker on their car: GET REVENGE! LIVE LONG ENOUGH TO BE A PROBLEM FOR YOUR CHILDREN! But —if you're lucky—that's exactly what will eventually happen.

Be glad if you're in a position to help when they need you. Toward that end:

- Scope out the government services available in their area with **eldercare.gov.**

- **Caregiver.org** is another good resource.

- If you live at a distance from your parents and they need help with things like driving, shopping, cooking, or laundry, there are commercial services that provide trained and bonded caregivers (Home Instead Senior Care — **homeinstead.com** — is one).

- If you are not in a position to determine the needs of your parents or monitor their care, you may wish to engage a geriatric care manager. To find one, try **aginglifecare.org.**

- If your parent can no longer live at home, **medicare.gov** has a section on long-term-care choices and another that rates specific nursing homes: **medicare.gov/nhcompare/home.asp.**

- Even harder than settling on the right long-term care is paying for it. Neither Medicare nor private medical insurance ordinarily will, and the long-term-care insurance industry has been plagued by inferior products, companies abandoning the field, and insurance rates that skyrocket after you sign up. Visit **com parelongtermcare.org** for help with this. But if you can afford it, best is simply to pay for this care directly, from your parents' savings or your own. Via insurance, you wind up paying also for the insurer's sales and administrative expenses and profit.

- It might not make sense to insure even if your parents *can't* afford to pay for long-term care, because Medicaid (known as MediCal in California) will cover it — but only once your parent is broke, or nearly so. The good news is that a person's house is exempt during his or her lifetime if that person is expected to return to it, or if his or her lawful spouse is still living in it. Additionally, a spouse may typically retain a car, household furnishings, personal effects (even jewelry), and a little more. See **elderlawanswers.com.** But before you start giving away assets to family and friends to qualify, be aware that the government is allowed to look back up to five years before the application date, reducing benefits by the amount transferred, and that there are penalties for fraudulent transfers intended to qualify for Medicaid. If you're planning to rely on Medicaid, consider consulting a member of the National Academy of Elder Law Attorneys (**naela.org**). For the official side of all this: **medicaid.gov.**

+ Visit **benefitscheckup.org** to be sure your parents are receiving all they're entitled to.

+ **Paytrust.com** can simplify their bill-paying and allow you to take it over easily if necessary. If they pay estimated taxes, help them enroll in the Electronic Federal Tax Payment System (**eftps.gov**) and all the year's payments can be scheduled in advance. Of course, they will also want to opt for direct deposit of Social Security and as many other checks as possible. Professional organizers listed at **napo.net** can come in once to help get things organized or visit regularly.

+ If your parents aren't wealthy enough to live off their investments and benefits, a reverse mortgage may provide extra cash every month, with the loan repaid only after the home is sold or when they die. Definitely worth an unrushed, careful look. Start with **consumer.ftc.gov/articles/0192-reverse-mortgages.**

+ They may also want to convert their tax-favored retirement accounts to lifetime annuities so as to remove the fear of outliving their income. A low-cost program is offered through Vanguard's Lifetime Income Program. It has an option that allows investments in mutual funds that will result in variable payments based on the performance of the investments, but still guaranteed to continue for life (this eliminates the biggest problem with fixed annuities, their failure to keep up with inflation). See **investor.vanguard.com/annuity.**

+ The same documents mentioned in the tips for unmarried couples should be recommended to your parents. In particular, a living trust can make it easy to transfer management of the assets to another family member if they become unable to manage their own affairs. And durable powers of attorney for financial decisions and health care, along with a living will, can avoid heartache and potential legal wrangling. A common problem, however, arises when nobody can *find* the documents. The U.S. Living Will Registry (**uslivingwillregistry.com**) offers to register living wills, organ donation authorization, emergency contacts, and health-care proxies so that they can be found quickly by health-care providers when needed (and to make sure your parents are reminded about these documents annually in case there is a need for them to be updated). A sticker affixed to their insurance card or driver's license will make it easy to immediately locate such documents in an emergency.

- If a parent who has prepared none of these useful documents needs someone else to take over, your family is going to have to go through the creation of a guardianship, which will make some lawyer very happy. Visit the National Guardianship Association website (**guardianship.org**) for help. Expect to come out of the experience angry, bitter, and determined to ensure that nobody else in the family makes the same mistake.

- Before any of these things comes to pass, buy your parents *The Beneficiary Interactive e-Book,* by **active-insights.com.** It will ask all the questions you'll desperately wish they'd answered before they were no longer able to (and not just on financial and estate matters). Then fill out your own copy! And print out copies of both to share with family members and trusted advisors.

- It's often almost impossible for parents and their children to discuss financial matters. In such cases, especially if your parents are likely to have more than $1 million in total assets, you should at least encourage your parents to speak with a "fee-only" financial planner (one who charges directly for her advice and doesn't make money from commissions on the sale of insurance, annuities, trusts, or mutual funds). Find one through the National Association of Personal Financial Advisors (**napfa.org**) or the Garrett Planning Network (**garrettplanningnetwork.com**).

Keep in mind that the worst part of dealing with aging parents is often not financial or legal but emotional. If an unfailingly polite mother spends her last few years alternating between obliviousness and nastiness, remember that she had to put up with much the same from you for your first few years (not to mention the nine months preceding). There's a good chance she can't control her behavior now any more than you could then.

Also, if multiple siblings are involved, and one of them is doing most of the work, make an *explicit* agreement on some fair compensation or reimbursement (presumably from the parental assets, but possibly from yours, depending on financial circumstances). Leaving it unstated is a recipe for permanent rifts or unofficial appropriation of assets that one child views as completely fair and the others view as theft. The idea is not so much to come up with the perfectly fair amount (who can say what that would be?) but to acknowledge the importance of the caregiver's time and effort, and the value of having a family member rather than a stranger making your parents' last years as comfortable and happy as possible.

Speaking of which, on the same theory that your house will burn down only if you fail to insure it and that Willow couldn't possibly have won if I had bet more than $3 on him (her?), perhaps the best reason to take all the precautions above is to make sure they all prove to have been — knock wood — *wasted effort*. There is every chance your folks will live long, happy, healthy lives, passing peacefully in their sleep with a neat folder of "final" documents in the top desk drawer.

Preparing for the alternative just makes good sense.

11

What to Do If You Inherit a Million Dollars; What to Do Otherwise

If I had put just two million dollars into that deal,
I'd be a rich man today!

— A REAL ESTATE MAN WE KNOW
(back when $2 million was what $10 million is today)

As TELEVISION VIEWERS of the fifties all know, coming into a million dollars, even if it is tax-free, is not all applause and confetti. In fact, it can cause all kinds of inner demons to surface.

Listen to Gail Sheehy, not long after publishing her huge bestseller *Passages*. Did coming into money cause her any problems?

"Yeees!" she cries plaintively. "It makes me sweat a lot more, it makes me embarrassed and guilty — I mean, truly, it's terrible.

"It's much more fun being the aspirant, because once you have gotten there, even if you are just there temporarily (as you must continually remind yourself you are), you're in a position of defending or protecting rather than aspiring or building.

"It's terribly uncomfortable. It's also a problem that is *totally* unsympathetic to anyone who has 5 cents less than you do. Right? So there's nobody you can talk to."

When it first became clear that *Passages* had hit the jackpot, Sheehy was chatting with Random House editor Jason Epstein.

Said he: "Yes, well. Money. You will find, Gail dear, that it will now be a dull ache in the back of your head. *Forever.*"

"It was so ominous," Gail says, "and it was exactly how I felt!"

Sheehy has been rich and Sheehy has been, if not poor, nearly so. "I can't say that I was happiest when I was living in a fourth-floor walk-up on East Seventh Street with a one-year-old baby, you know, carting her on one hip and the wash on the other when I came home from work." But neither, once she hit the top of the bestseller list, was she laughing all the way to the bank.

Many of us, needless to say, would have an easier time than Gail Sheehy "coping" with a fast million or five. Or think we would. Or would love at least the chance to try.

Still, the problem with sudden wealth seems less how to invest it than how to keep it from wrecking your life. You will notice that in movies and novels where the hero actually manages to pull it off—to steal, win, or discover a fortune—they always end the action there. As if to say that the happiness with which they lived ever after goes without saying. When, in fact, the screenwriter or novelist knows full well that this is not true, and can't think of a thing to write that wouldn't be anticlimactic.

Sheehy, with great good sense, has tried hard to avoid what she calls "that classic American trap—which is, you suddenly get a windfall and then, instead of living pretty much as you have, only a little better and with lots more security behind you —with money there to do something amazing every once in a while when it really counts—you suddenly leap up to meet that income level and always bubble up over it, and then are constantly running to keep up with this tremendous overhead you've established." It is a financial equivalent to the Peter Principle—getting yourself in, no matter how much you have, just a little too deep for comfort.

What to do, then, should you have the ill fortune to inherit a million dollars? Or, worse still, two?*

1. Go out for a very nice dinner.

2. Put about a year of normal living expenses someplace liquid, like a bank or money-market fund . . .

3. . . . and roughly equal sums into U.S. Treasury securities maturing in one, two, three, and four years.

4. Put the bulk of the remaining money into stock-index funds, split between domestic and foreign investments.

5. Buy a vacation home or bigger house, if you want one — but not so big that the cost of carrying it will in any way strain you.

    a. Do not buy a boat.

6. Be sure your will is in order.

7. Now relax and forget the whole thing. Review it once a year, mainly to roll over your Treasury securities as they come due. Don't spend any of the investment principal, but enjoy the extra income it throws off.

If even this seems too hard, just choose a no-load mutual fund family and split your windfall, a third, a third, a third, among a broadly diversified U.S. stock fund, a broadly diversified international fund, and a Treasury fund. Rebalance the accounts on your birthday each year to keep the amounts in each of the categories about equal. (That is, if your international stocks now represent 40% of the pie, because they've grown fastest, shift some of the gain into the other two slices, so they re-

---

* "A million" actually doesn't mean quite what it did when this book first appeared in 1978. The equivalent today would exceed $3 million — or $8 million if you want 1950s equivalency with *The Millionaire,* where John Beresford Tipton gave it away each week so you could sit back and watch (in black and white) as it wrecked someone's life. Yet the term "millionaire" will die hard, even if it now really means "five-millionaire" or "twenty-five-millionaire." You could find a single million stretched awfully thin with the list that follows. But do the best you can.

main about 33% each.) Or if you're really lazy, just draw your spending money, whenever you need it, from whichever account has the highest balance at the time. That's close enough.

This is not the way to get every last dollar from your inheritance — but isn't not-having-to-try one of the luxuries being a millionaire should bring?

Unless you want to switch from being whatever you were being to being a financier; unless you enjoy worrying about money and taking risks and paying taxes on profits and stewing over your losses; unless you are intrigued by the machinations of the Fed's Open Market Committee and the effects on the financial markets of the latest fiduciary fad — you should simply structure your assets, should you be so fortunate as to have them in such abundance, so as to give you security and peace of mind.

Life is not a business, as my father used to say. Why not set yourself up comfortably and stop worrying?

Now, until you do inherit that million, what to do in the meantime.

Mutual Funds

Far more practical for most investors than trying to go it alone in the stock market — which is at the very least time-consuming, and possibly a good deal worse for the financially suicidal among us — is the no-load, low-expense mutual fund.

Admittedly, for many investors profits are only part of the objective. Much of the reward is the fun — challenge — intrigue — of the game itself. I am such an investor, and I am the first to admit it. But that's not called investing, strictly speaking. It's called playing.

"The prudent way is also the easy way," counseled the late Paul Samuelson, Nobel Prize–winning economist, in a column he wrote for *Newsweek*. Someone else does the research, someone else does the worrying, someone else holds your certificates and provides a record of your dividends and capital gains for tax purposes. "What you lose is the daydream of that one big killing. What you gain is sleep."

Mutual funds provide wide diversification. Most allow you to have small amounts of money transferred from your checking account each month, so you can make steady investments automatically. Most are also geared to set up retirement accounts with a minimum of paperwork and expense. Many are part of "fund families" like Fidelity or Vanguard that allow you to switch your money from one to another—from their aggressive growth stock fund to their tax-exempt bond fund, for example. Just pick up the phone.

With mutual funds, the risks of the stock market are still there. Many funds declined 60% and more after the speculative binges of the late sixties, the late nineties, and the mid-naughties. But at least you don't have to make all the foolish decisions yourself. You need only decide which funds to invest in, how much, and when. In this very real sense, you are still managing your own money.

Mutual funds also make it practical to diversify globally. And while many people consider investing abroad dangerous, international diversification can actually *reduce* your risk. Stock markets of different countries move up and down at least somewhat independent of each other. A U.S. investor in 1929 wise enough to place 50% in foreign stocks would have needed only five years to recover from the worst crash in American history. A Japanese investor in 1990 who had 50% of his money outside of Japan —likewise. At the same time as it reduces risk, international diversification can actually boost returns. The rest of the world has discovered capitalism in a big way, and there is no reason that you shouldn't try to profit from that while reducing your exposure to the dangers of a bear market here.

The first step in choosing among mutual funds is about the only one that is at all clear-cut. There are funds that charge initial sales fees of 3% or more, known as the "load"; and there are others that charge no load.* *Choose a no-load fund.* To do otherwise is to throw money out the window.†

Numerous studies show that no-load funds perform just as well (and as badly) as load funds. This stands to reason, because the load goes not toward superior management of the fund but to the sales reps who sell it. And they have no influence over its performance. Yet most people still buy load funds. As long as there are people out selling, there will be people in buying. Don't be one of them.

(If you already own shares in a load fund, the load alone is no reason to sell—you've already paid it. But neither is it a reason not to sell. What's lost is lost.)

Sure, there have been some unbelievably successful load funds, such as Fidelity's famed Magellan Fund. But so, too, have there been unbelievably successful no-loads. A dollar invested in the American Century Growth Fund when it was founded in 1958 (shortsightedly, as the "Twentieth Century" Growth Fund) is worth more than $300 today.

In choosing a no-load fund, there are several things to consider. Two things to look at, for starters, are the management fees and the administrative expenses. These annual charges can total less than a quarter of 1% or climb to as much as 3% or more. You have to have a very good reason to go with a fund that charges

---

* Actually, they've gotten sneakier than that. Most load funds will omit the initial sales fee if you buy their B shares or their C shares. Don't be fooled. The B shares simply replace the front-end load with a back-end load that is charged when you sell the shares. The C shares are even sneakier. They charge no sales fee to either purchase or sell the shares, making them sound like a no-load fund. But they actually charge a level load in the form of a *continuous* load subtracted every year (actually, every day) for as long as you own the fund. If you hold a C share with a 1% level load for nine years or longer, you will end up paying a bigger load than you would on the worst front-end-load shares. Over an investing lifetime, you could easily pay more than a third of your original investment in sales fees. That's in addition to what you'll have to pay the people who actually manage the fund.

† In the old days, an 8.5% load was standard. And it was even worse than it sounds. When you sent $1,000 to such a fund, you gave up $85 in commissions, so you were really paying $85 to invest *$915*—fully 9.3%. Today, few load funds charge more than 5.75% (which works out to 6.1%), and many charge "only" 3% (which works out to 3.1%). But why start the race so far behind?

more than 1% a year for its management and administration. (Many funds will advertise their low management fee without mentioning other annual expenses and "12b-1" marketing fees. Be sure to dig for the total fees and expenses before investing.)

What really matters, of course, is not what a fund will charge you, but what it will *earn* for you. Here you can be much less certain.

If you knew which way the market was headed at any given time, it would be a simple matter of buying the highly volatile funds at the depths of a bear market, just as things were about to turn, and then switching to the conservative funds (or getting out of the market altogether) just as things were peaking.

However, if you do not have this happy facility—and who does?—then what you are looking for is that rare mutual fund that does better than average in both up *and* down markets.

Many elaborate studies have been conducted to identify such funds. None has worked. Morningstar, which knows as much about mutual funds as anyone, assigns funds "stars"—and fund families eagerly run ads touting their five-star funds. The only problem is that Morningstar's own studies show these ratings don't have a great deal of predictive value, except that one-star funds, the lousy ones, tend to stay lousy. And that's because they tend to have the highest expenses dragging them down, year in and year out. (Studies *have* shown that funds with low expenses consistently outperform funds with high expenses.)

People manage money, after all, not "funds"—and people who do a really good job often move on to new and better jobs, or retire. Who is to say that the money manager most responsible for a fund's success in a given two- or three-year period is even still at her desk?

Or that her firm will be honest? A dozen firms paid big fines a few years ago for allowing certain investors with clout (hint: not you) to invest hours after the market had closed, yet still get closing prices . . . and for allowing other little violations that, over time, chipped away at the returns to ordinary fund investors.

If you have mutual fund paralysis, just buy shares in one of Vanguard's index funds (800-662-7447, **vanguard.com**). Their hallmark is keeping expenses low. Over the long run, your performance will just about match that of the stock market as a whole — which is better than most mutual funds do, because most burden your investment with higher management fees. **This is a very simple concept but profound: just by investing all the money you have earmarked for the stock market in the Vanguard Index Trust, you will generally do better than most bank trust departments, mutual fund managers, and private investors — with far less effort!**

And, as described on page 162, you may do meaningfully better still in an "equally weighted" rather than "market-weighted" index fund.

One more advantage of index funds is that they do little trading. As a result, they generate few taxable gains. You have to pay tax on the dividends they earn each year, but most of the *growth* is tax-free until you sell the shares. That means "the government's" share of your money continues to work for you in the meantime. This doesn't matter within the shelter of a retirement plan, but it makes a big difference for unsheltered money.

Closed-End Funds

One kind of no-load mutual fund that particularly bears consideration is the "closed-end" fund. Such funds originally sold a set number of shares to the public, raising, say, $100 million to invest. Then they closed the doors to new money. Investors who wished to cash in their shares would sell them just as they would sell any regular stock, through a broker. Presumably, if the fund managers had turned the $100 million into $120 million, each share in the fund would be worth 20% more than it was at the outset. Or so everyone assumed. But things are only worth what people will pay for them, and shares in closed-end funds sank to discounts that ranged from a few percentage points up to 30%

and more. (A few rose to premiums.) As I write this, for example, you can buy a dollar's worth of assets in the Canadian World Fund for 70 cents. Or a dollar's worth of assets in the RMR Asia Pacific Real Estate Fund for 80 cents. (Visit the Closed-End Fund Association [**cefa.com**] to see current data.) The discounts won't do you much good if the managers of those funds have picked a dreadful assortment of stocks that all collapse — but it's just about as hard to pick bad stocks as good, so that's unlikely. More likely, you will have a dollar working for you even though you only had to pay 75 or 85 cents.

The risk is that the discount, irrational to begin with, could widen still further by the time you went to sell your shares. On the other hand, the discount could narrow — which at least makes more sense, even if it's not necessarily more likely to happen.

There's actually a sound reason for closed-ends to trade at a discount. They're burdened by a handicap: namely, the 1% or more in management and administrative fees many subtract each year. If the stocks in the fund grew by 10% a year including dividends, the net asset value of the fund itself would grow at only 9%, after that 1%. (Of course, that's true of open-end funds, too, and you can never get *them* at a discount.) Closed-ends may also trade at a well-deserved discount if their managers have demonstrated a consistent talent for making poor investments.

Then again, closed-ends offer two conceptual advantages over open-end funds. First, when trading at a substantial discount, a closed-end is like a *less-than-no-load* fund. You get $1 worth of assets working for you for 80 cents. Second, closed-end fund managers need not worry that, in a down market, they will be flooded with redemptions, forcing them to keep cash idle to redeem shares — or to dump holdings at what may be exactly the wrong time. So they may be able to do a better job managing the fund. True, they don't have the same incentive as with open-end funds. (With an open-end fund, good performance draws new investors, swelling the management fee; poor performance leads to redemptions and lower fees.) But they still have an incentive, because increasing the value of the fund also increases the management fee. And there is the ego factor, particularly with "personality" closed-ends, like the Zweig and Gabelli funds, that compete in the market alongside the faceless institutional funds.

♦ Never buy a closed-end fund when it is first issued (because sales charges will be built into the price and it will likely fall to a discount).

♦ Never buy a closed-end fund at a premium (because then you're paying $1.05 or $1.30 to get $1 working for you), unless you're convinced that the manager is so good he can beat the averages by enough to overcome both the drag of his management fee and the extra drag of having to make $1 do the work of $1.05 or $1.30. Which he can't.

Exchange-Traded Funds

These are closed-end funds that operate like index funds, often at an even lower expense fee. You buy and sell them just like stocks. In theory, they could fall to discounts or trade at premiums like other closed-end funds, but they include a management mechanism to prevent that.

Not surprisingly, the best ETFs come from Vanguard. You could go to Vanguard and invest directly in their Vanguard Total Stock Market Index Fund, incurring a microscopic 0.18% annual expense ratio. Or, you could buy shares in the Vanguard Total Stock Market ETF (ticker symbol: VTI), with identical investments, and an even lower annual expense ratio—0.07% —but a commission to buy or sell them. (Or *without* a commission through Vanguard Brokerage Services.)

ETFs offer the advantage that you can borrow against them (if you need a temporary low-cost margin loan to avoid high-interest credit-card loans). And ETFs can be shorted—but if you consider that an advantage, you must have started reading this book from the back.

You can also buy exchange-traded funds called SPDRs and iShares. Their expense ratios are usually a bit higher but most iShares can be traded at Fidelity without a commission, and you can find a very broad selection of options, such as "sector" iShares that invest only in telecommunications stocks or in oil service companies. Why you think you know how well the stocks of companies in these sectors will do is something for both of us to ponder.

There are ETFs that track various foreign market indexes as well. When these first came out, the annual expenses were ridiculous, and they sometimes even failed to track their respective indexes. (How could that happen? Did they lose the list of companies they were supposed to invest in?) Since then, they've improved, and all of them have expense ratios under 1%. The Vanguard Europe Pacific ETF (ticker symbol VEA) has an expense ratio of 0.09%. If you'd like to spice up your returns with emerging markets, the Vanguard Emerging Markets ETF (VWO) has an expense ratio of 0.15%. And there are similarly low-expense ETFs that cover the entire world except the United States (VEU), and the entire world *with* the United States (VT).

There are also now ETFs that index various parts of the bond market. The best broad index fund is the Vanguard Total Bond Market ETF (BND, with an expense ratio of just 0.07%).

Someone who wanted to follow the simplified wealth maintenance plan near the start of this chapter might reasonably use VTI to cover the U.S. market, VEA to cover international stocks, and SHY for the Treasury portion.

Which are better — mutual funds or ETFs? When all is said and done, it largely comes down to convenience: If you already have a deep-discount brokerage account, use ETFs. If you already invest with Vanguard, use its funds.

The Personal Fund (Play Money)

With ultra-low commissions, there is now the possibility for the ultimate fund. The one you put together yourself. The Personal Fund. It is no-load, of course, because you don't charge yourself a nickel. And not just low-expense, like an index fund — *no*-expense. But that's not the real reason to bother with this, because unless you have zillions of dollars, the tiny fee an index fund charges is insignificant.

The real reason to bother is tax management. With a Personal Fund, designed to more or less match one or another index, you get to control the tax consequences. The Dow may be flat one year; but *within* the Dow, one stock may have doubled while another is down 50%. That does you no good if, say, you own a Dow index fund. But if you owned all 30 Dow stocks individually, you could sell the loser for a tax loss — saving you real cash money April 15 — and use the winner to do your charitable giving.

There are a couple of ways to do this. One, as suggested, would be to buy all the stocks in the Dow Jones Industrial Average. The Dow may not be the best index to use, but it's the one everybody watches and, for the purposes of this exercise, has the virtue of containing only 30 stocks. Your total commission cost, if you used one of those $8-a-trade Internet brokers, would be $240. But you'd save the annual management fee. Now, say two years have passed and the Dow is up 10% — nothing much — but that within the 30 stocks, one of them is up 80% and one is down 50%. You could sell the loser and get a tax benefit, buying it back 31 days later to reestablish your position (remember, the IRS will disallow your tax loss as a "wash sale" if you don't wait that month) and use the winner to replenish your account at the Fidelity Charitable Gift Fund, buying *that* stock back moments later (no need to wait 31 days).

Or instead of the Dow, use the free stock screener you'll find at **magicformulainvesting.com.** The 30 stocks it picks for you might do even better.

An Overall Stock-Market Strategy: Put *most* of the money you want exposed to the very real risks of the stock market—which must be money you will not *need* to touch for many years—into equally or fundamentally weighted index funds. But if you want a little more excitement, and a chance to dream a little—and possible tax advantages—set aside a small portion of those funds to direct yourself, at Ameritrade or Fidelity. Split that cash among five or six speculative bets (not necessarily made all at once, by the way . . . no need to rush into this). Taking losses on those that crater could lower your taxable income by as much as $3,000 a year; gains from those that soar (if any ever do) could remodel your kitchen *or,* so long as you hold them a year and a day, fund all your charitable giving—again, see page 128.)

The Future

What you should do with your money naturally depends on what the future holds.

The conventional wisdom among best-selling financial writers of the seventies and eighties was that unemployment and recession would get so bad that the fiscal and monetary floodgates would be thrown open to avert depression, bringing on inflation. To fight it, the Fed would slam on the brakes and throw the country into an even greater slump requiring even *more* stimulus, causing even *worse* inflation, requiring even *tougher* brake-slamming . . . and around and around it would go, inflation, recession, inflation, recession, getting ever worse. The "malarial economy," Howard Ruff and others dubbed it—alternating chills and fever and, eventually, collapse. Ruff wrote *How to Prosper During the Coming Bad Years* and (when they didn't come) *Survive and Win in the Inflationary Eighties* (which proved to be highly *dis*inflationary). Douglas Casey cashed in with *Crisis Investing*. Ravi Batra hit #1 in 1987 with *The Great Depression of 1990* (unemployment was 5.6% in 1990), the same year James

Dale Davidson and William Rees-Mogg weighed in with *The Great Reckoning: Protecting Yourself in the Coming Depression* followed by *Blood in the Streets: Investment Profits in a World Gone Mad.*

And so it went.

"But there is another scenario which should not be dismissed out of hand," I wrote in this space in 1983, "unaccustomed though we've become to improvement: That this decade, if we keep our wits about us, could become what Paul Volcker has called the mirror image of the last one: falling energy prices, falling inflation, falling interest rates, rising productivity, rising real wages, rising employment. I make no secret of being partial to the optimistic scenario. I think we've laid a technological base that places us, potentially at least, on the brink of unparalleled prosperity."

And indeed the decade that followed worked out much that way. (One indicator: the Dow quadrupled.) And the generally positive trends continued well beyond 1993. Seven years later, in 2000, unemployment was 4%, the Dow had nearly tripled its quadruple, our National Debt had been shrinking relative to the size of the economy as a whole — we faced challenges, certainly, and had kicked cans down the road. But things were looking pretty good.

Then came 2001–2008. But *then* came 2009–2015, so things are again looking pretty good.*

---

* I don't mean to make half my readers crazy by pointing this out, but the stock market and the economy do better under Democrats than Republicans. During the 12 Bush years, net private-sector job creation totaled just 747,000 — versus 19.6 million during the Clinton years and 10 million so far under Obama — or 14 million if you don't count the first few horrific months he inherited. So that's 747,000 jobs under the 12 most recent years of Republican leadership, as deficits ballooned; 30 million under the 15 most recent years of Democratic leadership, as deficits were brought back under control.

Invested in the S&P 500 only during Republican administrations since 1929, and excluding dividends, $10,000 would have grown to only about $12,000 — versus about $600,000 if invested only during Democratic administrations.

The technological progress we can look forward to is, as I argued at the front of this book, *dazzling*. The resultant economic growth and prosperity—if we can find politically palatable ways to share it—could be *tremendous*. But as I also argued, the tide of falling interest rates has ebbed. So keep enough powder dry in banks or TIPS to endure what *could* be a nasty spill; and "average down" each time we have one.

Sermonette

Whether you choose mutual funds or a direct plunge into the stock market, bonds, or a savings account; whether you shelter your investments through an IRA or a SEP; and whether you spend now or save to spend later—you will find that, by the prevailing American ethic, anyway, you never have enough.

D. H. Lawrence wrote a wonderful story years ago called "The Rocking-Horse Winner." "Although they lived in style," Lawrence wrote of his fictional family, "they felt always an anxiety in the house . . . There was always the grinding sense of the shortage of money, though the style was always kept up . . . And so the house came to be haunted by the unspoken phrase: *There must be more money! There must be more money!* The children could hear it all the time, though nobody said it aloud. They could hear it at Christmas, when the expensive and splendid toys filled the nursery. Behind the shining modern rocking horse, behind the smart doll's house, a voice would start whispering: 'There *must* be more money! There *must* be more money!'"

One of the children began playing the horses. Before long, in league with the gardener, he had managed to turn a few pennies into a small fortune. The child arranged to have it given to his mother, anonymously. "Then something very curious happened. The voices in the house suddenly went mad, like a chorus of frogs on a spring evening." Debts were paid off and new luxuries lavished—"and yet the voices . . . simply trilled and screamed in a sort of ecstasy: 'There must be more money! Oh-h-h; there must be more money. Oh, now, now-w! Now-w-w—there must be more money!—more than ever! More than ever!'"

More is never enough. But there may be a way around this for some people, a way to be just as contented and happy if you don't inherit a million dollars as if you do. It is suggested by this passage from *Stone Age Economics* by Marshall Sahlins:

> By the common understanding, an affluent society is one in which all the people's material wants are easily satisfied . . . [But] there are two possible courses to affluence. Wants may be "easily satisfied" either by producing much or desiring little. The familiar conception, the Galbraithean way, makes assumptions peculiarly appropriate to market economics: that man's wants are great, not to say infinite, whereas his means are limited, although improvable: thus, the gap between means and ends can be narrowed by industrial productivity . . . But there is also a Zen road to affluence, departing from premises somewhat different from our own: that human material wants are finite and few, and technical means unchanging but on the whole adequate. Adopting the Zen strategy, a people can enjoy an unparalleled material plenty—with a low standard of living.

Or as a friend of mine once said: "It's just as easy to live well when you're poor as when you're rich—but when you're poor, it's much cheaper."

This is not to advocate Buddhism, asceticism, Spartanism —or, for that matter, poverty. I, for one, like living a little better every year. In fact, I believe happiness lies less in how much you have than in which way you're headed.* Which is a strong

---

* Consider two young families, one with an income of $200,000 but somehow knowing it is headed down to $150,000; the other earning $30,000 but somehow knowing it is headed up to $50,000. I submit that the family earning $30,000 a year, though it will never be as affluent, might well be the happier of the two. Things are looking up.

argument for saving something each year rather than see your net worth slip backward; and for *pacing* your acquisition of the finer things, lest the day come when you can't afford them. For remember: a luxury once sampled becomes a necessity. It's not so bad living on a low floor—until you've had a view.

And by the way? It's worth remembering that, however much we may sensibly delay gratification, most of us still live better than any Roman emperor ever did. They had no air conditioning! No antibiotics! No smartphones! No way to move themselves or anything else faster than seven miles an hour! Yes, they could get somebody with a lute to come play a tune. But you or I can command any philharmonic orchestra in the world to assemble—instantly—and play a symphony as we jog around the lake. Not all that bad, when you think about it.

Ultimately, how you should spend or invest your money depends not so much on price/earnings ratios or dividend rates as on those larger questions that forever lurk but generally go unasked: Who am I? What am I trying to do with my life? Is money the means or the end?

There is a good measure of self-knowledge required to choose the proper investment course. It has even been postulated that many small investors in the stock market, without knowing it, secretly want to lose. They jump in with high hopes—but feeling vaguely guilty. Guilty over "gambling" with the family's money, guilty over trying to "get something for nothing," or guilty over plunging in without really having done much research or analysis. Then they punish themselves, for these or other sins, by selling out, demoralized, at a loss.

In any event, whether or not they secretly want to, many investors, failing to seek out value and then hold it patiently, do lose. If this little book saved you $1,000 a year—on wine (by the case, on sale), on life insurance and finance charges, on brokerage commissions (trading less often, and with a deep-discount broker), on investment letters (not subscribing to them), and on taxes (particularly with a Roth IRA)—I would be delighted.

But if it saved you from getting burned in the stock market, or on even one seemingly surefire "investment" someone was trying to sell you — I would be thrilled!

(I hear, by the way, that the Mexican peso is now very strong again, and that you can get a hell of an interest rate south of the border.)

APPENDIXES

"I have no idea how much my interest rate is,"
says Suzanne Carver, a Chicago housewife,
as she paws through her purse to check her card.
"It doesn't say on here. Well, as long as I can
buy things with it, who cares?"

— *WALL STREET JOURNAL,*
March 19, 1987

Earning 177% on Bordeaux

THIS EXAMPLE HAS sort of evolved. The first time I used it was in 1978, on the *Tonight Show*. Say you bought a $10 bottle of wine for dinner every Saturday night but could instead get a 10% discount buying by the case. You'd "make" 10% on the extra money you tied up. And you'd "make" it in just 12 weeks — a bottle a week for 12 weeks equals one case of wine — which works out, I explained, to "better than a 40% annual return."

I didn't explain how *much* better. I figured 40% was dramatic enough. Where else can you earn 40% tax-free?

As the years passed, I found people were having trouble understanding this little shtick of mine. Why is it 40% if I just got a 10% discount?

So I tried explaining it in a little more detail. What actually happens, I explained, is that instead of going to the store and laying out $10 for one bottle, you are laying out $108 for 12 bottles (full price minus the 10% discount). That extra $98 is your "investment." By keeping at most $98 extra tied up all year, you save $1 a week on wine — $52 a year. And "earning" $52 a year by tying up $98 is earning 53%.

So now I was up to 53%, an even better tax-free return.

This confused people even more. That first $98 is gone, they would tell me, and now you have to come up with a new $98 to buy your next case of wine.

But think about it. If you were someone who planned to spend $10 a week on wine — $520 a year — and who would have LOVED to save 10% buying by the case but just couldn't scrape up enough money all at once to do it, how much financing would you need?

Would you have to go to a bank and ask for a $400 loan in order to change your buying habits?

No, you would need only a $98 credit line—and you would only fully draw it down that very first week. After that, you would replenish it by $10 a week (the $10 you would otherwise have spent on wine by the bottle), which means that after 12 weeks, when you needed to buy the next case, you would not only have replenished the full $98, you'd actually have an extra $12 to work with (the money you saved buying by the case). So now you'd have to draw down only $86 of your $98 credit line.

In other words, to finance this change in buying habits you'd need to borrow a *maximum* of $98. On *average,* over the course of the year, you need far less than $98 to finance this change in buying habits. So the return on your decision to tie up that $98 at first, and then gradually less, is actually much greater than 40% or 53%.

If my friend Less Antman has keyed all this into his Hewlett-Packard financial calculator correctly—and I've never known him to err—it works out to an annualized 177% rate of return (though try explaining THAT in 40 seconds on the *Tonight Show*).

It's still only $52 you're earning—$1 a week by getting the 10% discount. But applied to all your regular shopping, it can be the best "investment" in your portfolio.

Next step: find a vintage you like equally well that's only $8 a bottle.*

---

* In 2014 a dinner guest brought a bottle of wine that, as we drank it, even I could tell was really nice. (I know nothing about wine.) I went online to see whether I could afford it and was astonished to find it for $6.99 a bottle. Needless to say, as brilliant as is a 177% return on a $10 bottle of wine, it's even more brilliant (if fewer actual dollars) at $6.99. I bought four cases . . . excited . . . but nervously thinking—what do I know about wine? (Really: I know nothing about wine.) What if they hate it?

I poured a glass for a connoisseur without letting him see the bottle. He started speaking Wine—a language I do not—guessing it was French (it is South African), possibly from 2010 (it was 2013), and commenting on its notes and hints and palate (or was it his palate? Whatever). He may have said something about bacon. But the gist was that he liked it.

What might it cost, I asked?

He guessed it was in the $20–$30 range (I paid $6.29 with the discount, free shipping); $50–$60 in a restaurant. At which point I bought six more cases. Oracle Pinotage 2013. Enjoy.

How Much Life Insurance
Do You Need?

IF YOU'RE SINGLE with no dependents, you need little—to assist with burial expenses and, posthumously, pay off a few debts—or none. The great push to sell college students life insurance is not entirely unlike the selling of ice to Eskimos, except that a lot more insurance is sold that way than ice.

If you're married, with a hopelessly incompetent spouse, a family history of heart disease, and a horde of little children, you should carry a great deal of insurance. Less if your spouse has a reliable income. Less still if you have fewer children or if those children have wealthy and benevolent grandparents. And still less as those children grow up.

If you're very rich, you need no insurance at all, except as it is helpful in providing liquidity to settle your estate. If you *live* richly off a high income but own outright little more than a deck of credit cards and a Rolex, it will take a lot of insurance to keep from exposing your dependents to an altogether seamier side of life when you're gone.

What you want, ideally, is enough insurance, when combined with other assets you may have, to pay for what are euphemistically called "final expenses"—deathbed medical expenses not covered by other insurance, funeral expenses, possible postmortem emergencies like an illness of the surviving spouse, payment of bills—and then enough in addition to replace the income you had been kicking into the family till. So that, financially anyway, you will not be missed.

Of course, you don't have to replace all your income, just the after-tax portion you were actually taking home. And not even that much, because with you gone, there will be one fewer mouth to feed, one fewer theater ticket to buy. Not to mention the savings on the second car or commuting expenses, medical and dental expenses, gambling losses, your NRA membership, life insurance premiums, charitable contributions, clothing, laundry, shaving cream—and the cigarettes that did you in in the first place. Your surviving dependents will need perhaps 75% to 85% of your current take-home pay in order to live as well, or nearly as well, as they were before. So if you were earning $60,000 a year and taking home $45,000, your family might maintain roughly the same living standard on around $35,000 to $40,000 a year.

To figure your life insurance needs, estimate what your heirs would need if you died this afternoon. A typical calculation goes as follows:

1. Estimate how much your heirs would need to replace if you died. For most families, as I've said, this number falls somewhere around 75% to 85% of your annual take-home pay. If you take home no pay, but merely do 80 hours a week of cooking, cleaning, day caring, and shopping, estimate the cost of your replacement.

2. Subtract the annual Social Security benefits your family could expect to receive (most likely someplace vaguely in the $30,000 ballpark, if you have young kids—but use **ssa.gov/es timator** to find out).

3. The difference—if there is a difference—is the annual income gap you'll want life insurance to make up. But for how long? This depends on the ages of your children and spouse, and whether you'd expect your spouse to remarry. Choose a time period from the following table and multiply the annual income gap by the figure on the right. The result is an amount of insurance that should last the number of years you require, if invested sensibly, and keep up with inflation. For example, to provide an additional $10,000 for 25 years, you'd multiply $10,000 by 18 —$180,000.

	Multiply by:*
5 years	4.7
10 years	9
15 years	12
20 years	15
25 years	18
30 years	20
50 years	26

4.   Add a lump sum as a cushion for funeral expenses, grief-induced family illnesses, the payment of worrisome debts—at least half a year's salary and in no event less than $25,000. And another (giant) lump sum if you would like to leave enough to put all three kids through college and medical school.

Now you have a grand total of your insurance needs. But wait!

5.   Subtract whatever assets you've amassed such as savings accounts, stocks, bonds, and retirement accounts (including whatever pension benefits you'd be entitled to from work). Subtract still more if there's a wealthy and loving grandparent in the picture who would want to help out or whose wealth would eventually pass on to the family. And subtract the value of the group life insurance you have at work—but make a mental note that you may have to replace it if you switch jobs and that, in the event of a long terminal illness that forces you from your job, you will have to promptly exercise your (very expensive) option of continuing the policy on your own.

---

* This assumes your heirs could invest the proceeds to earn 3% after taxes and inflation. If you think they could earn more, you'd need less insurance—but you're probably not being realistic. The 3% assumption I've used may actually be optimistic. (Beware online calculators that purport to help you determine how much life insurance you need but don't tell you the rate at which their calculations assume your insurance proceeds will grow.)

6. Round up to the nearest $50,000, and there's your answer. If it looks overwhelming, remember that you can stretch your coverage by purchasing term insurance instead of whole life, and by shopping for it carefully (see page 27). Remember, too, that your spouse could remarry; your spouse could go to work; once the kids are grown, *they* could provide support as well. Furthermore, it is not inconceivable that your family could be happy with a more modest lifestyle than they now enjoy.

How Much Social Security Will You Get?

A MUCH-PUBLICIZED 1994 POLL, still oft-cited, found more young people believing in UFOs than in the possibility they'd actually get anything back for all their Social Security contributions. This view is nuts but perhaps healthy—at least it means they're not counting on Uncle Sam to provide for their retirement.

When Social Security was launched in the thirties, there were 40 people working for each person receiving benefits. But then something awkward happened. People started living longer. And having fewer kids. Today there are fewer than three people working for each current recipient. With Baby Boomers now retiring, it will approach two.

At the same time, Congress kept upping the benefits.

With payroll taxes already sky-high, something's got to give. Three things, actually. And the good news is that by doing just a little bit of each, the equation can work just fine:

♦ The age at which you can retire with full Social Security benefits is already being gradually pushed back from 65 to 67 by 2027. Having the full-benefits age *continue* to rise by a month per year, perhaps to age 70 by 2063 (while keeping 62 as the early-retirement age), would go a long way toward righting the balance of the system—while giving today's workers plenty of time to adjust their plans.

♦ It would be rotten to raise the already-hefty payroll tax *rate* (currently 6.2% each from you and your employer plus a further 1.45% each for Medicare). And politically explosive to remove the income ceiling on which the tax is levied—currently $118,500 (although they've *already* removed that ceiling on the Medicare portion). But what if all income above the ceiling were nicked by just 1%? Annoying, but hardly a killer; and perhaps worth paying so that Grandma—much as we love her—doesn't have to move in.

♦ Benefits need to rise with inflation. But a small change in the way we account for inflation can have a very large impact. In setting the initial benefit that today's 30-year-old will receive when she retires, the system currently adjusts for a thing called "wage inflation," which is slightly higher than the more familiar price inflation. "If we were to switch from wage to price indexing of earnings in calculating initial benefits," wrote Robert Pozen, former head of Fidelity Investments and an expert in this field, "this switch alone would effectively close Social Security's long-term financial gap." Doing this even just partially, as Pozen recommends, would have a huge impact.

So that's it. A bit of pain around the edges, with plenty of time to prepare for it, and the Social Security problem is entirely solved.*

And do you know what? With the productivity gains continued technological progress will likely bring us in the years ahead, Congress might well be in a position to *roll back* those adjustments before they've even much kicked in; or even once again begin to *increase* benefits from time to time, as for decades they regularly did.

So there may well be room here for a "grand bargain" after all—a much higher minimum wage that would help those at the bottom (and boost the economy and cut the defi-

---

* An oft-proposed alternative is to privatize Social Security: have each of us invest for ourselves. But it has huge problems. First, what do you do for old folks who've failed to invest wisely? Or who live unusually long? (No need for *everyone* to save enough to live to 103; but what if *you* live that long?) Are you going to let them starve in the street? You'd still need a safety net. Second, how do we get from here to there? It's fine for today's workers to say, "Just stop withholding FICA from my pay and I'll provide for myself!" But where, then, do we get the funds to provide for the millions of grandparents *currently* subsisting on Social Security? And there are other big problems (call me). But listen: to the extent Social Security benefits *are* so modest—the bare essentials—we've *already* privatized America's retirement system. It's called IRAs and 401(k)s. Social Security is, and will remain, just the safety net.

cit) now . . . **urgently needed infrastructure investment that would provide good domestic jobs now . . . and adjustments to Social Security that might never need to take effect by the time they were scheduled to kick in years from now.**

Grand bargain or not, the long and the short of it is that —whatever it may be called by the time you retire—there is almost sure to be a meaningful Social Security safety net. In real dollars, real buying power, monthly checks won't *sharply* rise (how could we afford it?) nor *sharply* shrink (how could Congressfolk, seeking reelection, allow it?).

Either way, you're wise to be thinking about this, and to put all you can—starting now!—into your Roth IRA, your SEP, your profit-sharing plan at work, and, on top of that, into two or three carefully selected no-load, low-expense, stock-market mutual funds. Because no matter what, Social Security alone will never be enough to provide a comfortable retirement—nor was it ever meant to. It has always been designed to provide only the bare essentials.

Social Security benefits are tied to how much you have paid into the system (over a minimum, cumulatively, of ten working years). You should be mailed a statement from the Social Security Administration three months before your birthday each year showing you the history of wages on which you've been taxed with guidelines for estimating your benefits.

In the case of death benefits, the payout to your surviving spouse will depend in part on your age at death and on the composition of your family.

To get a rough idea of the annual benefits you'll be entitled to —likely someplace vaguely in the $15,000 to $35,000 ballpark —visit **ssa.gov/estimator.**

A Few Words About Taxes
and Our National Debt

*If the Bank runs out of Money, it may issue as much Money of its
own as it may need by merely writing on any ordinary paper.*

— THE RULES OF MONOPOLY, PARKER BROTHERS, INC.

CAN I JUST say something about taxes?

I hate them as much as the next guy, and I'm all for being
smart about minimizing them, individually. (See, for example,
Chapter 6.) But if we weren't so pathologically averse to them as
a nation, we'd not be *in* this mess.

Let me start with a story.

A long time ago, I was sent to Washington to interview the
Secretary of the Treasury. I was 20-something, and he was Bill
Simon, known to be one scary guy.

It was 1974, and the country was in crisis over OPEC's oil
price hikes, and at the end of the interview I couldn't help myself. "I know it's probably crazy," I stammered, "and I must be
missing something. But why don't we just start adding a dime a
gallon to the gasoline tax every year, and use every penny of that
to lower the income tax? So we *dis*courage the thing we want to
discourage—gasoline consumption—and *en*courage the things
we want to encourage—work and investment and greater fuel
efficiency?"

There was a long pause. "Well, of *course* we should do that"
—("You moron," his voice said, "any *idiot* knows that")—"but
it's not politically feasible." This is America after all. And indeed,
when Clinton hiked the gas tax by a paltry 4.3 cents, people
howled. I remember a TV newscast that featured a large woman
at a gas pump who said it would *wreck her life*. It worked out

to maybe $30 a year, but this woman—representing America—was incensed.

Yet think about it. The dime-a-gallon annual gas tax hike—every penny of which would by law have gone to lower the income tax—could have been announced in 1974 but not kicked in for five years to give people time to adjust. And it would have been voluntary! To avoid it, all people would have had to do was buy more-fuel-efficient vehicles!

Had we somehow found the will to take this path, we might well be leading the world in fuel-efficient auto production (hurray for Detroit and the manufacturing sector); but would, in any event, have burned literally trillions of dollars less imported oil into thin air, keeping that money at home instead. We'd be a stronger, richer, healthier nation. Just by changing what we taxed.

What does it say about our democracy that we couldn't do the obvious, way back in 1973 or 1983 or even 1993?

One can blame the politicians; but one can also blame the electorate that goes wild at a 4.3-cent gas tax hike and that has come to accept as a given that all tax cuts are good, all tax hikes are bad.

For a long time, no question, taxes were too high—especially on the wealthy. Under the strains of World War II, the top federal income tax bracket was set at 94% on income above $200,000 (which would be about $3 million in today's dollars). It remained at 90% for all eight Eisenhower years, was cut to 70% under Kennedy—and remained at that still-preposterous level through the administrations of Johnson, Nixon, Ford, and Carter.

In his first term, Reagan cut it to 50%—still too high, if you ask me—but then to 28% in his second term, which, combined with a major military buildup, led to big deficits and a growing National Debt.

Clinton bumped the effective top rate back up to 39.6% (but lowered the long-term capital-gains rate from Reagan's 28% to 20%). George W. Bush cut the top rate on work to 35% and the top rate on wealth—dividends and capital gains—all the way down to 15%.

If those tax cuts for the wealthy had not overshot the mark, the nation would not today be saddled with such a staggering debt; and there would have been more revenue to renew our decaying infrastructure.

And *speaking* of our staggering National Debt, it's likely to be the topic of so much debate over the next few years—and your own share of it is so large (in the ballpark of $60,000 for each member of your household)—it's worth having the tools to get your head around it.

In the first place, all that matters is the size of the debt *relative to the economy as a whole*. If the debt is relatively small—like a $175,000 mortgage on a $2 million home owned by a billionaire—it's not a big concern. If it's large—like the same $175,000 mortgage on a $160,000 home owned by a nurse—it can be devastating.

So imagine we ran a $200 billion deficit each of the next 100 years, while our economy grew at 5% a year—half from real growth, half from inflation. Terrible, no? A century of $200 billion deficits!

Actually, that scenario would be wonderful. A century from now, the debt would have grown to $40 trillion. But the GDP would have grown to $2.4 quadrillion. So the debt would have shrunk from today's ratio of roughly 100% of GDP to less than 2% of GDP.

All this is fanciful, to be sure, but illustrates the point. Deficits are OK, so long as the overall debt is—at least in most years—growing slower than the economy.

That's the first thing to understand. We don't need to "pay off the debt." Healthy businesses—and nations—can carry debt. In fact, it usually makes sense to do so.* *Modest* deficits each year are not a terrible thing. And in an economy as large as ours, gigantic numbers like "a hundred billion!" are actually modest.

Sometimes, though, a crisis comes along that requires *enormous* deficits—like winning World War II. What choice did we have? We had to do whatever it took to win. And in so doing, we took the National Debt—which had been roughly 30% of GDP at the start of the Depression and had risen to roughly 40% by the time we entered the war—all the way up to 121% by 1946.

Over 35 years that ended with Ronald Reagan's inauguration, we gradually shrank it back down to 30%. Not by paying it down; simply by having it grow more slowly than the economy.

That was our strongest debt/GDP ratio—30%. It soon shot skyward. Only between Bush Senior and Junior was the annual deficit tamed, as Clinton handed off what *Fortune* called "surpluses as far as the eye could see."

Clinton worked with a Democratic Congress that in 1990 had established a system called PAYGO (as in, "pay as you go"), requiring new budget items to be paid for with cuts elsewhere or new tax revenue. When the Republicans regained control of Congress, they ditched PAYGO. In 2010, the Democrats reinstated it, over unanimous opposition from Senate Republicans.

I would never argue that Democrats are uniformly and always perfect on this issue (or any other), or that Republicans are uniformly and always wrong. But to suggest there are not huge differences between the parties—to tar them both with

---

* Another piece of this is the way the accounting is done. The government does its accounting on a cash basis. All would agree that when we borrow to issue unemployment checks (say), that's money we are *spending*. But most would agree that when we borrow to build the Interstate Highway System, that's *investing*. Well-managed businesses borrow to make capital expenditures all the time. (And some would agree that when we spend money on education, that, too, is investing: in human capital.)

So part of the annual deficit would not even show up as a deficit if Uncle Sam did his accounting the way a modern business does, amortizing its investments over a number of years. In that sense, fairly considered, our annual budget deficit is smaller than it appears.

the same brush—is to miss some deeply ingrained themes. The Republicans of old—the Eisenhowers and Nixons and Rockefellers—would have been horrified.*

Clinton left office urging his successor (and anyone else who would listen) to "save Social Security first." It was his way of saying, "Don't blow the budget surplus I've left you on tax cuts —we need it to shore up the national balance sheet."

Bush, by contrast, told anyone who would listen that the surpluses were large and real—your money, not the government's. "Elect me, and I'll give it back to you." But what he really did was borrow the Social Security surplus—paid *in* by average working stiffs—and pay it *out* in the form of tax cuts that mostly benefited the very wealthy.

Obama cut taxes for 95% of working families but raised them for the best off. That this made Joe the Plumber so angry is a testament to the skills and resources of the folks who hope to manipulate him into supporting candidates who will put the interests of the wealthy ahead of his own.

---

* Full disclosure: As I write this, I'm treasurer of the Democratic National Committee. But I only get $1 a year—17 so far!—and the last thing in the world I'd want to be is an ambassador, so however wrong-headed my views may be, they are at least truly my own, advanced for no other reason than that I believe them.

Cocktail Party Financial Quips to
Help You Feel Smug

1.   If you are fully invested in the market (or wish to pretend you are), you can say: "I'm betting the Fed'll ease up." This means you think the Federal Reserve Board will ease up on interest rates, allowing them to fall and the stock market, as a consequence, to rise. Either this is the general consensus, in which case you will seem au courant; or it is a contrary opinion, in which case you will appear a shrewd man or woman of independent thought. No matter what "the Fed" is really doing, or how little you know of it or care—that you should have an opinion at all is impressive. If someone tries to pin you down, look genuinely uncomfortable, which won't be hard under the circumstances, and say, just a bit mysteriously: "Forgive me, I'd rather not discuss it just yet." (If rates are at or near zero already, and someone shoots back, "How could the Fed ease any *further*?" just smile . . . "Helicopters." If they fail to get the reference, just say: "Former Fed Chair Ben Bernanke. Google it.")

2.   If you've cautiously avoided the stock market but someone asks you what you're into these days, you can say: "Gee, Bill, I really don't have much of a mind for stocks. I know I must be missing out on some terrific opportunities, but I'm happier just sticking to municipals." This will be taken as a display of false modesty—it will be assumed you really do have a mind for stocks—and it will indicate that you are a high-bracket taxpayer of considerable means. You will be envied.

3.   Or: "I'll tell you the truth, Phil. I used to play the market until I totted up how much time I was spending on it—you know what an obsession it can become. After the Dow hit 18,000 in 2015, I took my profits and got out. I decided I'd rather spend the time with my kids." This is bound to make Phil feel guilty.

4. If someone is waxing philosophical about the market, you can say: "The great mistake made by the public is paying attention to prices instead of values." If that raises an eyebrow, because it sounds a bit more formal than you usually sound, you can continue: "Charlie Dow said that back at the turn of the last century [which he did], and it's as true now as it was then [which it is]." If you now have them in the palm of your hand, you could end the riff with, "Not sure what *Jones* was thinking." If you get puzzled looks and need to explain — "Dow *Jones*" — all the better.

5. If someone is boasting about a stock that's really zoomed, you can say: "Gosh, that's terrific! Sounds like time to short some."

6. Or (if you're really fed up) you could say: "Gee, a regular Hetty Green!" Chances are, your companion will have no notion who Hetty Green was. And you may want to leave it at that. ("The Witch of Wall Street," Hetty Green died in 1916, leaving $100 million to children who despised her. In 1916, $100 million was a lot of money.)

Selected Discount Brokers

You MAY HAVE noticed that I dedicated this book "to my broker." Forty years later, he is still my broker, charging $356 per trade. But having helped put his kids through college, I've long since moved most of my business to TD Ameritrade (**ameritrade.com**) and Fidelity (**fidelity.com**), who charge $8.

The savings are phenomenal and the service, I've found, more efficient.

There are firms that charge even less. But beyond a point, who cares? I bought 100,000 shares of a 31-cent stock through Ameritrade for an $8 commission. My full-service broker would have charged $2,006 (its 2-cent-a-share minimum plus its $6 "transaction fee"). Paying $5 instead of $8 would have made no difference at all. But paying $2,005 (with the prospect of another $2,005 to sell it)—that *does* make a difference.*

I have no doubt there are many other really good firms out there, but let me mention just two—E*TRADE (**etrade.com**) allows taxable individual accounts to trade foreign securities on six exchanges at an almost equally low commission. Vanguard

---

* I know, I know. What was I doing blowing $31,000 on some wild speculation? When this book first came out, I was barely *earning* $31,000, and it was only a few years earlier that I had bought 100 shares of Leisure Dynamics at $8 a share—my first trade with the above-mentioned full-service broker—and fell into a gloom spiral as that $800 disappeared. Well, the truth is that 40 years of frugality and compounding—combined with a great deal of good fortune for which I count my blessings daily—have paid off. I don't consider myself rich. I have met people with five times more money than me, and people with five times more money than that—and five times more money than *that*—all of whom feel truly dirt poor in the presence of my friend Warren Buffett. But if you are in your twenties, as I was when I started saving and investing in earnest, you too may be able to risk $31,000 in some dicey but not completely ill-considered speculation. Generally, if you do, you will lose your money. I do. That is in the nature of dicey speculations. But once in a while, it may work out, and with enough oomph to more than make up for the losses.

Brokerage (**vanguard.com**) offers commissions as low as $2 a trade.

The big decision isn't which discount broker to choose. It's whether to go the discount route at all. And whether, in fact, to try to choose *individual securities* at all. Should you just use mutual funds instead? They are the subject of the next appendix.

Selected Mutual Funds

THE SIMPLEST WAY to outperform most amateurs and professionals in most years—especially after tax considerations are included (see page 243)—is to buy an index fund with a very low expense ratio, like one of those described below. Better still, make that *two* index funds: one that invests in U.S. stocks and one that invests abroad (or a global fund to cover both).

When you think about it, isn't this remarkable? With just a few clicks of your mouse and a steady habit of periodic investing, you can set yourself up to outperform most professional money managers for the rest of your life.

Who says investing has to be complex or time-consuming?

That said, here are a few more ideas. Please note that I have absolutely no financial ties to any of these firms. Note also that in not discussing the literally thousands of other funds available to you, I am doubtless omitting some that will do spectacularly well. (If only I knew which!) But deluging you with alternatives is counterproductive. What you need are a few good choices and then, simply, to *get going*.

Vanguard (877-662-7447, vanguard.com). John Bogle founded this group in 1974 with the clear intention of making it the low-cost provider. He succeeded brilliantly. The average Vanguard expense ratio is around 0.2%, less than a fifth the industry average. The Vanguard Total Stock Market Index Fund (symbol: VTSMX) owns practically the entire U.S. stock market. The Vanguard Total International Index Fund (VGTSX) covers the rest of the planet. Vanguard's Total World Stock Index Fund (VTWSX) combines the two to save you the hassle but charges a slightly higher fee; and Vanguard Global Minimum Volatility Fund (VMVFX) attempts to provide a smoother ride without sacrificing performance. Each requires a $3,000 minimum to start, but Vanguard offers index ETFs that parallel many of these funds, with no minimum share purchase required.

WisdomTree offers several fundamentally weighted ETFs, including the WisdomTree Total Earnings Fund (EXT) for the United States; its World ex-US Dividend Growth Index (DNL) for everything else; and its Global Equity Income Fund (DEW) for both.

Charles Schwab (866-855-9102, schwab.com) recently took aim at Vanguard and started offering index mutual funds and ETFs with even lower expenses (time will tell whether this is a permanent strategy). Schwab currently has five market-weighted and six fundamentally weighted index funds, all with $100 investment minimums. To cover the world, use the Schwab Total Stock Market Index Fund (SWTSX) and Schwab International Index Fund (SWISX) for traditional weighting or the Schwab Fundamental US Large Company Index Fund (SFLNX) and Schwab Fundamental International Large Company Index Fund (SFNNX) for alternative weighting.

Tweedy, Browne (800-432-4789, tweedy.com). This fund family suggests that some funds really can beat the market. It began as a partnership in 1920 and counted none other than Benjamin Graham, the dean of modern investing, among its number. The partners learned from Graham the principles of value investing and practiced them for decades for their private clients. In 1993, the Tweedy, Browne Value Fund (TWEBX) and Tweedy, Browne Global Value Fund (TWGVX) were formed and opened to the general public. They buy stocks the old-fashioned way: hunting for the best bargains around. Both of their funds possess two characteristics that rarely go together: above-average performance and below-average volatility. During the slaughter that took both domestic and global stock averages down nearly 50% between March of 2000 and October of 2002, Tweedy, Browne Value was down only 19% and Global Value only 17%. When the global market dropped nearly 60% between October 2007 and March 2009, an equal split between the two Tweedy funds would have lost "only" 48%, which—though horrendous—would still have left your account balance around 25% higher than other funds. Overall, their "beta" (see Chapter 9) is less than 0.7. One nice touch is that the personal wealth of the partners is virtually all invested along with that of their clients. The minimum investment is $2,500 in a regular account but only $500 for an IRA. The taxable distributions from these funds make them best suited for tax-sheltered retirement money.

RSP and ACWV. Last on this short list: shares in Guggenheim's equally weighted S&P 500 index exchange-traded fund (symbol: RSP) and in MSCI's global minimum volatility exchange-traded fund (ACWV). One of the smartest financial planners I know keeps virtually his entire liquid net worth in ACWV. It is essentially the ETF equivalent of the Vanguard Global Minimum Volatility Fund mentioned above.

Fun with Compound Interest

IF YOU HAVE not yet learned how to work the compound interest key on your pocket calculator, or boot up a computer, but wish to astound your friends anyway, here is how $1 (or any multiple of $1) would grow at varying rates of interest, compounded annually. Unfortunately, if you are able to earn a very high rate of interest over a long period of time, it is likely to be because inflation is running at nearly as high a rate. Net of inflation and taxes, it's no cinch to earn 3% to 4% consistently, let alone any more. Still, it's fun to think about.

(A $2.99 iPhone app, Compoundee, puts the basic tools of compounding—allowing adjustments for inflation and taxes—in a user-friendly format. **Dinkytown.net** offers a complete suite of personal finance calculators, free.)

How a Dollar Grows

Year	3%	5%	6%	7%	8%	10%	12%	15%	20%
1	$1.03	$1.05	$1.06	$1.07	$1.08	$1.10	$1.12	$1.15	$1.20
2	1.06	1.10	1.12	1.14	1.17	1.21	1.25	1.32	1.44
3	1.09	1.16	1.19	1.23	1.26	1.33	1.40	1.52	1.73
4	1.13	1.22	1.26	1.31	1.36	1.46	1.57	1.75	2.07
5	1.16	1.28	1.34	1.40	1.47	1.61	1.76	2.01	2.49
6	1.19	1.34	1.42	1.50	1.59	1.77	1.97	2.31	2.99
7	1.23	1.41	1.50	1.61	1.71	1.95	2.21	2.66	3.58
8	1.27	1.48	1.59	1.72	1.85	2.14	2.48	3.06	4.30
9	1.30	1.55	1.69	1.84	2.00	2.36	2.77	3.52	5.16
10	1.34	1.63	1.79	1.97	2.16	2.59	3.11	4.05	6.19
11	1.38	1.71	1.90	2.10	2.33	2.85	3.48	4.65	7.43
12	1.43	1.80	2.01	2.25	2.52	3.14	3.90	5.35	8.91
13	1.47	1.89	2.13	2.41	2.72	3.45	4.36	6.15	10.70
14	1.51	1.98	2.26	2.58	2.94	3.80	4.88	7.08	12.84
15	1.56	2.08	2.40	2.76	3.17	4.18	5.47	8.14	15.41
20	1.80	2.65	3.21	3.87	4.66	6.72	9.65	16.37	38.34
25	2.09	3.39	4.29	5.43	6.85	10.83	17.00	32.92	95.40
30	2.43	4.32	5.74	7.61	10.06	17.45	29.96	66.21	$237
35	2.81	5.52	7.69	10.68	14.79	28.10	52.80	$133	$591
40	3.26	7.04	10.29	14.98	21.72	45.26	93.05	$267	$1,469
50	4.38	11.47	18.42	29.47	46.90	$117	$289	$1,083	$9,100
100	$19	$132	$339	$868	$2,200	$13,780	$83,523	$1.17 million	$82.8 million
200	$369	$17,292	$115,125	$753,849	$4.8 million	$190 million	$7.0 billion	$1.4 trillion	$6.9 quadrillion

To see how $3 or $1,000 or any other figure would grow, simply multiply by 3, or 1,000, or that other figure.

Still Not Sure What to Do?

I<small>F EVERYTHING YOU</small>'<small>VE</small> read so far leaves you unsure what to do, let me grab you by the hand and make it this simple:

Short of inheriting or marrying wealth, the surest way to become rich is to save all you can and invest it for long-term growth.

If you save at least 10% of each paycheck and earn a 7% annual return, it will take just over 30 years to grow your nest egg to equal ten years of income. You can then quit work and, with a little kick from Social Security, stay at approximately the same standard of living for the rest of your life. Or keep working (or save even more) to build a yet more comfortable margin of safety.

+ **How do I save 10% of income?** If you have a retirement plan at work, just have a portion of your pay automatically shunted to it (namely, whatever portion the company matches with a contribution of its own). For the rest, instruct your bank to set up an automatic monthly transfer from your checking account to your investment account or Roth IRA. There are people in the world making 10% less than you who are not ragged and homeless. Live like them.

+ **How do I earn 7% a year?** This is the hard part, because the 7% has to be the *real* return, after taxes and inflation. But 7% is not a pipe dream—over long periods, it's been the average real return for common stocks.* Of course, that's before sales charges, commissions, and management fees, which is all the more reason to try to keep expenses to a minimum.

---

* Well, 6.7% is the latest figure I have. But with the benefit of dollar-cost averaging, described on page 155, and regular rebalancing between domestic and international stocks, described on page 238, the return for someone saving each year would actually have been significantly higher.

Want just one idea? A couple hundred dollars a month is enough to open two accounts with Schwab: their Total Stock Market Index Fund to cover the United States and their International Index Fund to cover the rest of the world. A portfolio split equally between the two will have an expense ratio of 0.14%, an efficient way for the small investor to share in the growth of the world economy.

◆ **Because that 7% assumption *is* aggressive, try to save more than 10%.** If your employer matches a portion of your retirement-plan contribution, this can be relatively painless. And a Roth IRA will help, because it will eliminate the drag of taxes at withdrawal.

◆ **Is that it?** Yes. If the stock market collapses, look at it as a great opportunity to make subsequent purchases at bargain prices. As much as possible, act as if the 10% you are investing has been spent, and don't touch your treasure until it reaches at least ten times your annual salary. Then start spending up to 7% of it per year and, if it keeps growing at that rate, it will never be exhausted. If you can, wait even longer to touch it, and spend even less than 7% at first — try to spend 4% or 5% and let Social Security make up the difference. (Try, especially, to refrain from dipping into your nest egg when the market is low, lest you achieve what is in effect the *reverse* of dollar-cost averaging, selling more shares when the market is low and fewer when it is high.)

In real life, of course, it may not be this neat. You may not be able to amass a trove, and earn a return, that would last forever. But neither may *you* last forever, so this could be less of a problem than it seems. And it's possible that you could supplement dwindling income with a reverse mortgage on your home (page 233) or with a little help from those kids you trained so well (page 219), or that to avoid worry about outliving your money you might invest some of it, someday, in an annuity (page 121).

- **Can I get rich any faster?** Aiming for higher returns is a good way to get lower returns. The hardest part of making this system work is patience. Focus on your career, your family, your friends, and enjoying life to the fullest with the other 90% of your pay, so the process of building wealth is as much fun as the result.

- **What if I'm 63 — is it too late to start?** Yes. But in my experience, the overwhelming majority of 63-year-olds who buy books about investing are those who've amassed a pretty good nest egg already. Good for you! Give this book to your kids.

- **What if I have more questions?** I've told you everything I know — and then some. This sponge is dry. Still, the world changes. Feel free to visit **andrewtobias.com,** which, at least as of this writing, has more than its share of daily comments to annoy you, along with a feature called "Ask Less," where you can ask more.

Index